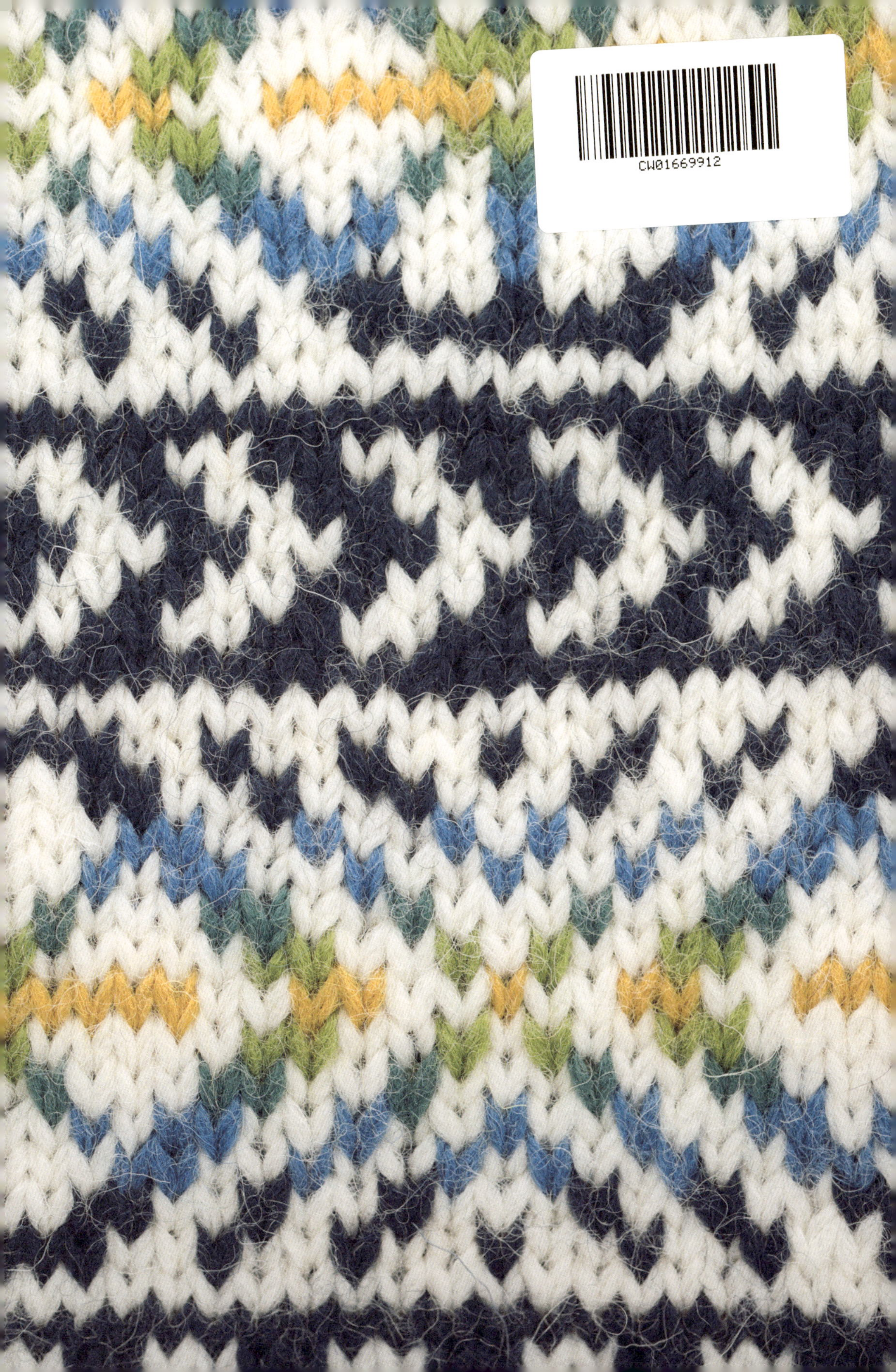

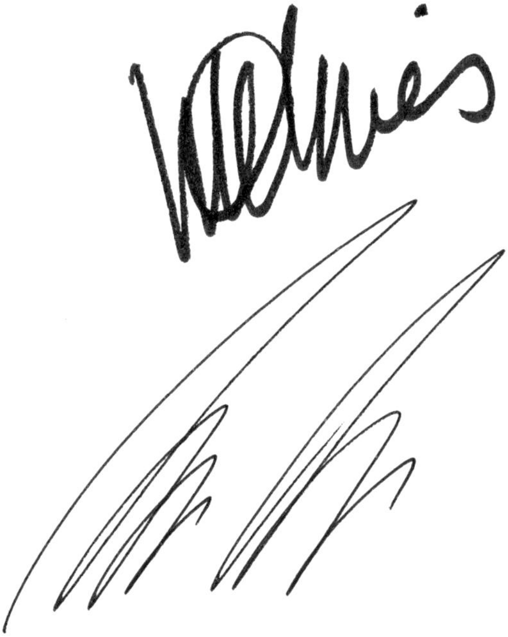

Limited Edition
54 of 500

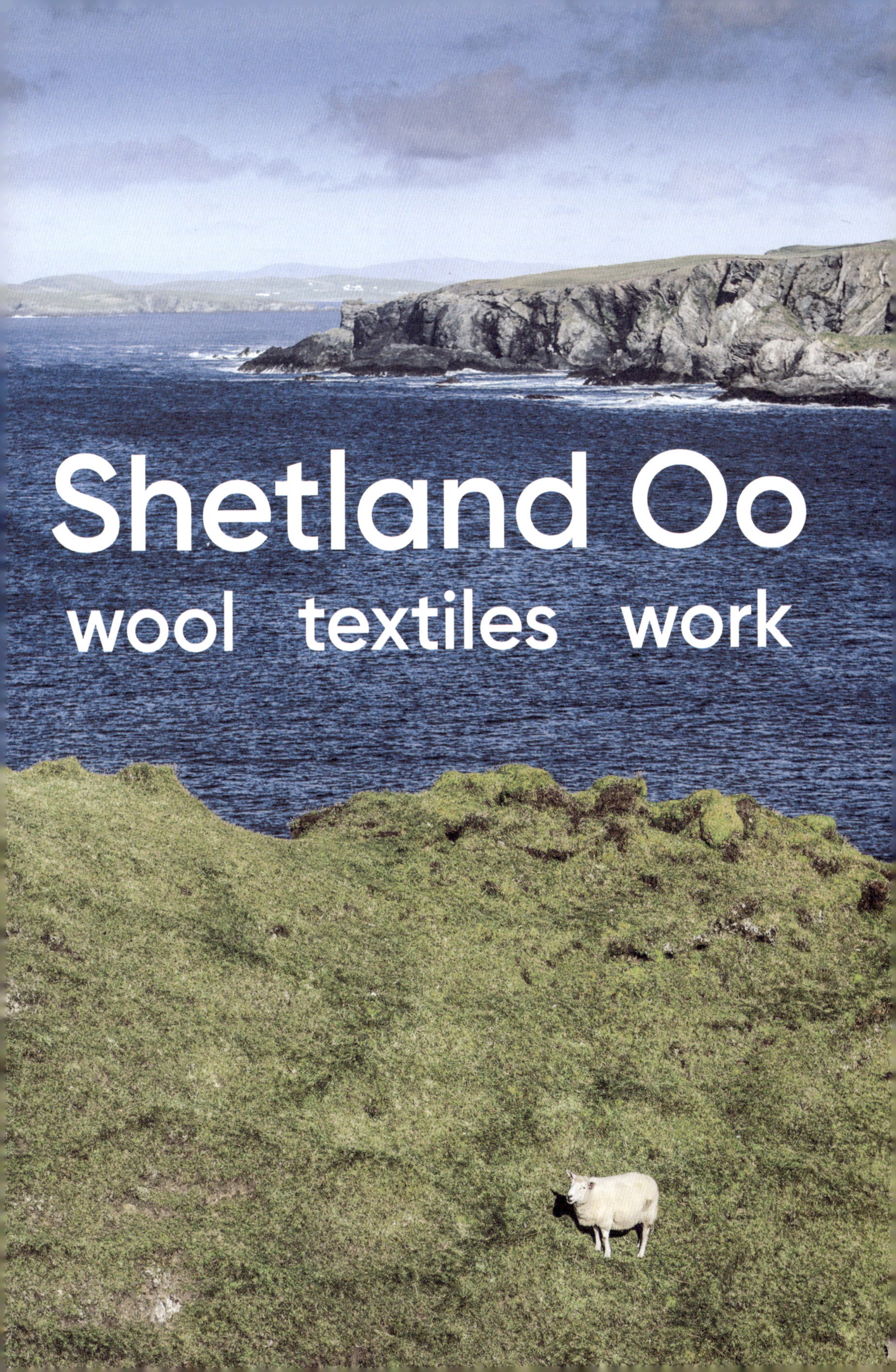

# Shetland Oo

## wool textiles work

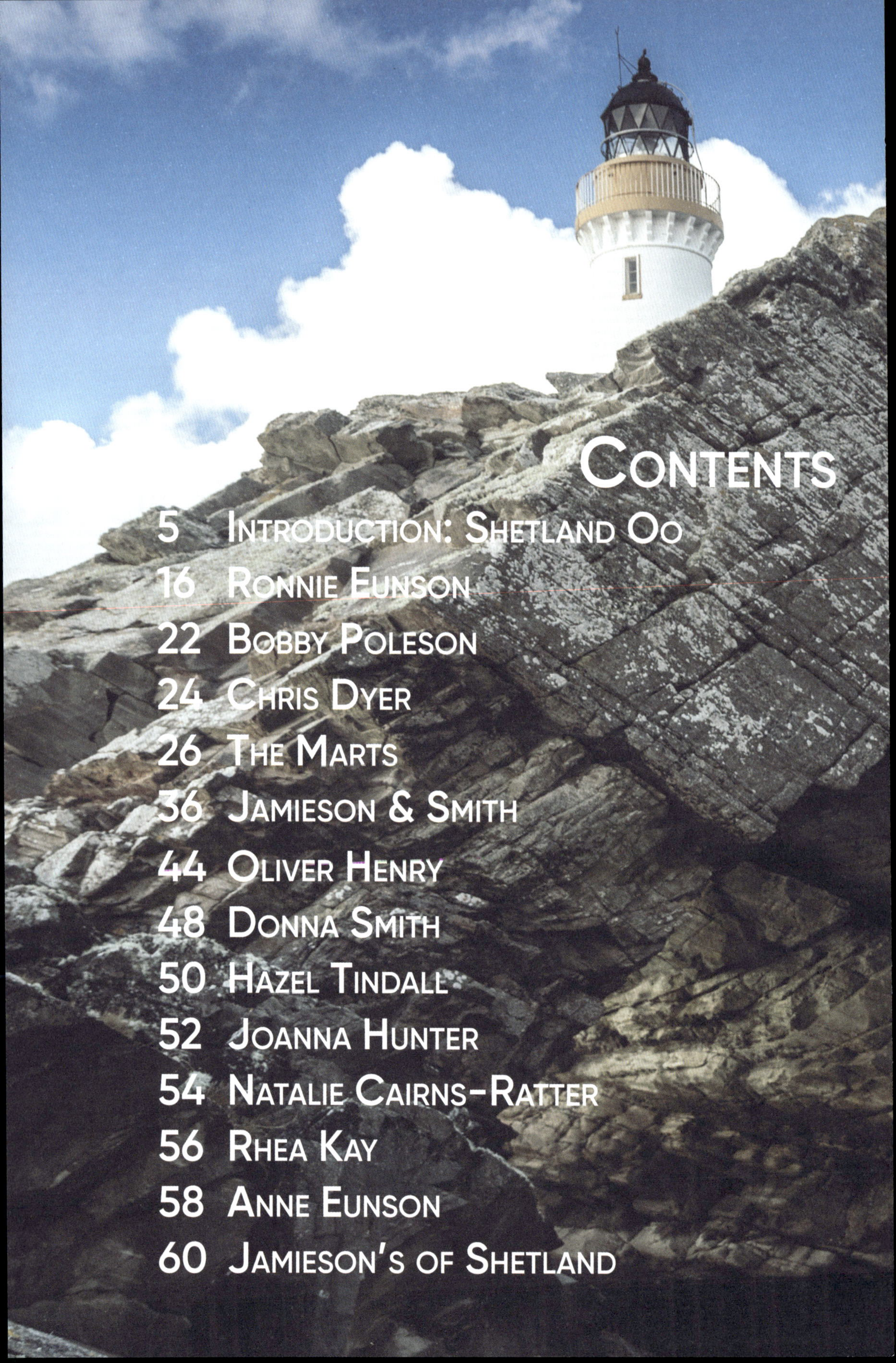

# Contents

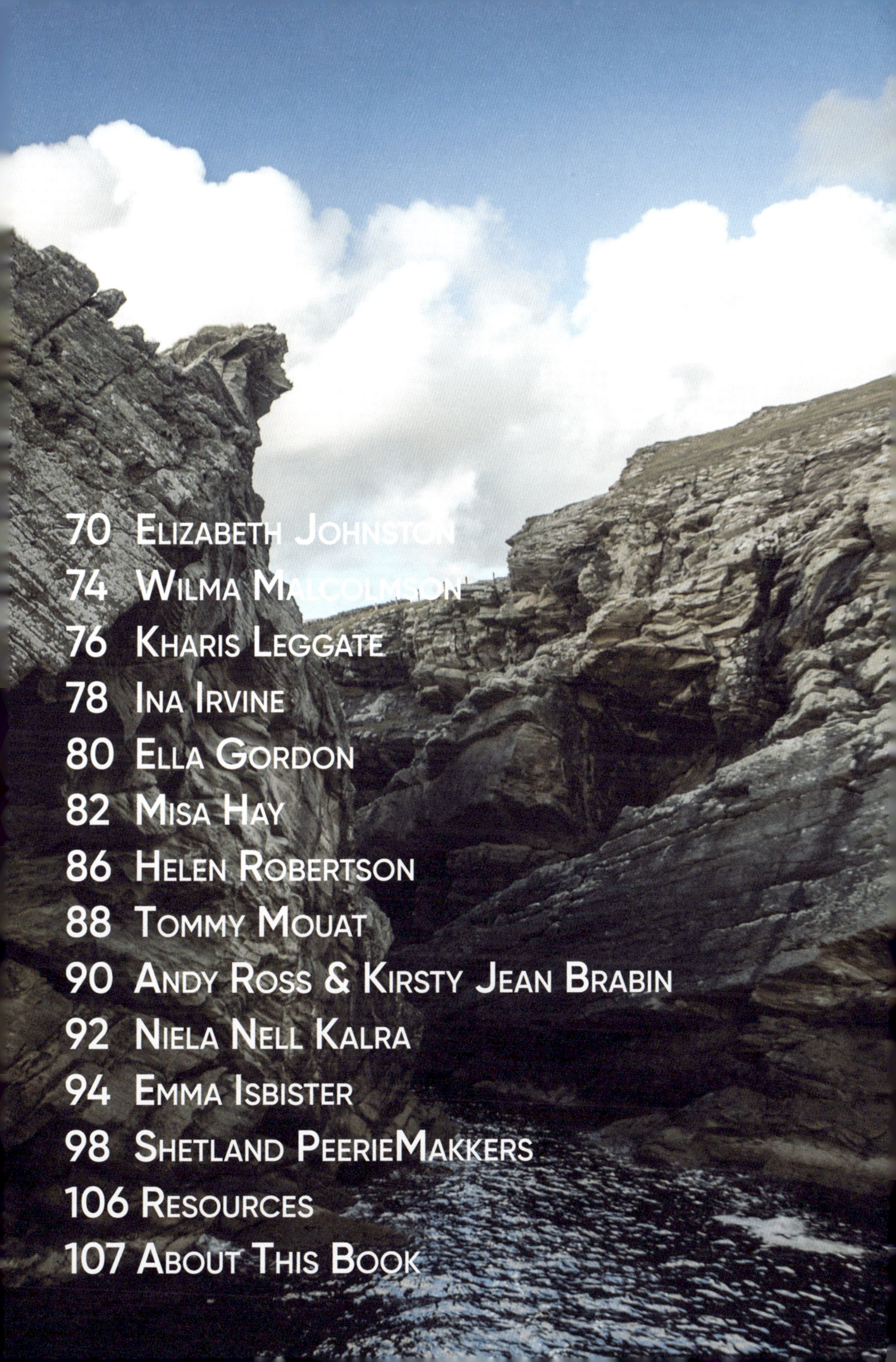

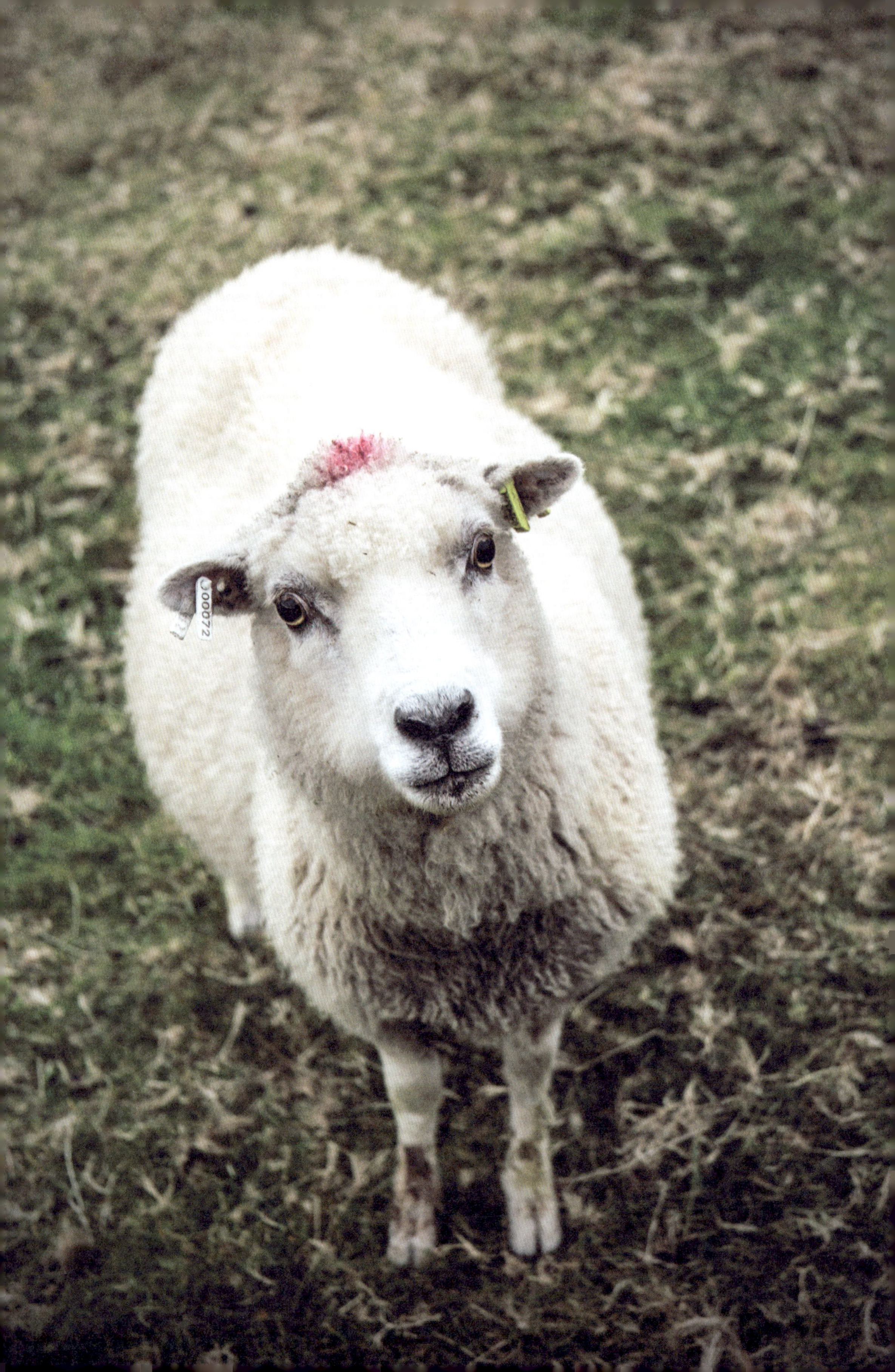

# Shetland Oo

## A Brief History of Work with Wool

In Shetland, wool has a very important and highly distinctive story. Nowhere else in Britain, and few places in the world, has wool—and the hard work that it involves—played such a significant continuous role for the life of a landscape, and the people that inhabit it, from prehistory to the present day. Wool once served as a form of currency, provides warmth, makes work, and has always supported an impressive range of Shetland professions and practices from croft to creative enterprise. Hardy, colourful, characterful sheep have lived alongside the islands' inhabitants for millennia—and, through the skilled labour of the hands of Shetland's craftswomen and men, their fleeces have been transformed through the centuries into countless things both beautiful and useful. As the raw material of fine textiles that are rightly the focus of world-wide renown, wool (or in Shetlandic, oo) is the very fibre of Shetland's being.

Sheep have existed in Shetland since the Neolithic period. The archaeological evidence of Bronze and Iron-Age finds—such as textile tools like loom weights and spindle whorls—suggests the multiple uses Shetland's early inhabitants found for processed wool. From the ninth century, Scandinavian settlers radically transformed many aspects of island life, possibly introducing sheep stock with different fibre characteristics, and new techniques of spinning yarn and cloth production, such as tablet weaving. In Norn—the language spoken in Orkney and Shetland prior to the transfer of the Northern Isles from Norway

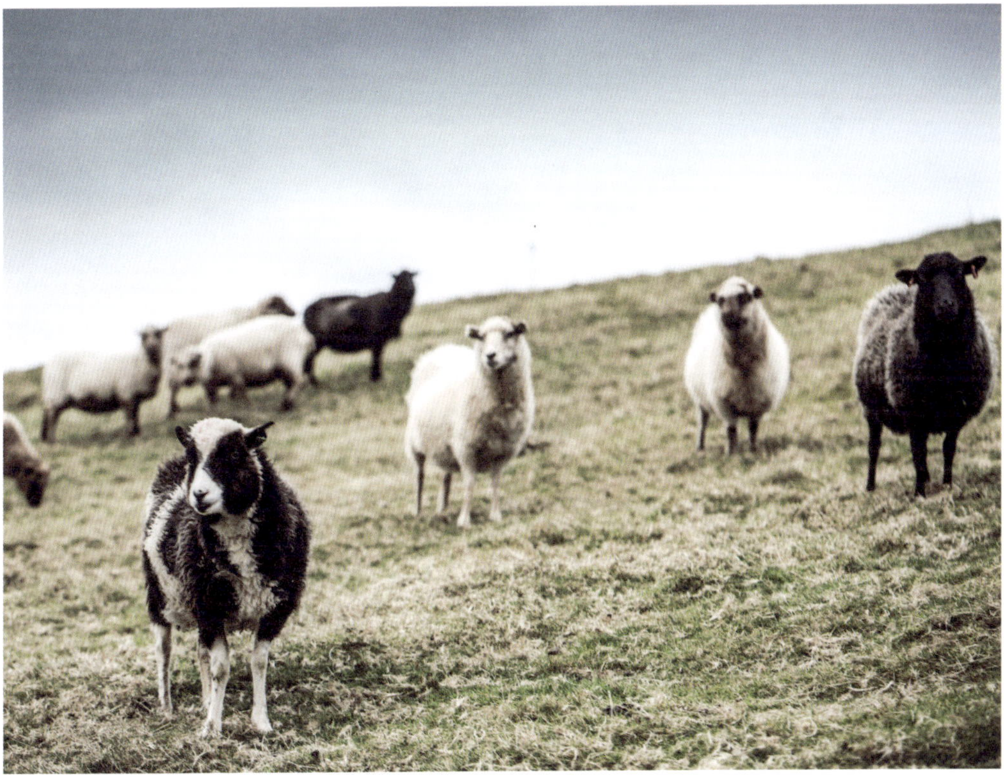

to Scotland in 1469—over fifty distinct terms are recorded in reference to fleece shades and markings. Part of the defining language of the island landscape, sheep and wool have long featured centrally in Shetland life and culture. In the words of Ronnie Eunson: "the native Shetland sheep breed has a wide genetic base adapted to Shetland's climate, the vegetation, and the challenges of living on a rock in an ever heaving ocean. This adaptation has taken at least 5000 years and could never be created simply by humans. Their ability to produce healthy meat and exciting wool amidst the many challenges of this environment makes them one of the world's pre-eminent breeds of domestic livestock. They deserve our total respect."

## A Fine Yarn

Over the centuries, Shetlanders have produced many different kinds of woollen textiles for many different purposes. From the earliest times, the keepers of sheep in Shetland have continually improved and changed the nature and character of the wool their animals produce to best suit the purpose for which their fleeces were intended. Until the sixteenth century, wool was primarily used for weaving, and what was woven in Shetland was wadmal: a naturally coloured textile ubiquitously used to fashion garments for ordinary folk around the North Atlantic region. To create wadmal, Shetland women spun yarn by hand before using warp-weighted looms to produce cloth which they fulled at one of the many natural rocky basins around the islands' shores. Wadmal wasn't just cloth but cash or specie: the medium through which Shetland's tenant population were compelled to pay rent or taxes to their landlords. As the cloth declined in popularity (and for the lairds became less profitable) so hand knitting began to replace weaving as a craft through which Shetland women supported home and family. For hand-

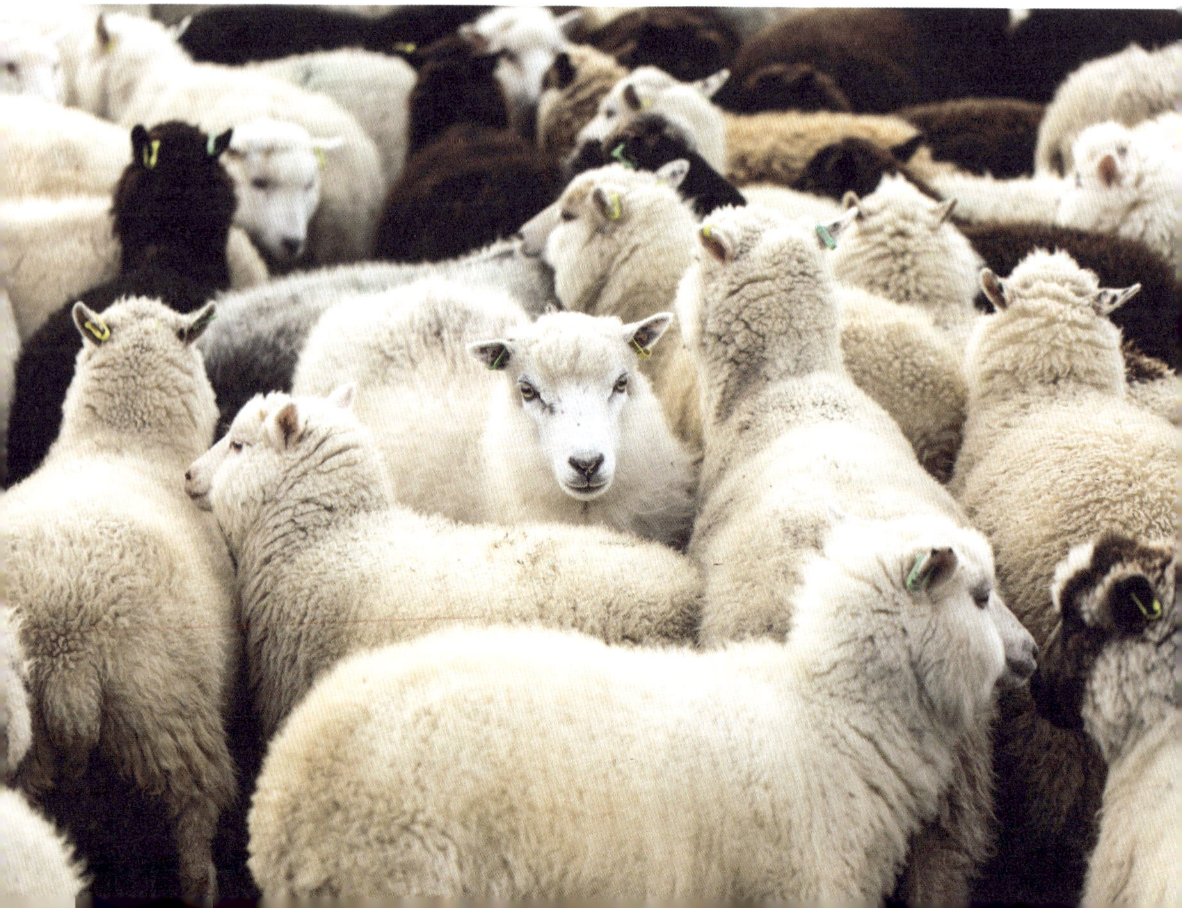

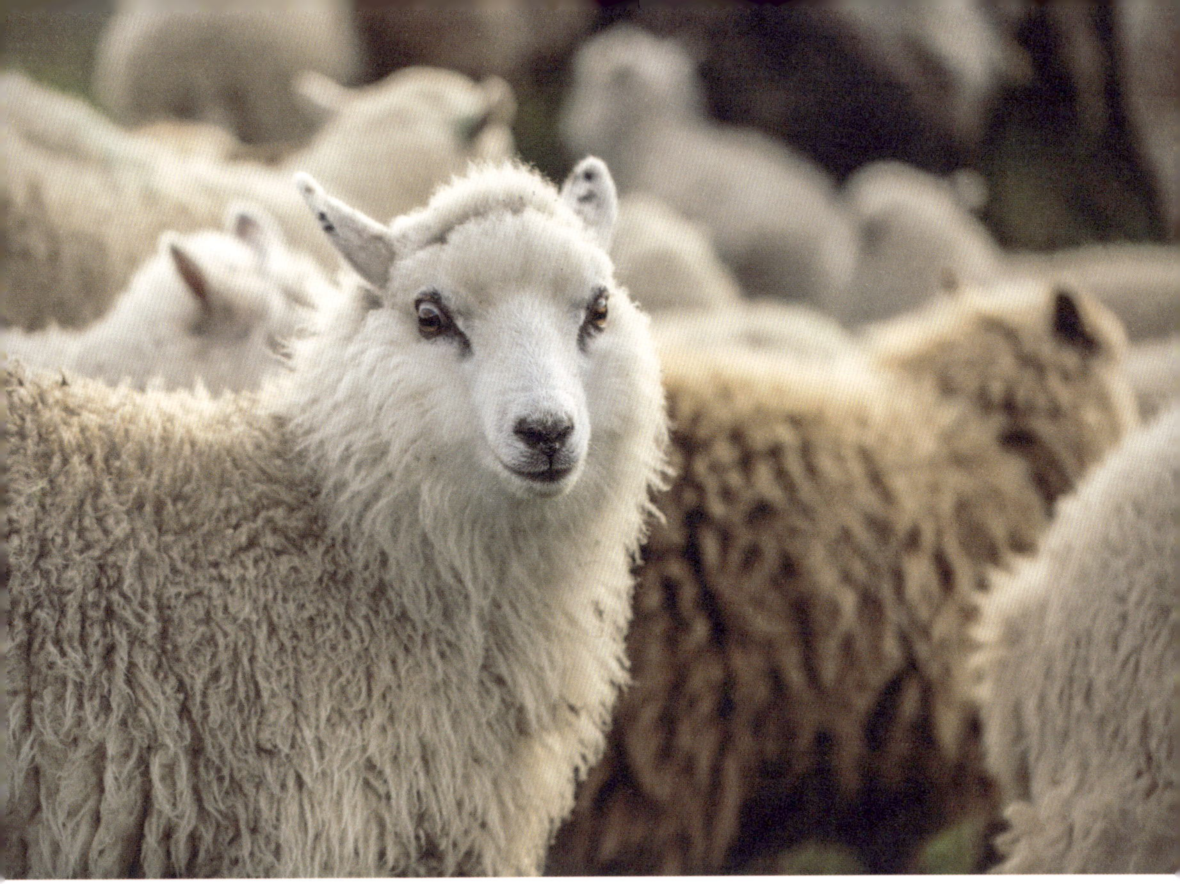

knitted toories (hats), gloves and stockings, a yarn of different quality was required, and Shetland knitters began to choose softer fleeces of a finer quality to spin, strategically breeding stock capable of producing fibre with these characteristics. Shetland knitters traded their wares at the Lerwick quayside with Dutch and German merchants, and, by the early 1700s, knitted items were routinely used, as wadmal had once been, in lieu of rental payment. Lairds and merchants cashed in on the new trade as thousands upon thousands of pairs of hand-knitted stockings left Shetland to warm feet in Scotland, England, Europe and the American colonies. Knitting made Shetland's industrious craftswomen even more productive. While wheel spinning and loom weaving were highly focused seated activities, knitting was eminently portable and could be accommodated between other tasks and on the move. Working as they walked between peat hill and lamb house, well and croft, knitting steadily through long winter evenings, creative eighteenth-century Shetlanders transformed the fibre their sheep produced into textiles of increasing fineness and complexity.

During the final decades of the eighteenth century, the fineness of Shetland's woollen textiles began to draw increasing external interest. Wars with the United States and France had eroded overseas exports of Shetland handknits, but the domestic market thrived, and agriculturalists were eager to develop British wool products that might rival those of the ubiquitous Spanish merino. "I have received the lock of Shetland wool," Joseph Banks wrote to John Sinclair in 1790, having been deeply impressed with a fine pair of hand-knit Shetland stockings in the possession of George III. "It is the softest I ever felt," he enthused, "and has long been known to be the best wool for hosiery." Through the activities of the Highland Society, and later the British Board of Agriculture (of which he became the first president), Sinclair and others sought to investigate, and attempted to standardise, what they referred to as "the real kindly breed" of Shetland sheep. This "kindly" fleece—which could be hand-spun to form a cobwebby yarn and knitted up into lace of breathtaking complexity and fineness—was distinct from the "coarse" yarn from which ordinary Shetland stockings were created (much to Sinclair's chagrin). In his distinction between "kindly" and "coarse," Sinclair was highlighting the fact that the composition of a Shetland fleece might vary mercurially between heterotype (hairy) fibres and soft, pure wool. The fact that these small, primitive eighteenth-century animals generally possessed far "kindlier" fleeces than those of their wirier-coated cousins around the North Atlantic region suggests the creative husbandry of several generations of Shetlanders in carefully selecting animals for the fineness of their wool. The Shetland Flock Book Society was formed in 1927 with the aim of preserving and promoting the "kindly" fleece in all its colourful diversity— together with the health and hardiness of the breed, a role which it continues to this day.

## Women's Work

As Lynn Abrams' important research has shown, nineteenth-century Shetland differed markedly from mainland Britain in the complex nature of the roles of the islands' women. The long-term effects of wars, migration and deaths at sea on the male population meant that by the middle of the century the islands had the highest female-to-male ratio of any region in northern Europe and an extraordinarily high proportion of female-headed households, often containing several generations. Married or unmarried, young or old, Shetland women worked the land, maintained crofts, crops and animals, and supported children and elderly relatives. Everyday life was economically precarious, and Shetland women found it necessary to be continually productive. Over the latter half of the nineteenth century, more than two-thirds of Shetland women are estimated to have been involved in the wool and hosiery industries—in other words, in knitting. On the one hand, the work of wool brought Shetland women an important and unusual degree of collective autonomy: the fleeces they spun into yarn were often clipped from their own sheep, and they chose what that yarn became. Stockings and plain haps might be fitted in around other household chores and worked up very quickly, or if a member of the household had the skill, exceptionally fine work, such as the lace shawls then in vogue, could command a high return, especially if working to commission. But though Shetland knitters were essentially independent producers who retained control over the work of their hands and what those hands created, their economic position was extremely insecure. Bound by an exploitative system of barter-truck through which finished goods were swapped for groceries and store-specific credit notes rather than cash, and operating in a saturated market where the majority of knitted goods were produced for exactly the same reasons of basic economic need, nineteenth-century Shetland knitters were at the raw mercy of the Lerwick merchants with whom they exchanged their wares.

Despite the findings of the 1872 truck commission, the perfidious system continued well into the twentieth century. But one interesting effect of the First and Second World Wars in Shetland was the erosion of the power of the merchants: new mainland connections and servicemen happy to pay for knitwear with ready cash meant that knitters might deal personally with customers, respond directly to market demand (such as the modernist trend for Fairisle garments) and work on well-paid independent commission. By the 1950s, the economy of knitting in Shetland

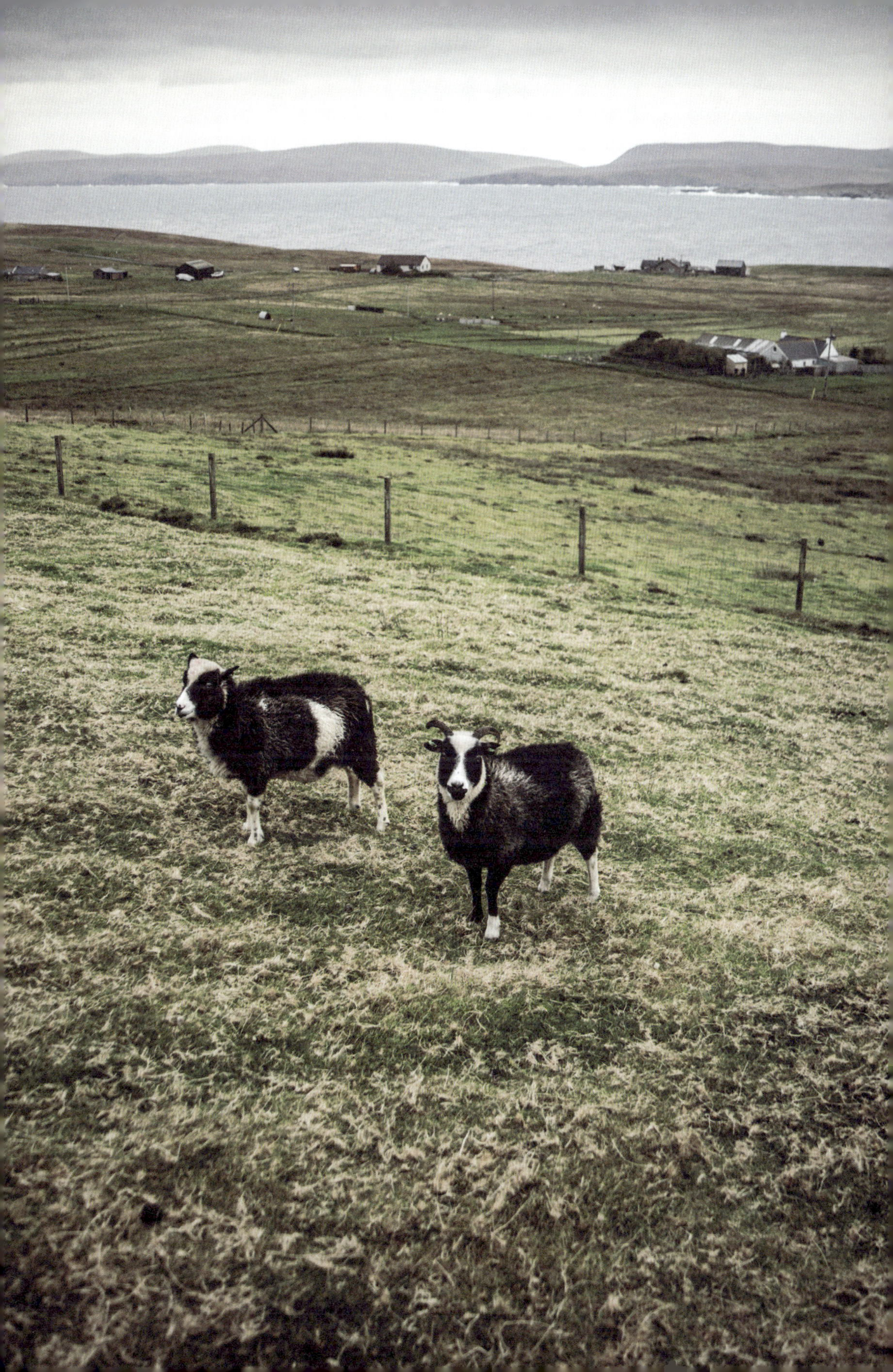

had radically changed: the market for fine-lace shawls and haps had fallen while that for Fairisle items rose, and the commercial spinning and dyeing of wool by mainland mills, such as Hunters of Brora, heralded a decline in the use of natural fleece shades and the production of fine hand-spun yarn. The structure of the work had altered too. New knitwear companies burgeoned, for whom Shetlanders acted as outworkers, acquiring knitting machines to produce garments swiftly at home. Where once one woman might have experienced all the stages of processing wool from fleece to finished garment, now there was a much greater division of labour, as both male and female knitters specialised in a single task, such as machine-producing jumper sleeves and bodies, hand-knitting Fairisle yokes or finishing cardigan ribs and cuffs.

## A Changing Landscape

Important changes were afoot in the work of raw wool as well. In 1950, Shetland wool producers voted to secede from the newly formed British Wool Marketing Board in order to retain maximum control over the islands' wool clip and this arrangement remains in place today. With Cheviots, Suffolks, and crosses of various kinds all playing their vital role in Shetland sheep farming alongside the more familiar native breed, the annual wool clip is now highly varied and various. In mainland Britain, fleeces of lower grades fetch little to nothing at auction, and are frequently destroyed or burnt. But, because of the work of local companies such as wool brokers Jamieson & Smith, lower-grade fleeces produced in Shetland can be transformed into woven products, carpets, bedding and home furnishings, with the higher grades reserved for the production of the fine hand-knitting yarns for which Shetland is still renowned. Effectively maintaining a variety of sheep on the hill, and allowing crofters to retain a high degree

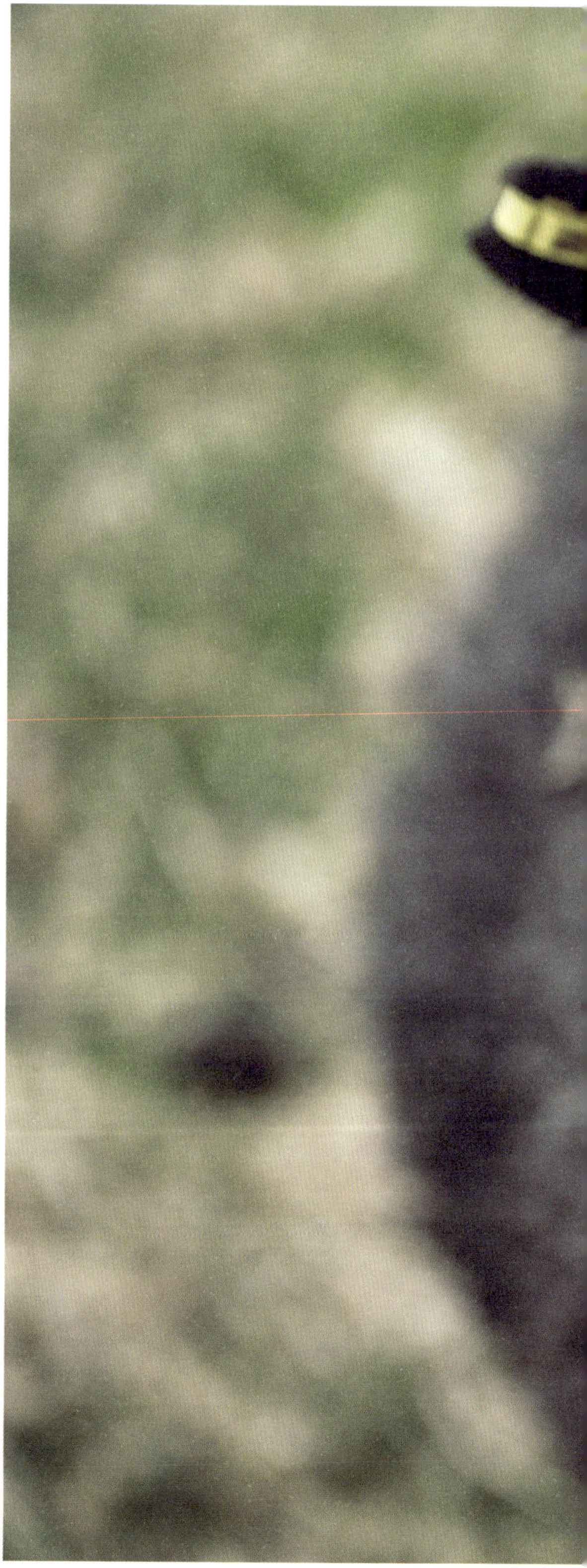

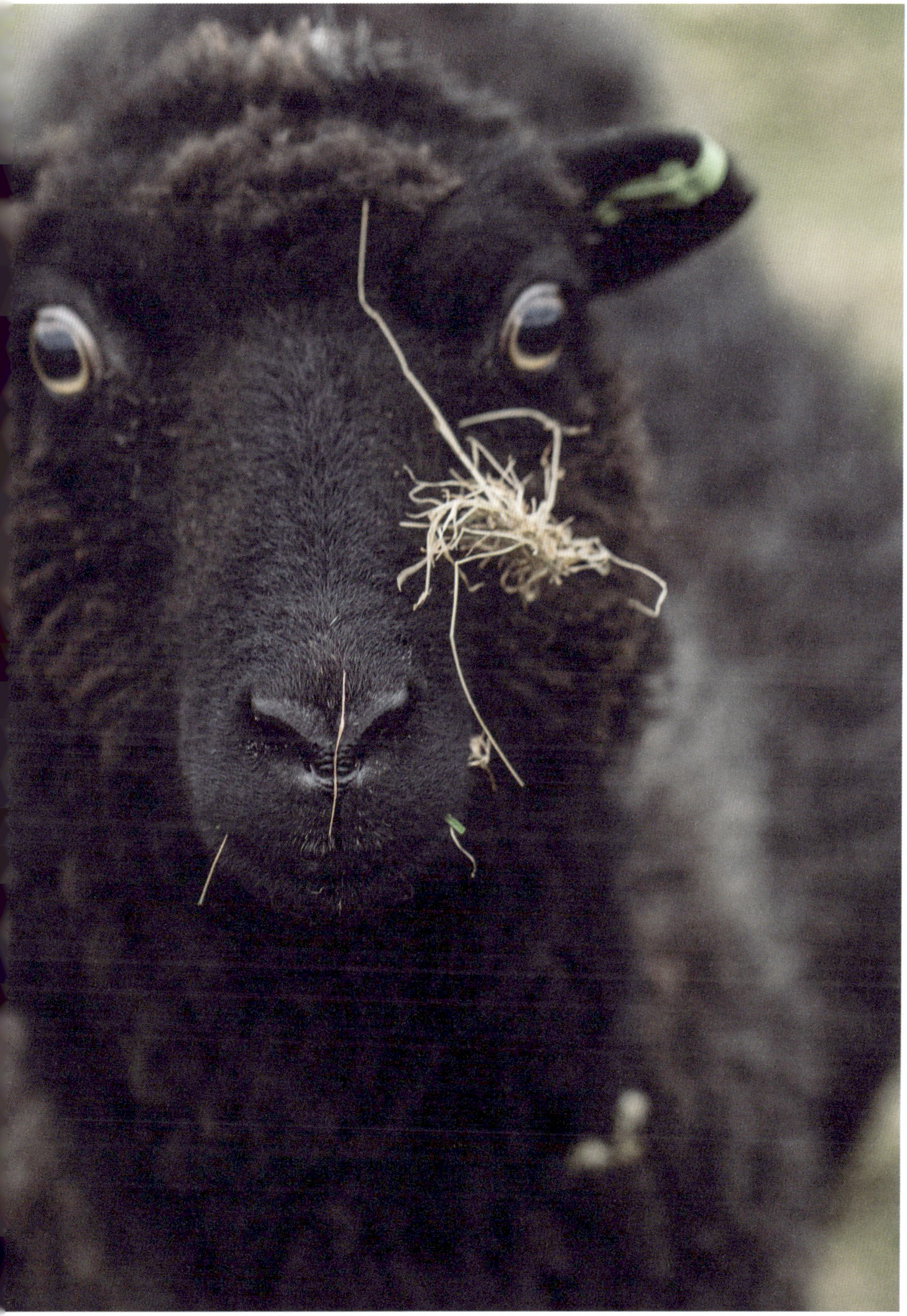

of autonomy in relation to their labour and economic interests, one might argue that this direct connection between wool producer and wool broker is far fairer than current relationships that exist between the BWMB and many small wool producers in mainland Britain. The vertical operation of Jamieson's Shetland mill, and the involvement of Shetland Organics at every stage of their wool's progress from fleece to finished skein, means that much of the work of processing and selling wool is still performed by those living in the islands, and that that work greatly benefits the local economy. Shetland's unique arrangement for wool's sale and processing also means that the exceptionally skilled and important work of fleece sorting and grading rightly commands enormous local respect. Not for nothing is Jamieson & Smith's chief wool man, Oliver Henry, fondly known as ooey (woolly) Ollie.

Following the discovery of North Sea oil, and the development of the new pipeline terminal at Sullom Voe in the mid-1970s, Shetland's cultural landscape was transformed. By then, Shetland textiles were associated by many of those who worked in the industry with a particular kind of drudgery, as skilled craftswomen like Hazel Tindall and Elizabeth Johnston found themselves compelled to work with limited palettes, reproduce standardised patterns, and knit uninspiring designs rather than follow their own creative paths. Many Shetland women stopped knitting entirely when they discovered new employment opportunities and, with them, greater economic independence. Meanwhile, in a fashionable world increasingly dominated by neon-bright acrylics, chunky knits and fancy yarns, the more traditional markets for Shetland wool came increasingly under threat. It was in this context that the Shetland Handknitting Trades Association was developed, with the aim of promoting and protecting the skilled crafts that had traditionally supported the Shetland wool industry. The SHTA played a vital role in assisting creative Shetland entrepreneurs like Wilma Malcolmson to establish thriving knitwear businesses in what might otherwise have seemed like difficult times, and disseminating international awareness of the unique nature of Shetland wool and knitwear design through trade shows and marketing campaigns. Organisations like the SHTA encapsulated the interesting spirit of the times: on the one hand, Shetland enthusiastically moved forward into a new more prosperous modernity, but on the other, it kept one eye on the past, developing a renewed appreciation of its unique cultural heritage and the vital role that wool continued to play in island life. Following Shetland's carefully negotiated financial compensation by the oil industry, new public bodies and resources were formed, such as Shetland Amenity Trust, whose work over the past three decades has proved vital in communicating the distinctive importance of Shetland's history and heritage, including that of wool. In 2007, the magnificent Shetland Museum and Archives opened at Hays Dock in Lerwick. In this beautiful airy building, researchers draw on impressive archival resources to develop a wide range of projects related to Shetland wool, while the world-class textile galleries, curated by Dr Carol Christiansen, tell the story of the difficult lives and extraordinary achievements of the many skilled folk who have worked with oo.

## The New Work of Wool

The past decade has seen renewed interest in both hand knitting and husbandry, and Shetland oo thrives in its new contemporary life. A popular textile degree at UHI / Shetland College has created a professional context and springboard for local design talent like Anne Eunson and Ella Gordon, while the phenomenally successful annual event of Shetland Wool

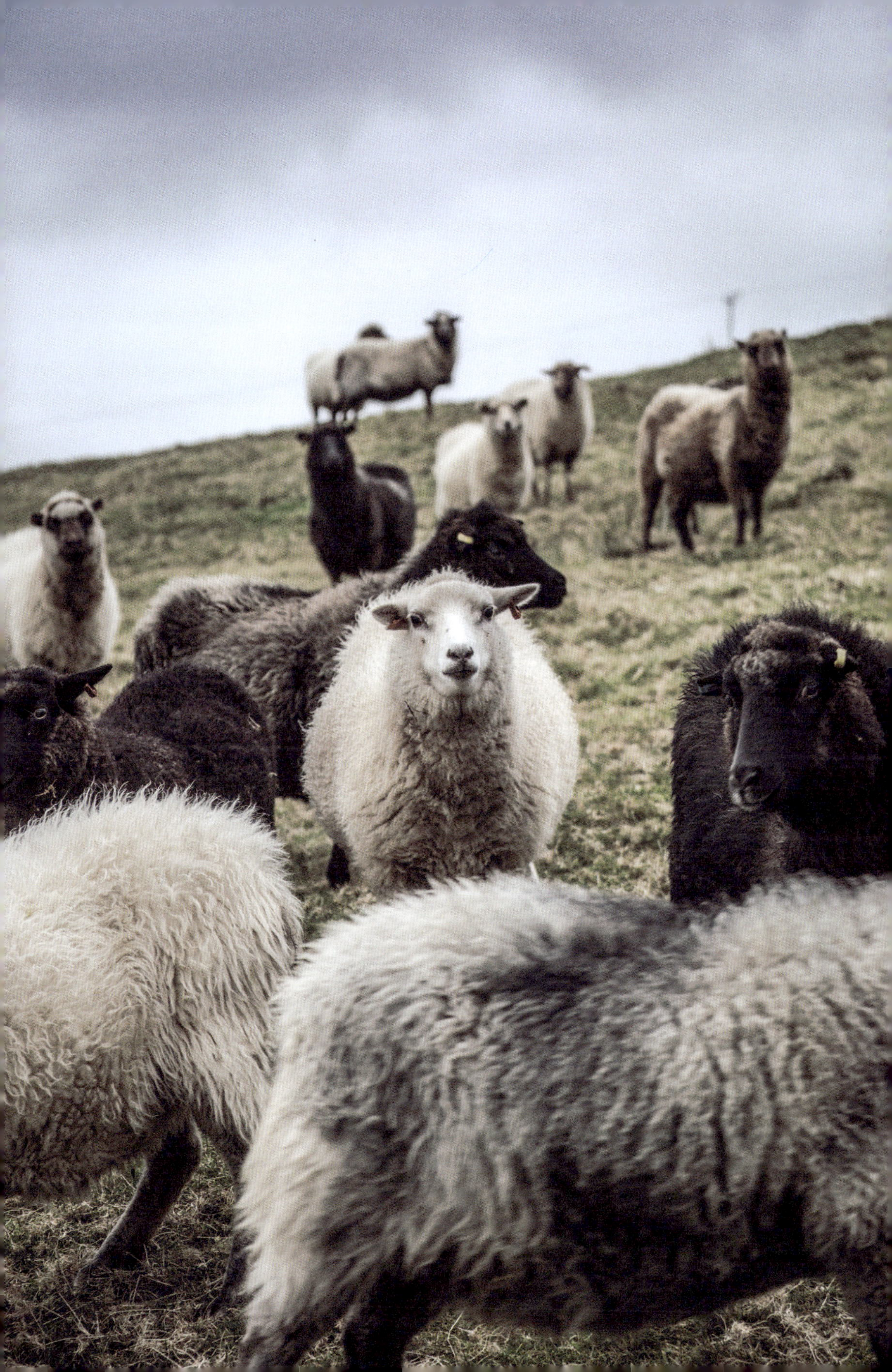

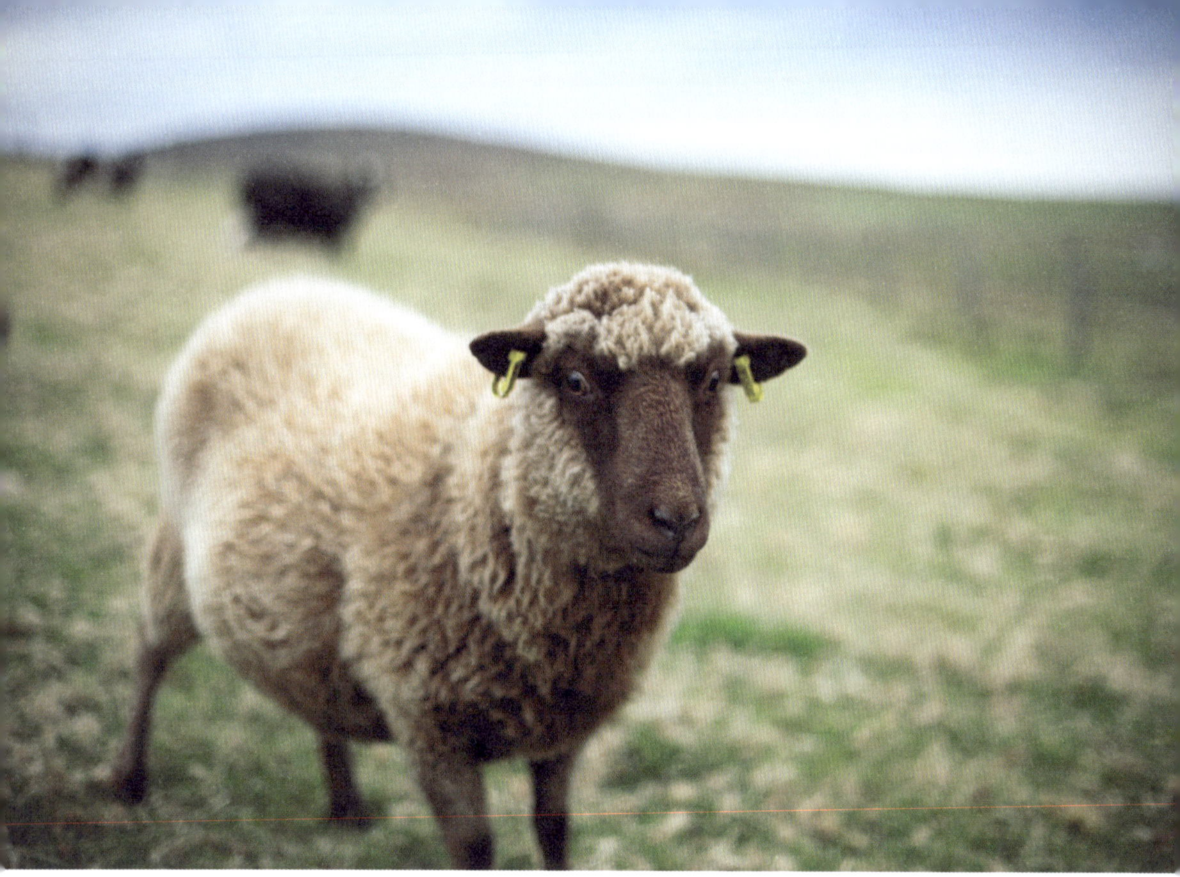

Week brings thousands of global visitors to the islands to soak up the woolly atmosphere and learn from the world's best knitters. Interest in Shetland wool is keen and widespread and textile tours and workshops organised by Andy Ross, Misa Hay, and the dynamic team of Gudrun Johnston and Mary-Jane Mucklestone sell out as quickly as they are advertised.

In many ways, the contemporary landscape of oo in Shetland is completely different, and yet some things don't change at all. "Wool and sheep are just a way of life here," says Joanna Hunter, knitwear designer and owner of successful Shetland brand, Ninian. Like her neighbour Donna Smith, Joanna combines her professional work in knitwear design and manufacturing with raising Shetland sheep on her croft on beautiful Burra Isle. As they have always done, the women and men of Shetland slot in husbandry around their many other jobs. When he isn't hard at work as an Amenity Trust archaeologist, Chris Dyer is building a new life for himself on his Bressay croft, raising traditionally coloured Shetland sheep (which can be seen on this and the preceding pages). In Northmavine, meanwhile, Bobby Poleson (who first formed an interest in stock improvement at the age of 8) now combines his full-time job as a marine engineer with breeding and judging champion Cheviots.

Shetland is a place where the business of wool and its cultural heritage are now mutually self-supporting. Local company, Jamieson's, provides yarn for the clubs in which young knitters learn their craft, Uradale Farm and Shetland Organics regularly sponsor the work of local designers, and Jamieson & Smith have collaborated with the Shetland Museum in the development of a beautiful new range of worsted-spun yarns. All around the islands, from Unst to Fairisle, a wide range of artisanal woolly businesses are flourishing, showcasing an impressive number of different crafts and skills, and headed up by a refreshingly diverse group of individuals (the majority of whom are women) of all ages. "It is a very inspiring place to be," says hand weaver Kharis Leggate, whose beautiful woollen textiles won a national award in 2015. In the increasingly global context of contemporary textiles, those who now work with wool in the islands possess a keen awareness of the important histories of the creative Shetlanders who went before them. "What inspires me most is my ancestors' perseverance," says textile student Rhea Kay: "they knitted endlessly, but still found time to be experimental and creative with the little that was available." "I try to express an appreciation of their struggle in my work," says innovative artist and designer Helen Robertson of her Shetland forebears, "and to tell their story to a wider audience." In a landscape that has been shaped for centuries by the difficult, fascinating and inspiring story of wool, Shetland designers, spinners, knitters, weavers, tanners and jewellers all variously describe the extraordinarily powerful effect of their environment on their creative psyche: for some the effect is direct, and for some almost subliminal. Even Niela Nell Kalra (whose contemporary textile work boldly defies received notions of tradition) has found a distinctly local sense of place creep into her recent knit collections. "Shetland just tends to get you in the end," she says.

*With thanks to Ronnie Eunson and Chris Dyer for allowing us to photograph their sheep.*

*"Shetland repays patience and those who take time to explore."*

*Andy Ross, GlobalYell*

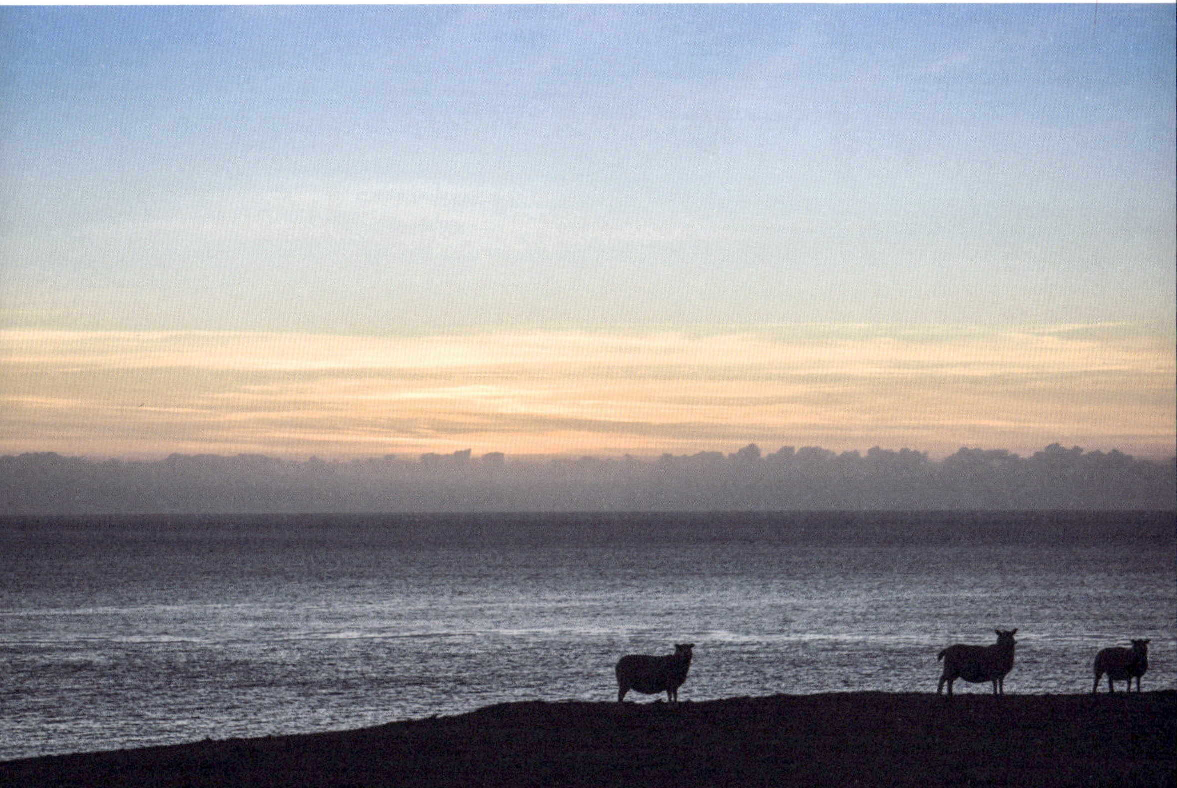

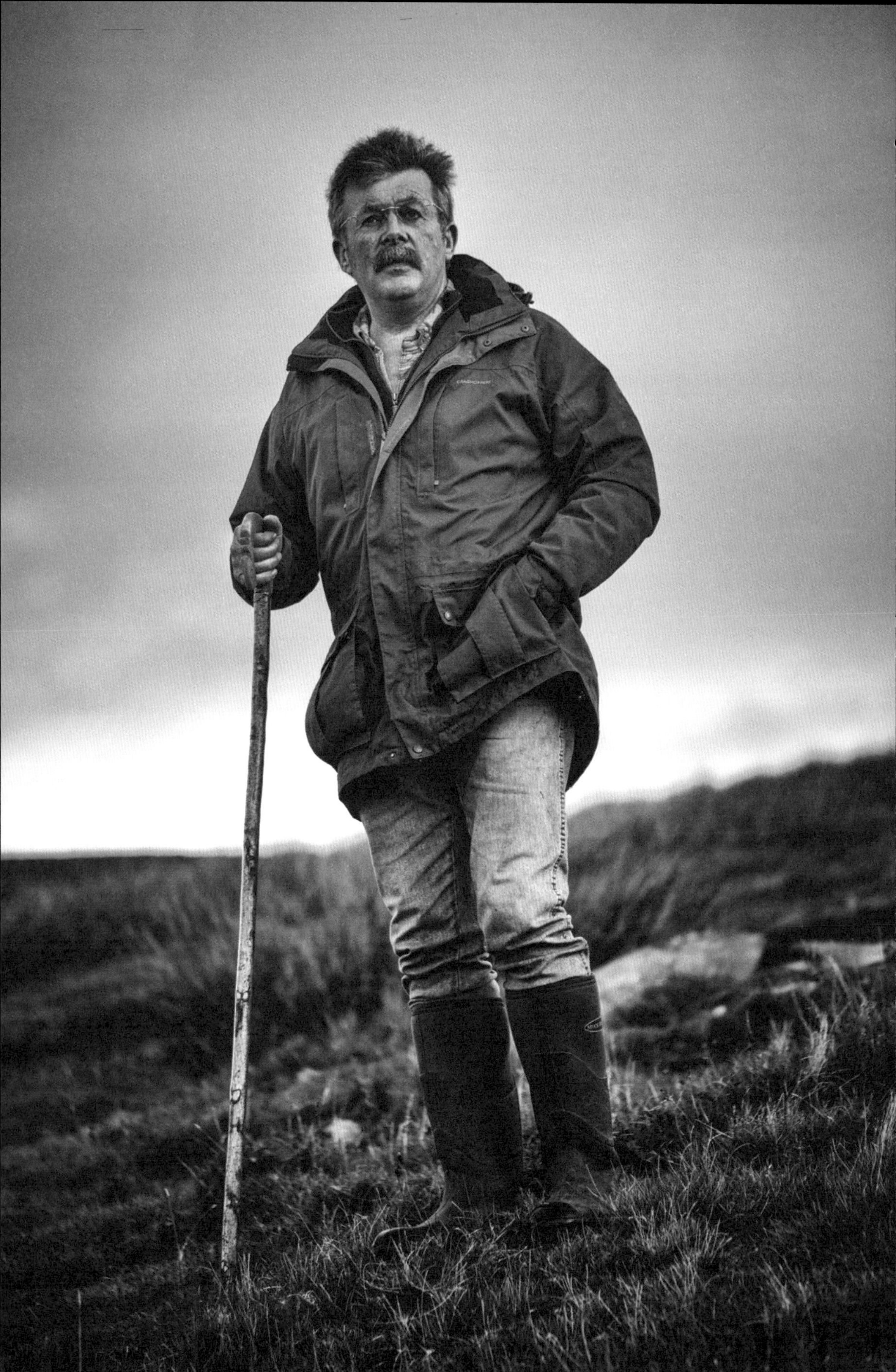

# Ronnie Eunson
## Uradale

Sustainability is at the heart of Ronnie Eunson's husbandry. Uradale crosses a typically dramatic Shetland landscape that rises from sea level to peat tops, and, sixteen years ago, Ronnie reflected on the scale and nature of farming to best suit the challenges of this environment. He halved the size of his flock, focused on native Shetland sheep rather than crosses, converted to organic farming, and diversified production to include wool as well as lamb. "Our sheep thrive here," Ronnie says, "their genetic base has adapted to attune to the island climate. They really are part of the landscape." Uradale's customers enjoy the flavour of organic lamb, and its yarns are developing a growing international fan-base too. Ronnie grades the wool right on the farm, while partner Sue draws inspiration for her palette from the wild plants in the valley below. "What we have here is as near to a holistic system as is possible in Shetland," Ronnie says. "You start with sustainable flocks, sustainable environments and accountable systems. Every step of the process enables traceability. Every step is organically certified, from scouring through spinning and dyeing. The world of fast fashion raises ethical questions every day. Why shouldn't customers demand this level of assurance?" Away down the hill, Ronnie surveys his wonderfully diverse flock, the expanse of peat and vegetation, the rocks, and then the sea. "It can be tough pursuing your own path, but I believe there is true merit in authenticity," he says. The living landscape of Uradale is certainly proof that is the case.

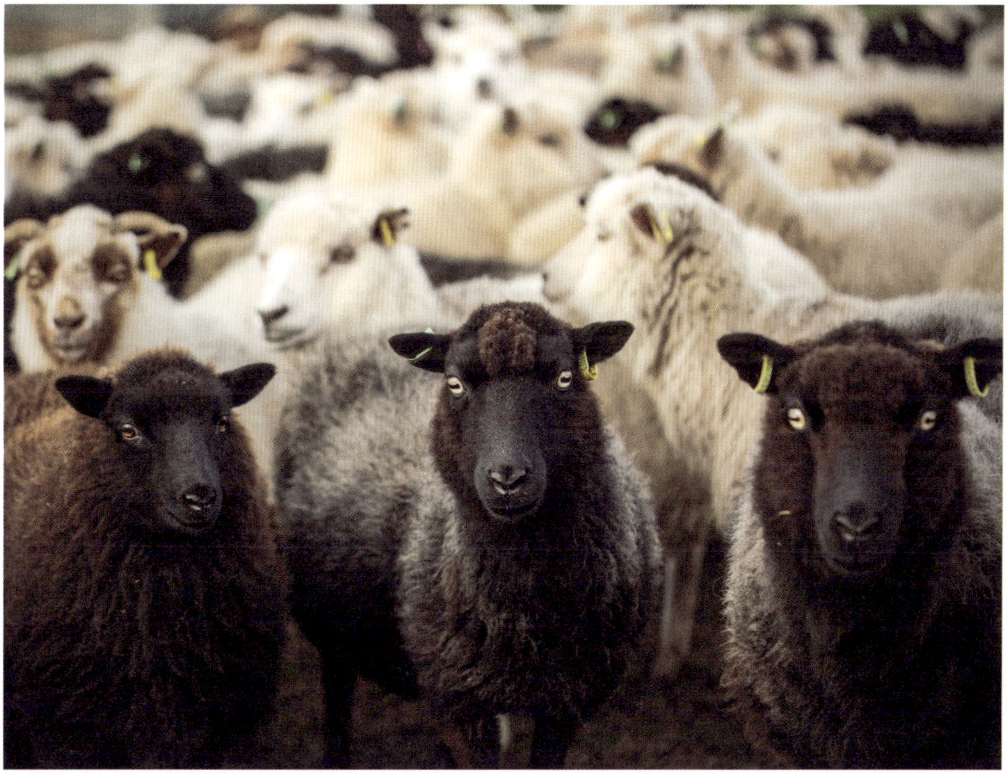

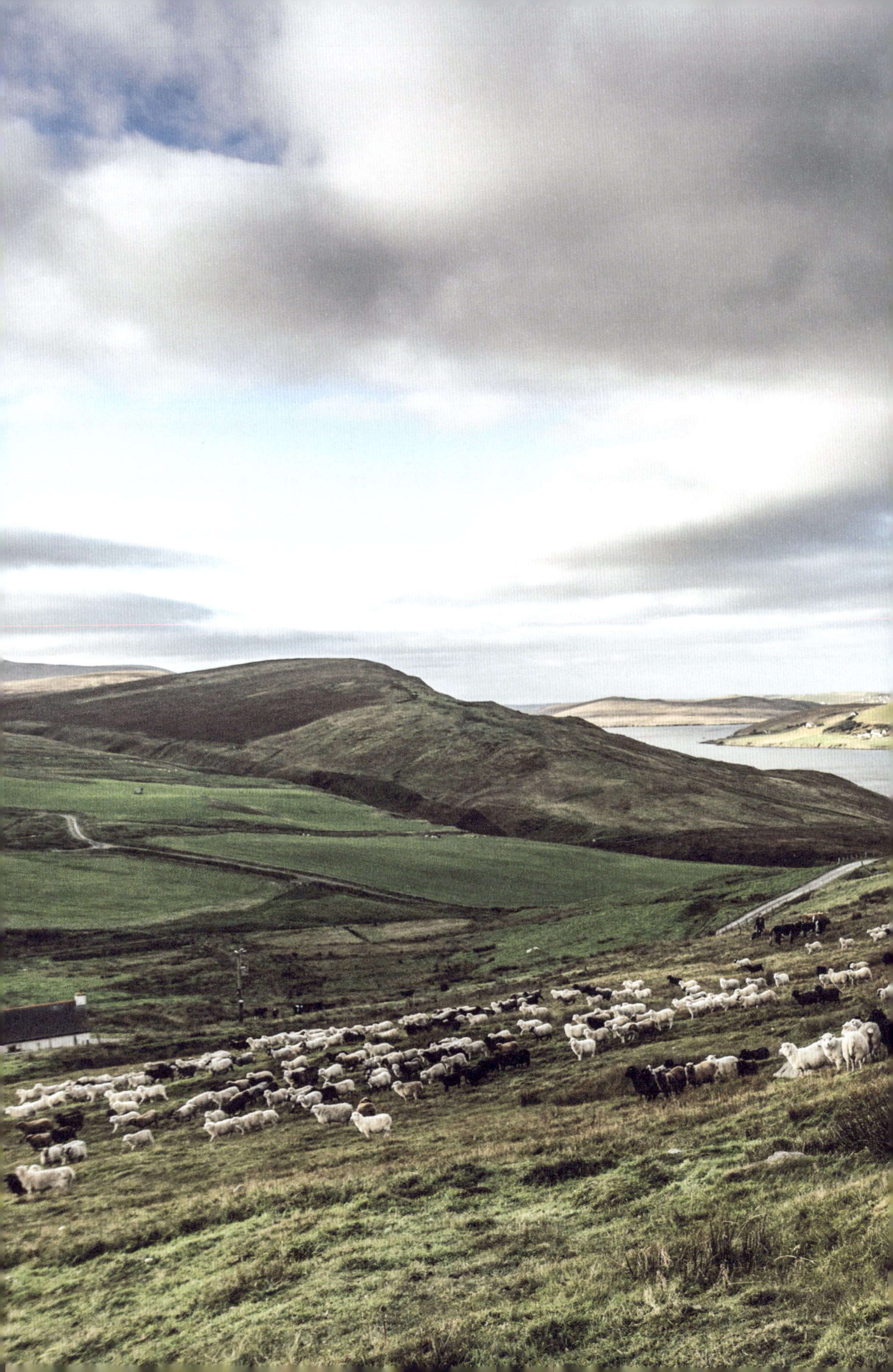

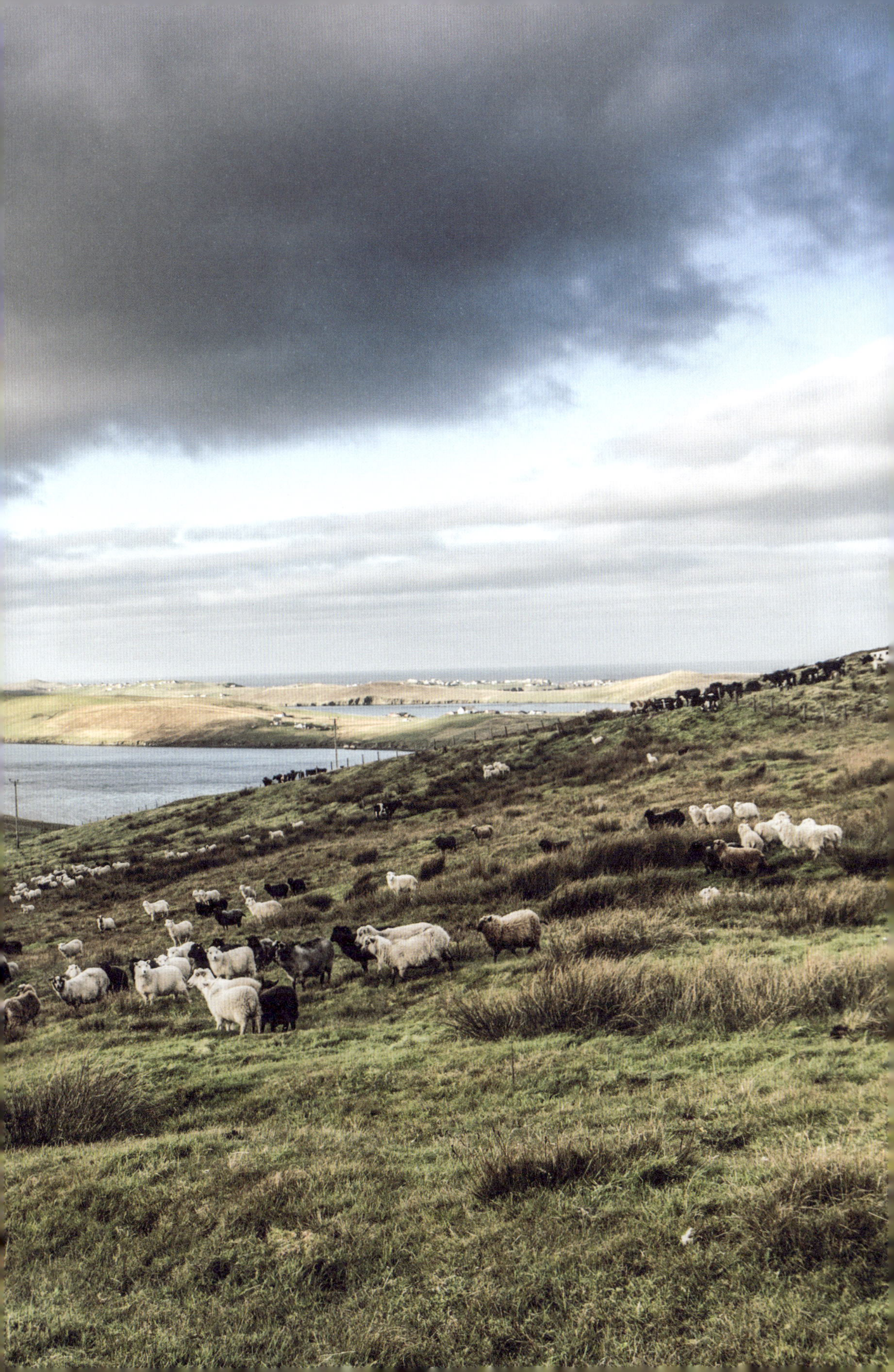

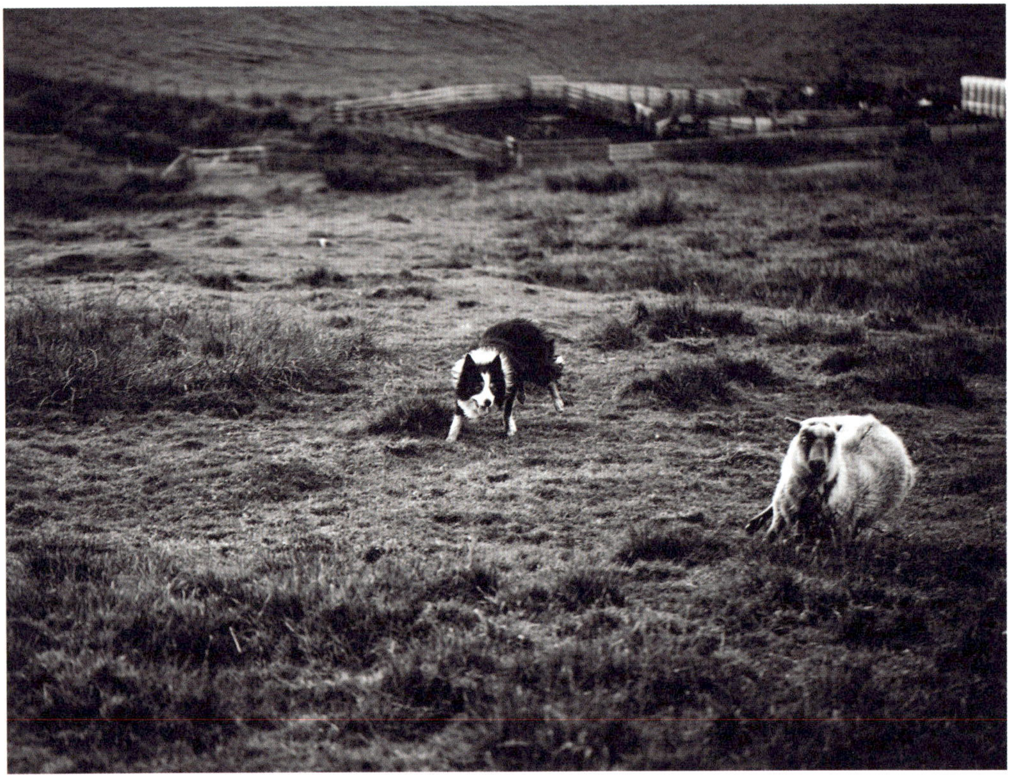

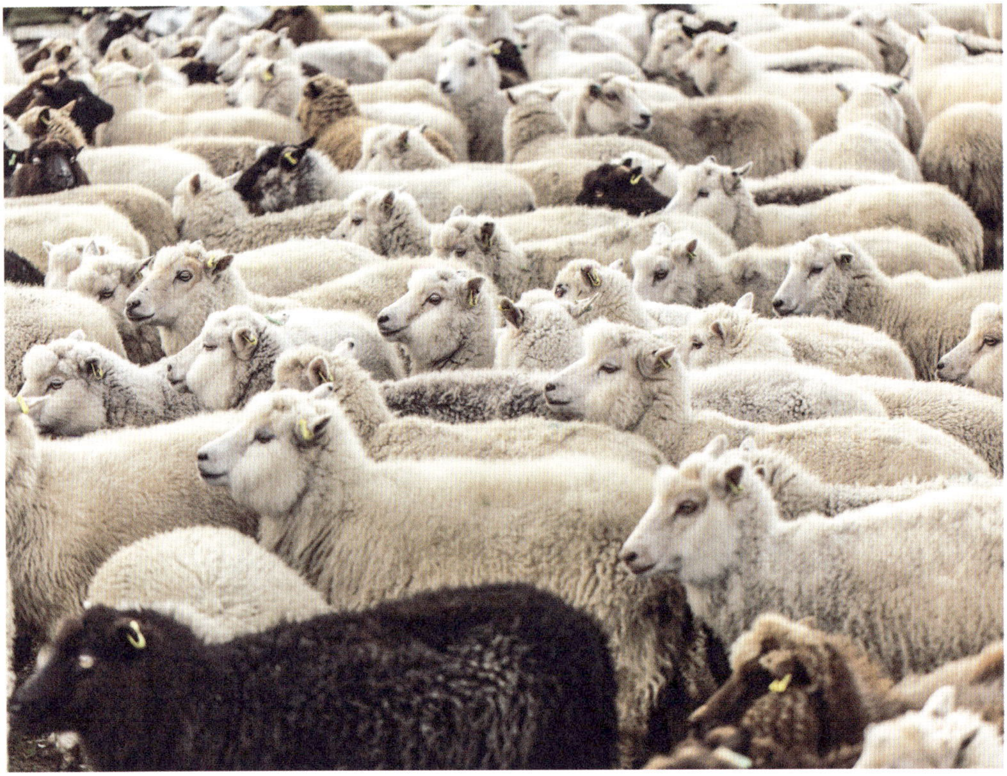

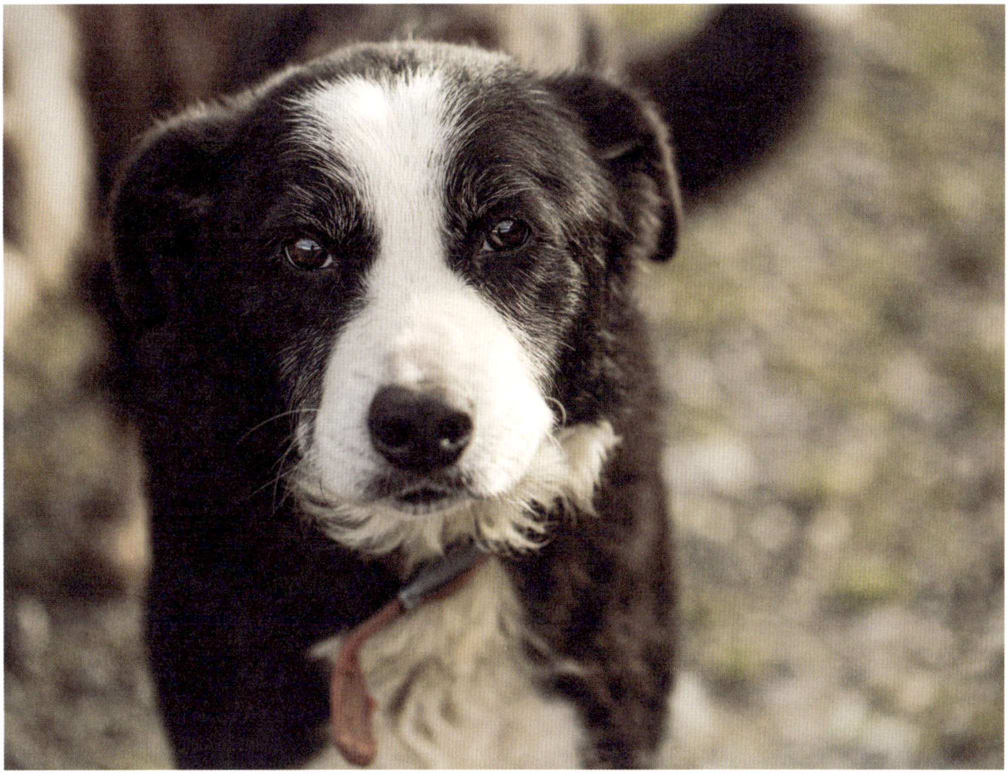

*"The adaptation of our native sheep to Shetland has taken at least 5000 years and could never be created simply by humans. Their ability to produce healthy meat and exciting wool amidst the many challenges of this environment makes them one of the world's pre-eminent breeds of domestic livestock. They deserve our total respect."*

*Ronnie Eunson*

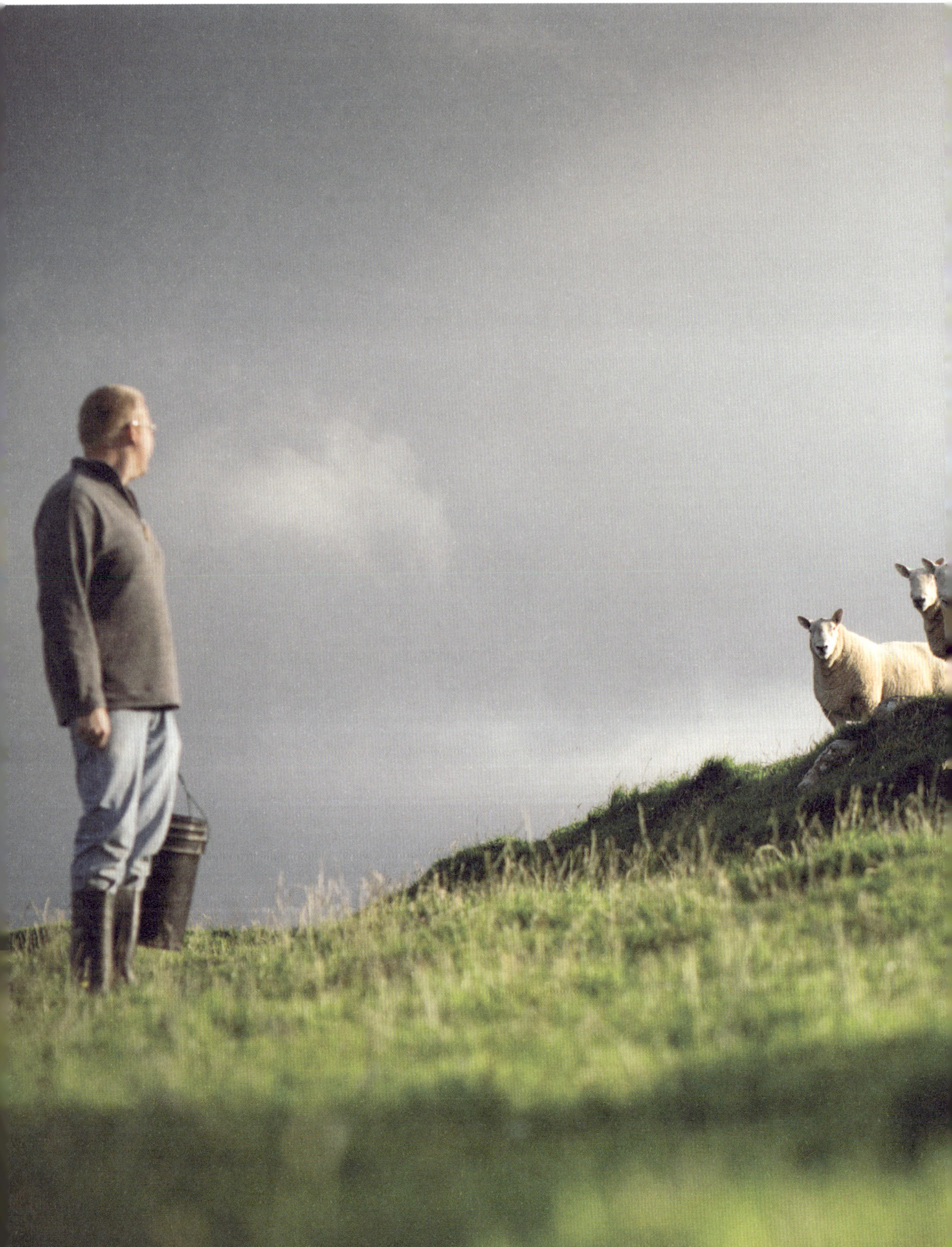

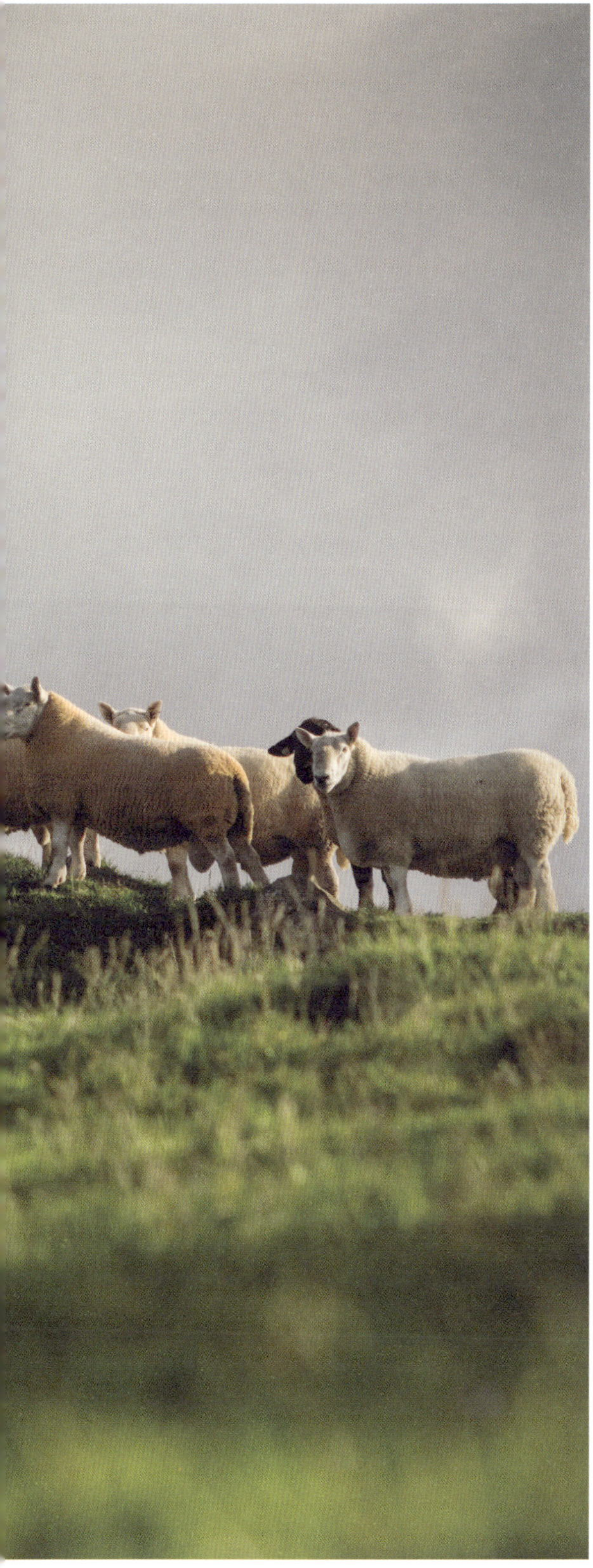

# Bobby Poleson
## Sheep Breeder

From the Blackfaces and Shetlands with whom he won his first prizes at the age of 14, Bobby Poleson has always been interested in showing and breeding fine sheep. Between the full-time demands of his work as a marine engineer, Bobby researches agricultural developments, improves his stock with care and rigour and spends every spare moment that he can with his animals. Now 27, Bobby has won Shetland-wide respect for his focused energy as a breeder of champion Cheviots. Sought after as a judge at any Shetland country show he does not enter, Bobby is pictured here with his rams (left), and gimmer (below) who won awards in 2016 as Shetland's champion and reserve champion Cheviots.

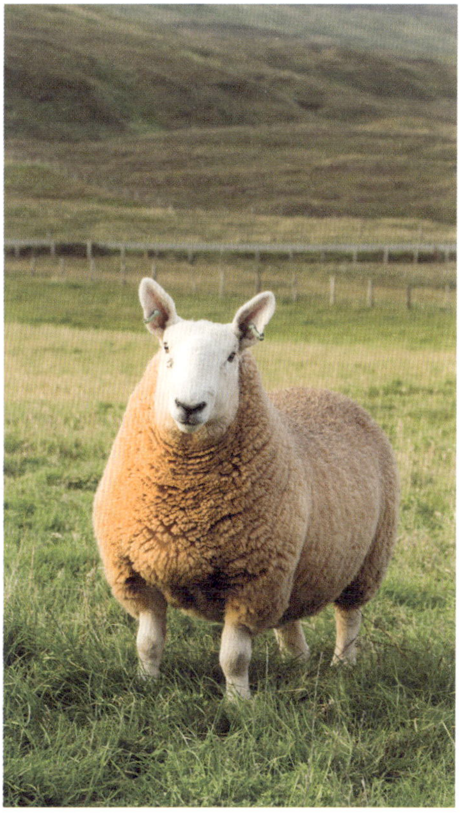

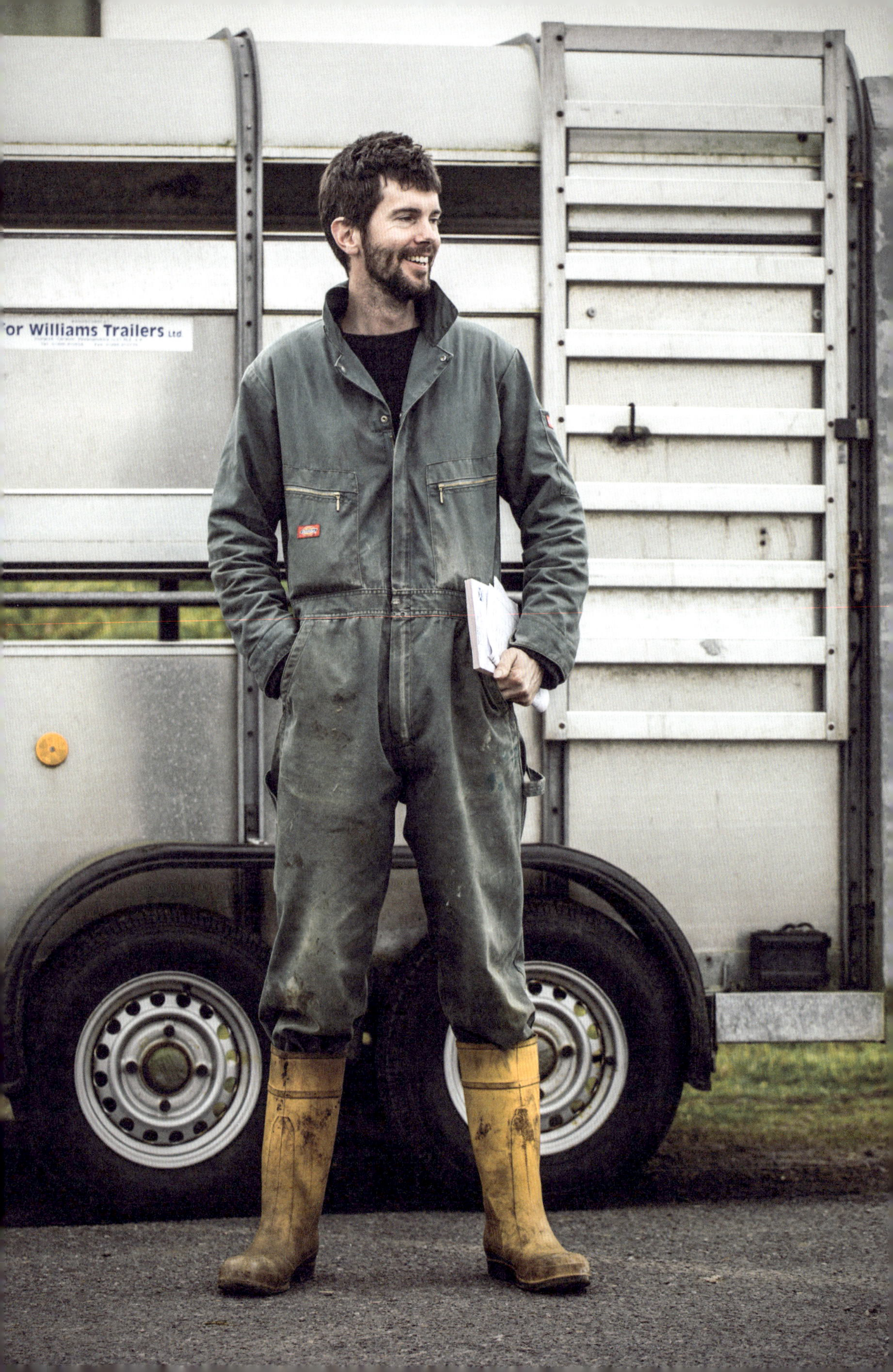
or Williams Trailers Ltd

# Chris Dyer
## Archaeologist & Crofter

Growing up in Hertfordshire, and studying in Yorkshire, Chris Dyer always felt drawn to animal husbandry, as well as to an outdoor life. Moving to Shetland, where he was appointed as an Amenity Trust archaeologist, Chris immediately appreciated how landscape, history and farming traditions were uniquely intertwined in the islands, from vernacular architecture to the environmental adaptations of the native sheep. Chris made his home on the island of Bressay, where he often worked at the Keldabister Farm during busy lambing periods, gratefully drawing on local expertise and receiving friendly advice and practical assistance about all matters sheep and croft. When the opportunity arose to purchase the croft at Garths of Kirkabister, Chris jumped at the chance. There, he and his wife, Afra, now run a small flock of Shetland sheep, together with pigs, turkeys, hens and a thriving vegetable garden. "It is incredibly rewarding for us to produce our own animals, knowing, on an almost individual basis, the quality of life that they enjoy," he says. Chris is a great admirer of the hardy character of Shetland sheep, and has a particular fondness for their diversity of shades and markings. "One winter's evening, shortly after we'd moved in, a neighbour arrived with a croft-warming present. I asked him and his wife inside, anticipating a bottle of something, but he said 'no, it's in the trailer.' There I found two fleckit Foula ewe lambs from Lynn Robertson (fleckit sheep are white with large spots and splodges of darker colours). To our delight, this spring both had fleckit lambs."

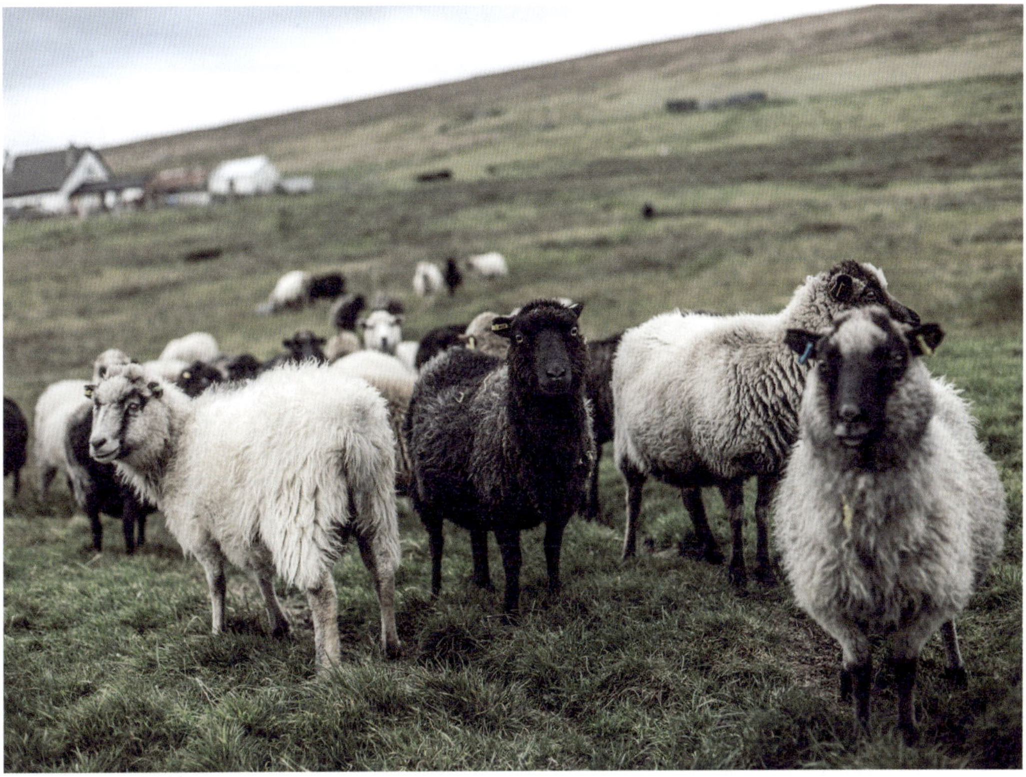

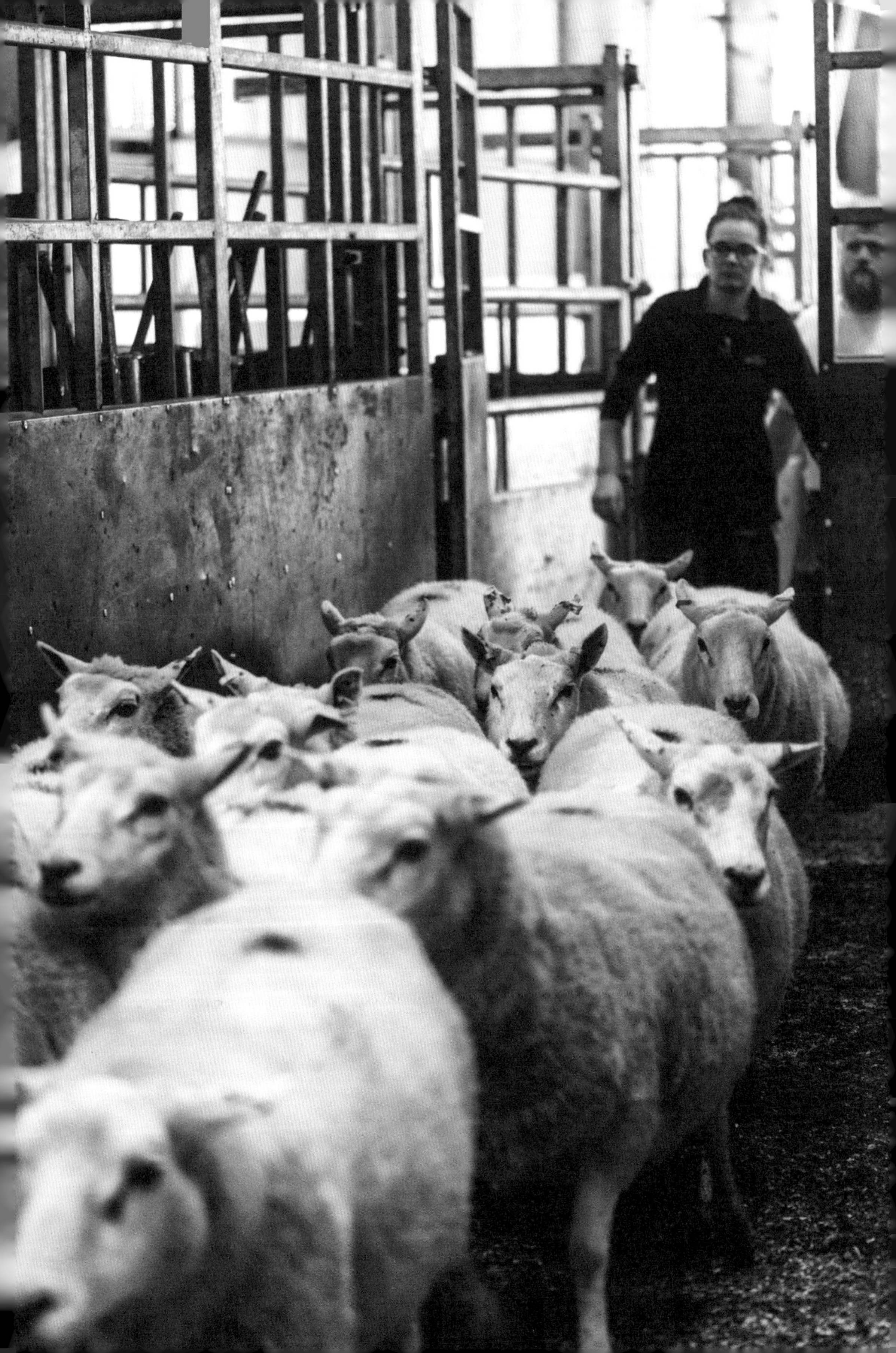

# The Marts

## Shetland Livestock Marketing Group

As the season of Shetland country shows and prizes draws to end in August, so that of livestock sales and marketing begins. Every autumn, the marts on Staney Hill spring to life, with the activity and noise of sheep and trailers, sellers and buyers. The voice of auctioneer, Rod Mackenzie rises above the excited hubbub, controlling the crowd's rising interest and keeping orderly business moving through a busy sales day which, on any single Saturday, might see more than 3000 animals exchanged. Gates clank open, sheep enter the ring, a lone escapee is caught and returned to its rightful pen. The ring bristles with atmosphere. Talk flows on stock improvements, prices and condition. Animals are marked with the initials and colours of their new owners, and the sale moves on. The diversity and range of sheep sold at the marts suggest how broad a field now exists in modern Shetland husbandry: Texels, Suffolks, Cheviots, crosses of all kinds. But with 30,000 Shetland sheep in the islands, and a long history of traditional crofting, it is the native breed that still attracts most attention here. National regulations mystifyingly now classify wool as a by-product of the industry, but this official devaluing of the fibre does nothing to reduce its importance in Shetland and beyond. Here, the Shetland Flock Book holds its annual hotly contested competitions for fine Shetland fleeces and wool on the hoof. Animals are carefully scrutinised to assess the fineness of their wool, and prize-winning fleeces are keenly sought after by interested craftspeople from around the globe.

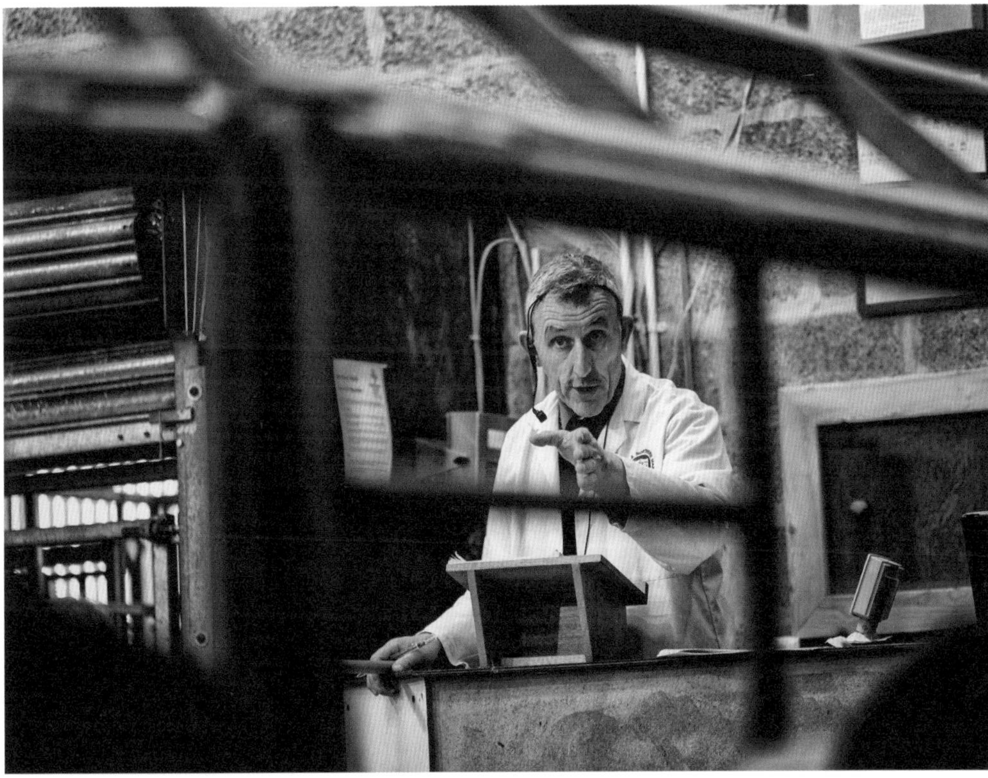

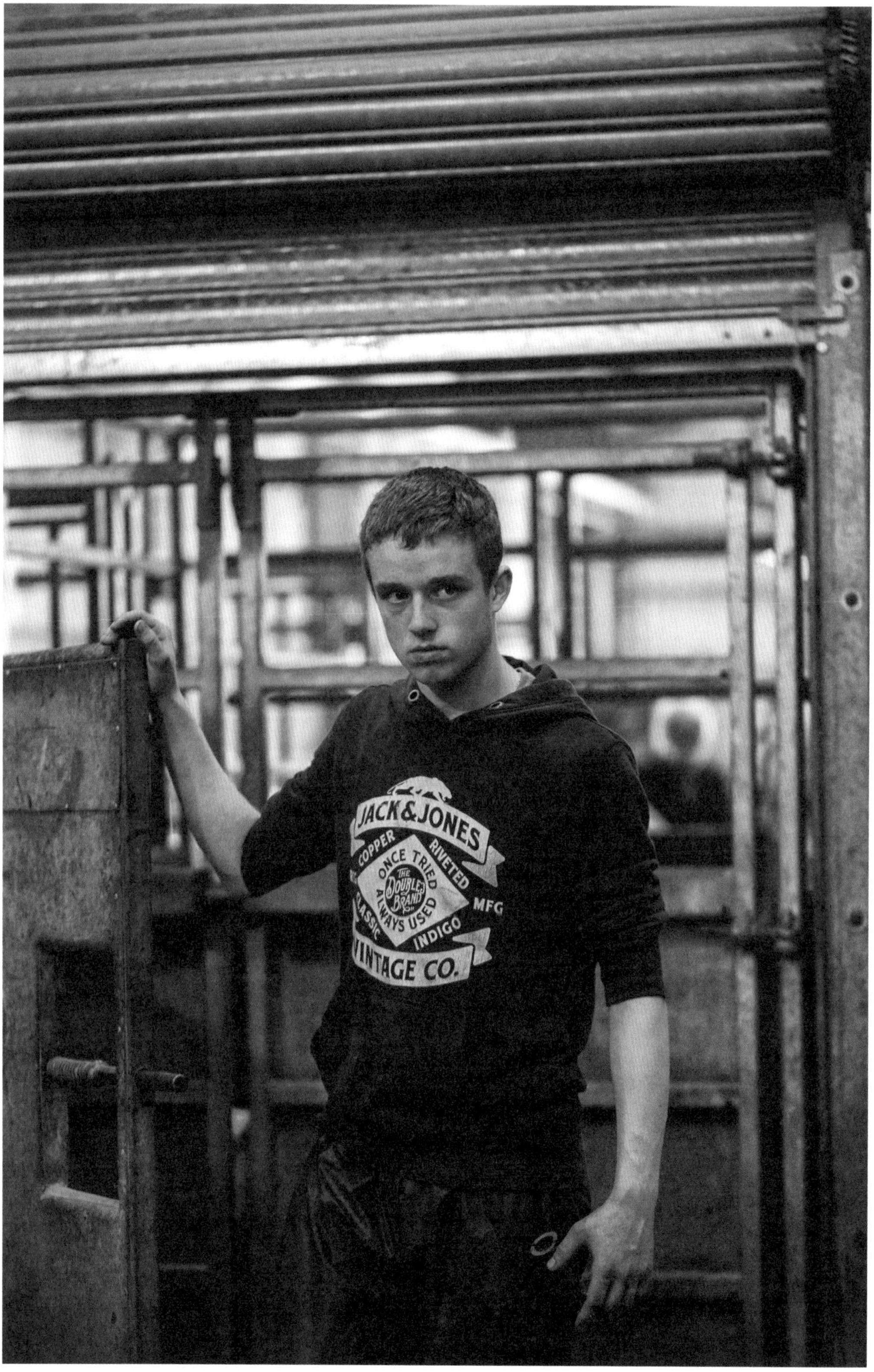
JACK&JONES
COPPER
RIVETED
ONCE TRIED
ALWAYS USED
CLASSIC
INDIGO
MFG
VINTAGE CO.

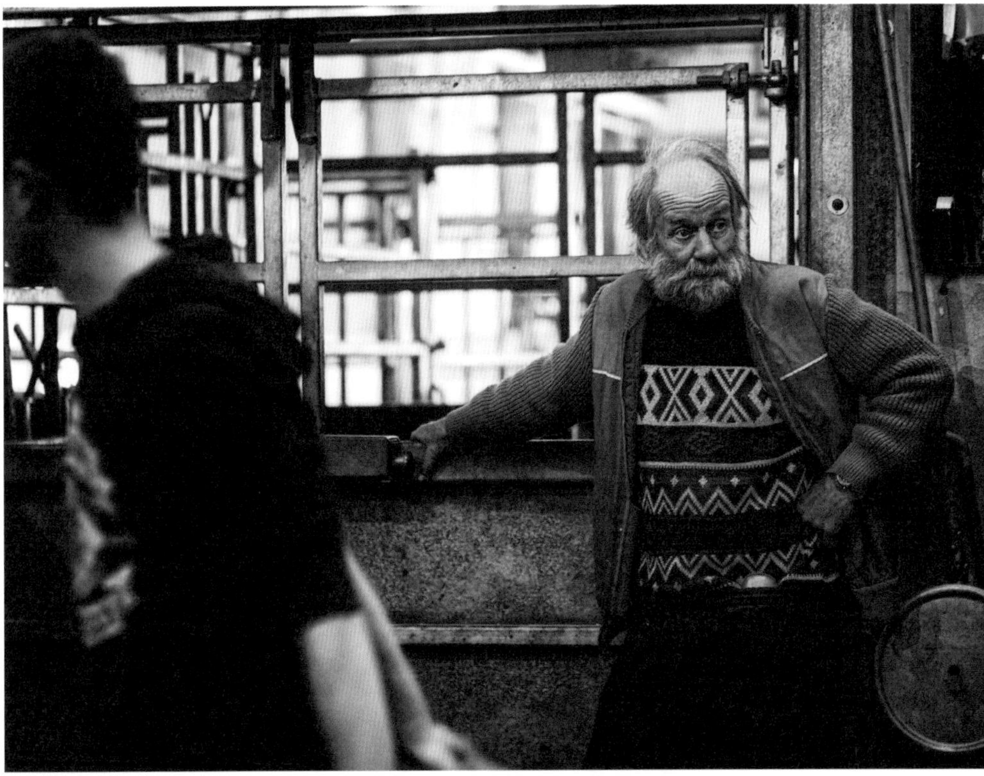

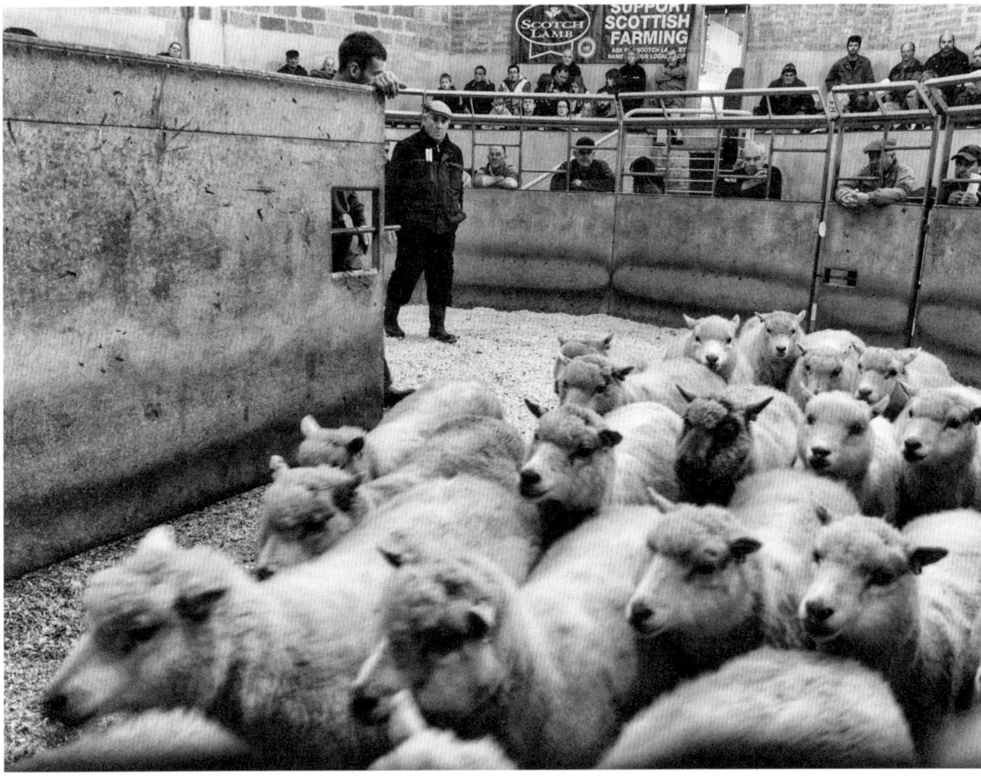
SCOTCH LAMB
SUPPORT SCOTTISH FARMING

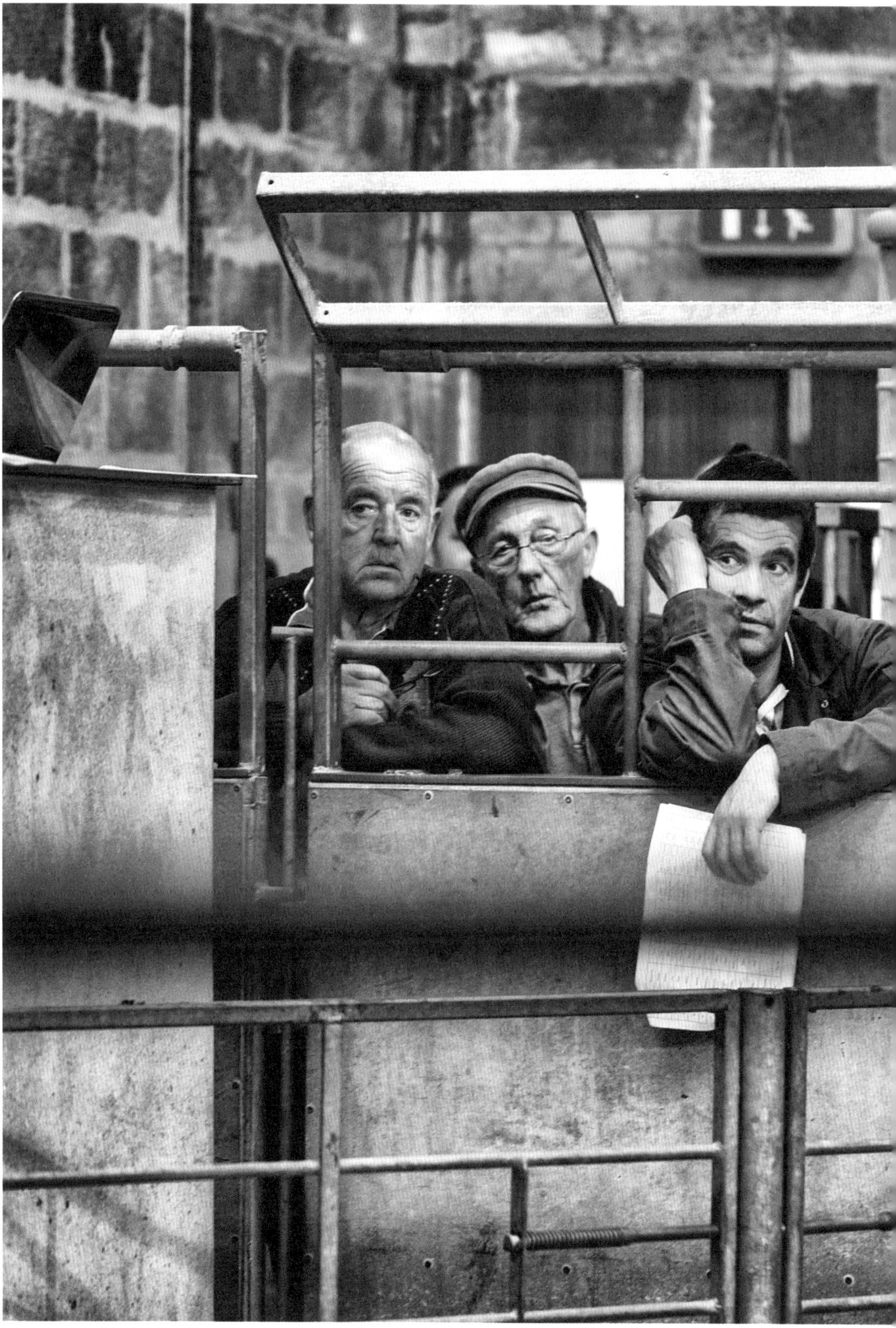

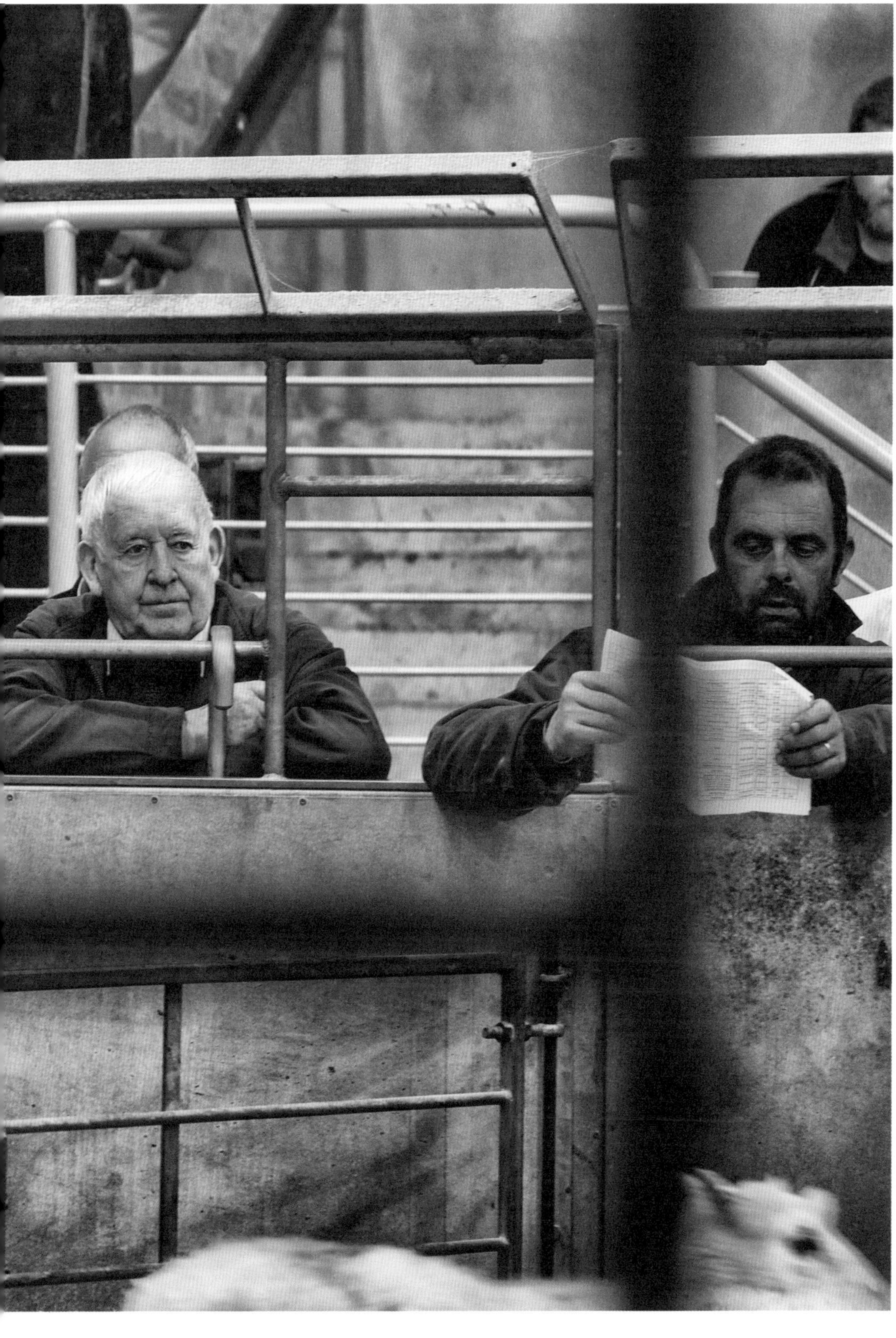

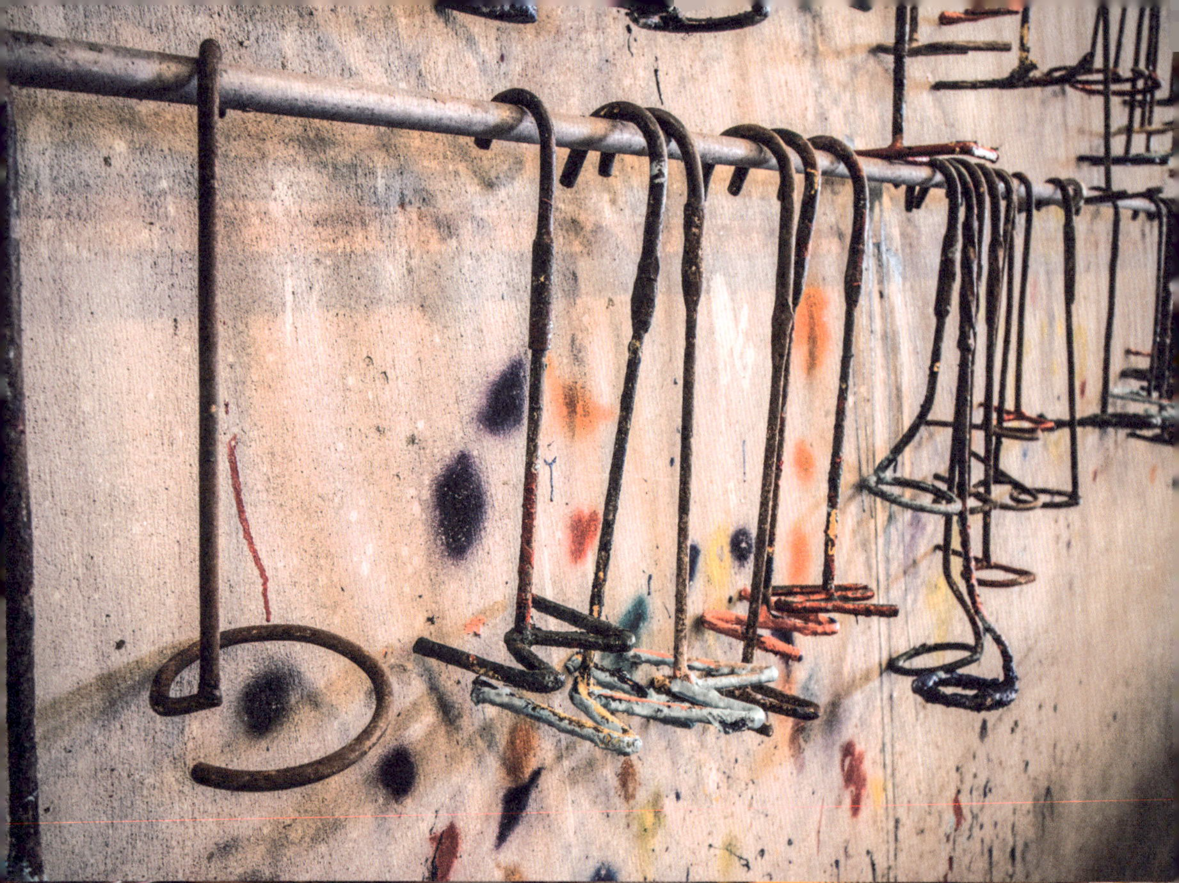

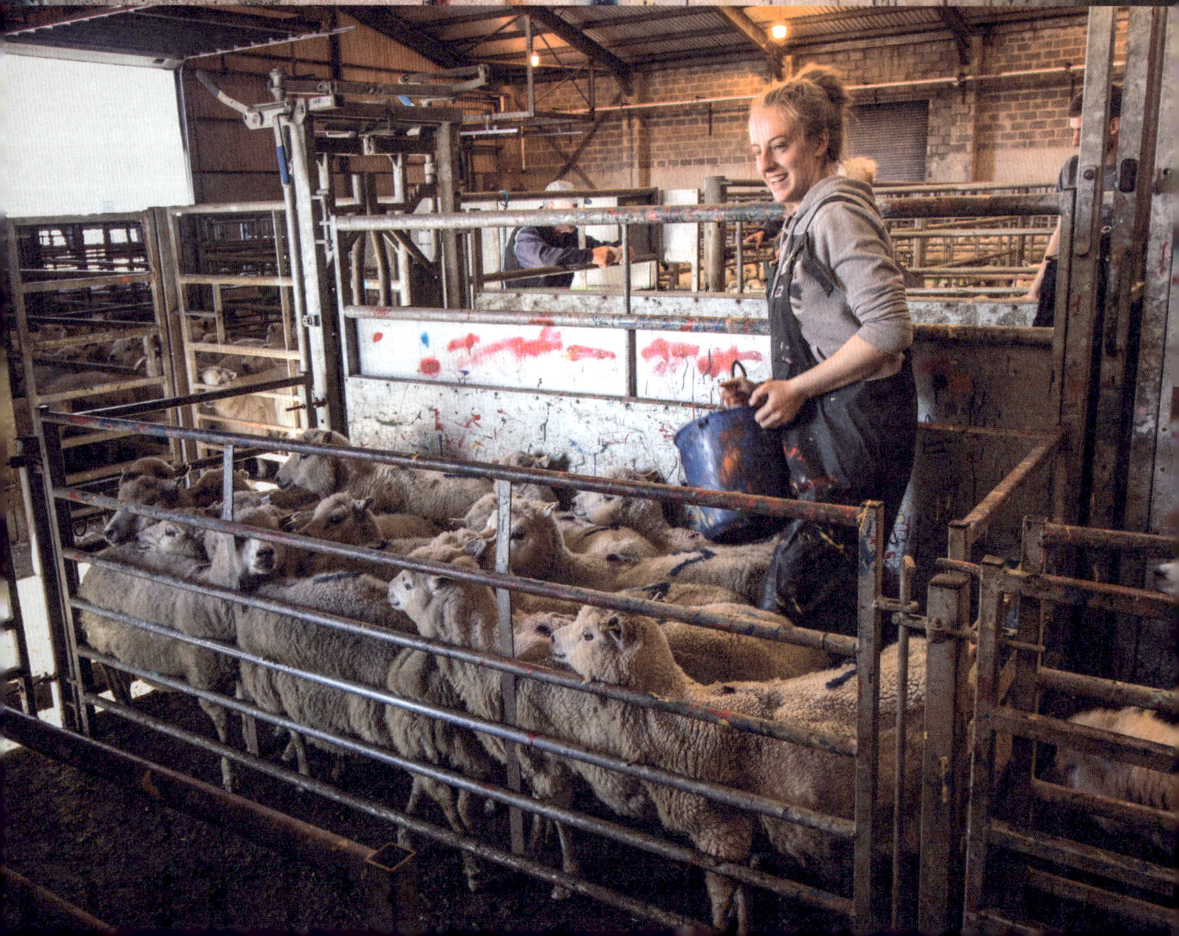

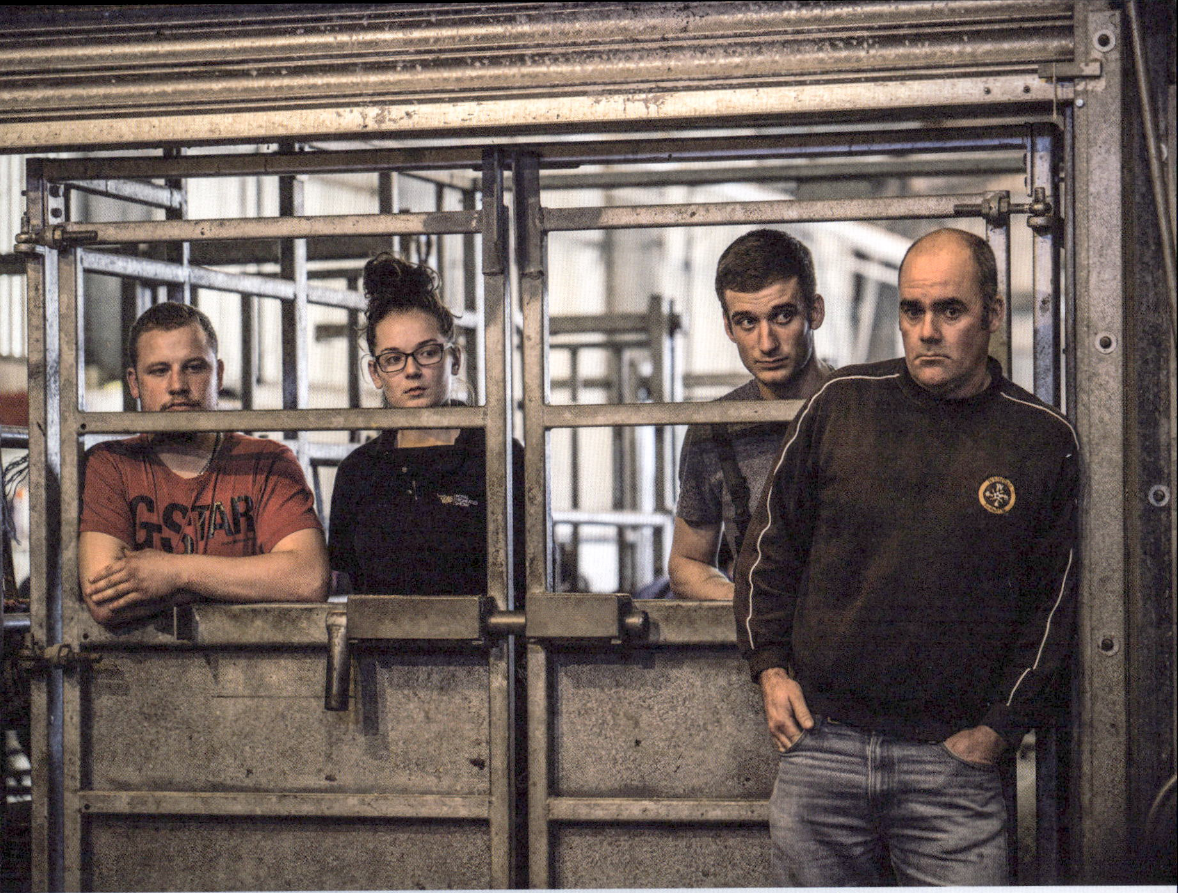
G-STAR

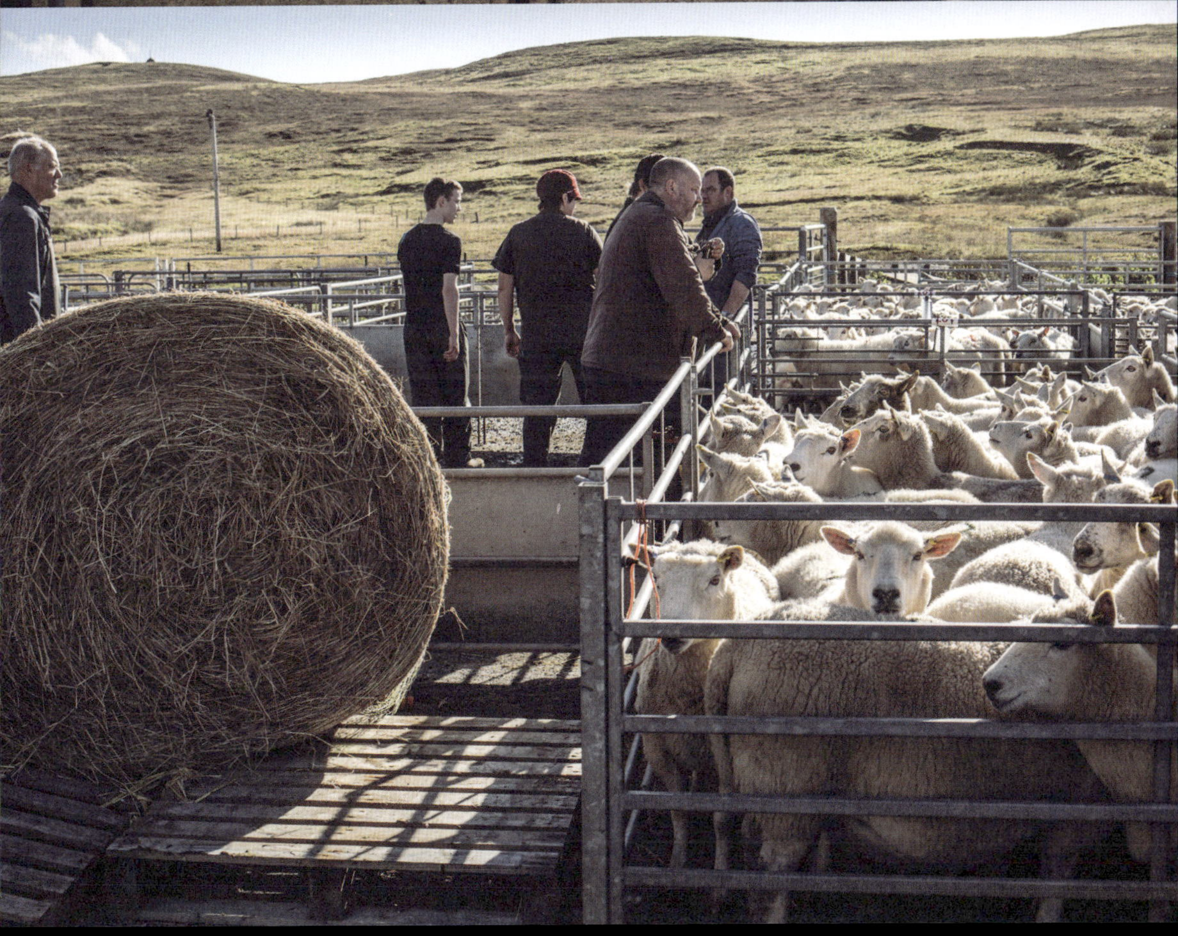

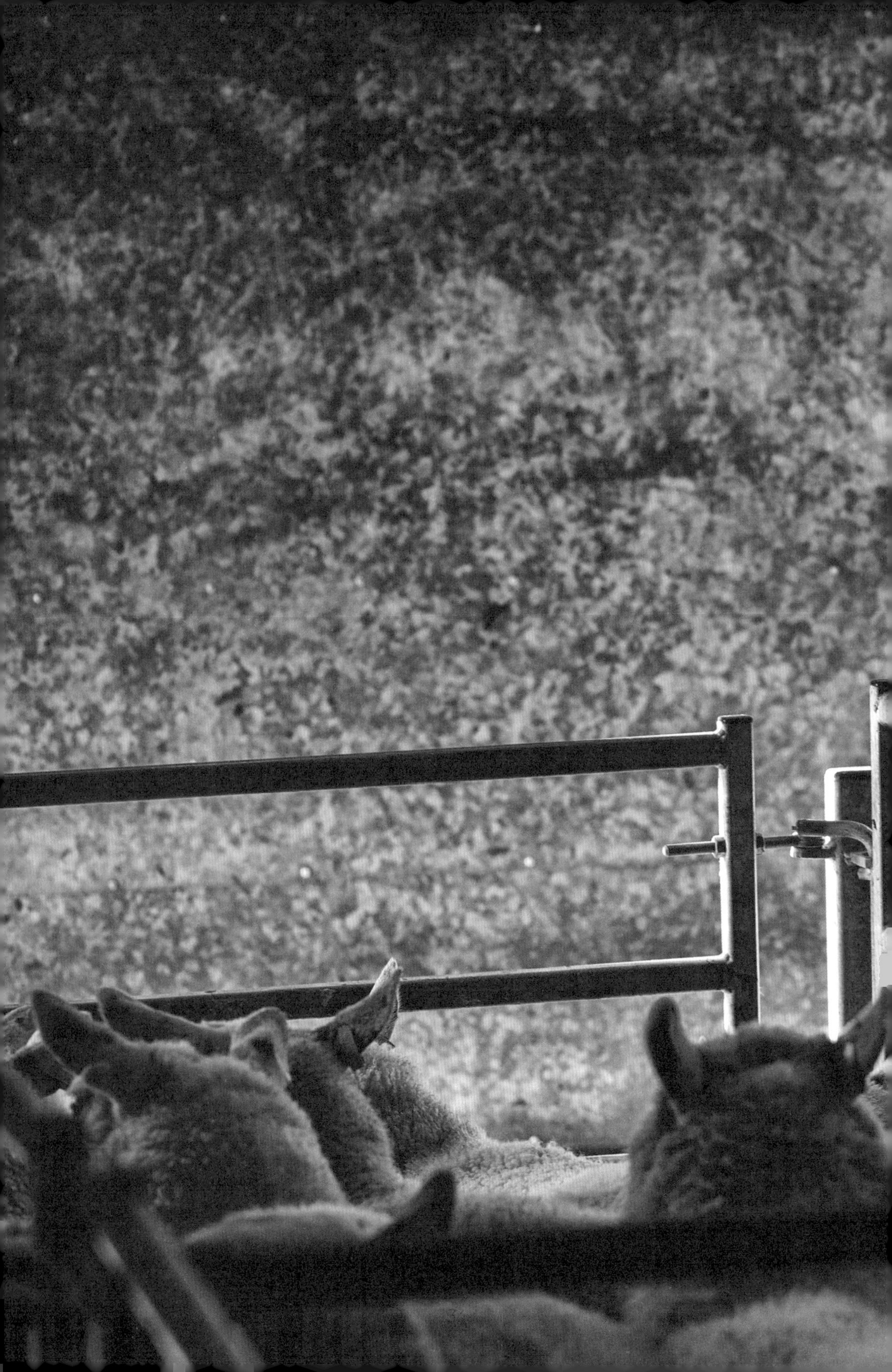

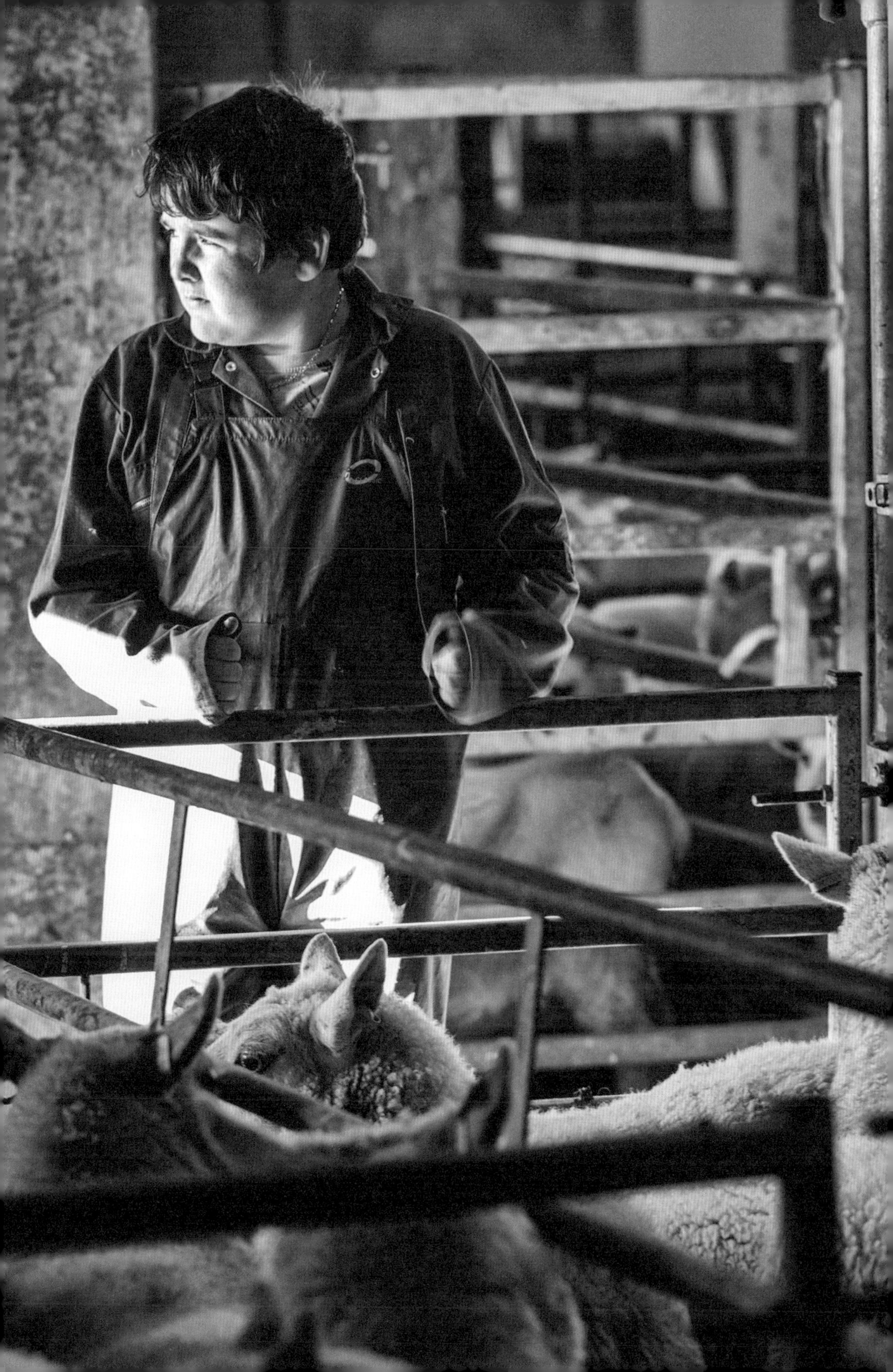

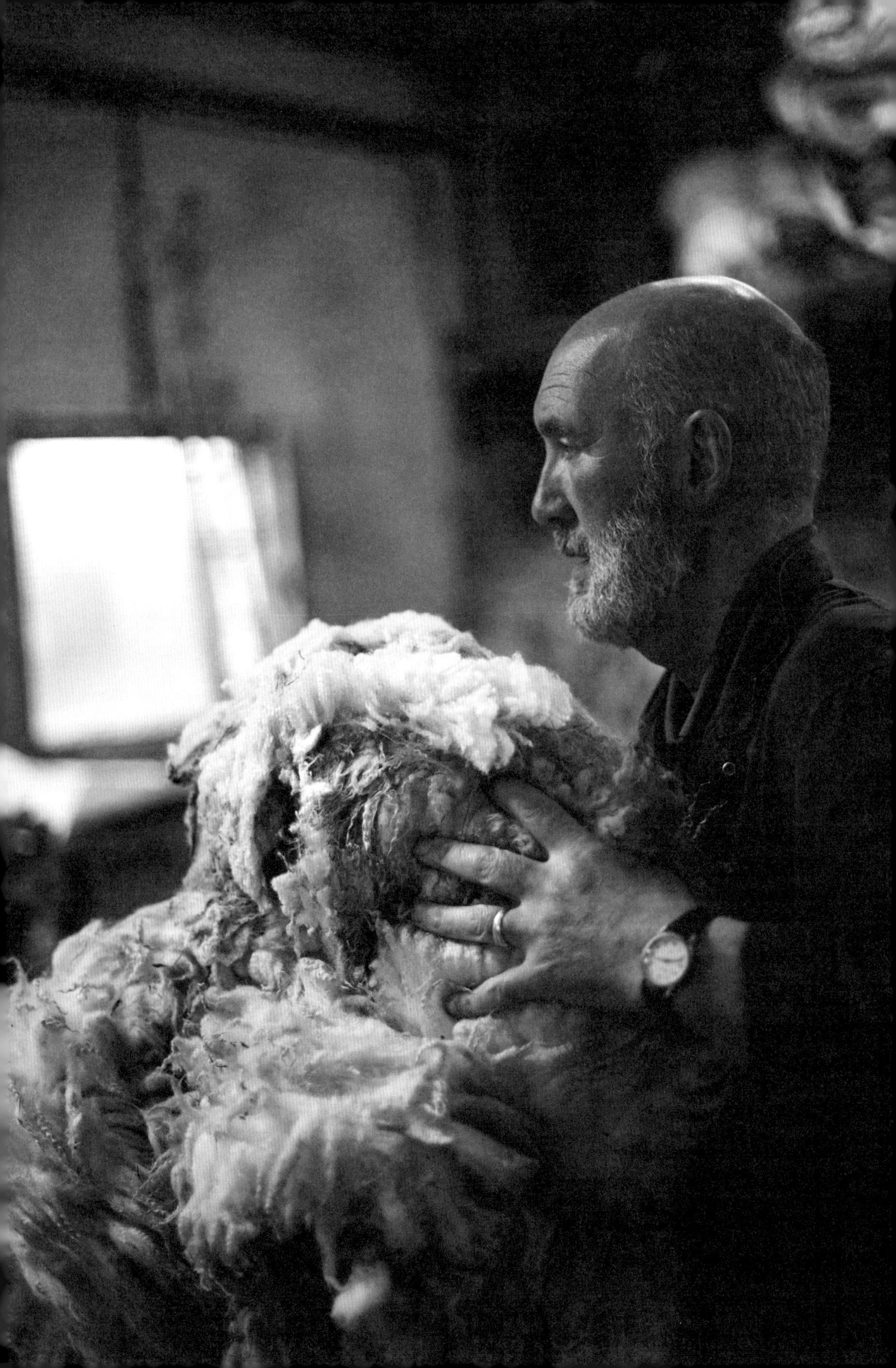

# Jamieson & Smith
## Shetland Woolbrokers

John "Auld Sheepie" Smith had a keen knack of discerning coarse from kindly wool, and it was under the hands of this talented Scalloway crofter, and later those of his children, Jim and Eva, that the company known in Shetland simply as "the brokers" was formed. Founded with the skilled work of wool sorting and grading at its heart, by 1955, Jamieson & Smith had grown to handle around 75% of the Shetland wool clip. Today, 80% of Shetland's fleeces, supplied by between 600 and 700 crofters, pass through the iconic green doors on Lerwick's North Road to begin a journey of transformation into wonderful wool products from carpets to fine-lace shawls. In association with their parent company, Curtis Wools, and working with innovative brands like Vi-Spring and the Real Shetland Company, Jamieson & Smith has radically diversified the uses for all grades of Shetland wool, in products such as duvets and mattresses. The brokers employs a dedicated local team including June Moulder (who from her office has kept the company shipshape for over a decade), Sandra Manson (a talented knitter and designer who was commissioned to knit a fine lace christening robe for the royal family) and Jan Robertson (who grades fleeces, raises her own Shetland sheep, and wins prizes with her loyal collie, Sally). Supplying beautiful yarn to the world's handknitters and supporting a wide range of local industries from design to crofting, Jamieson & Smith is a Shetland institution whose important work draws worldwide appreciation.

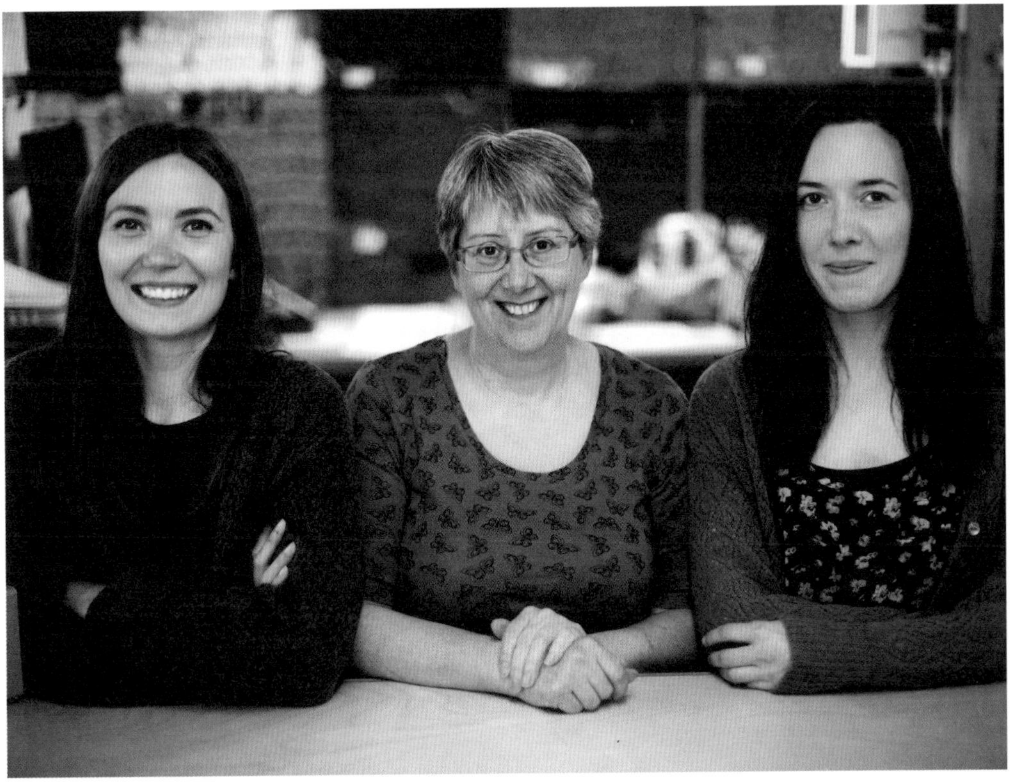

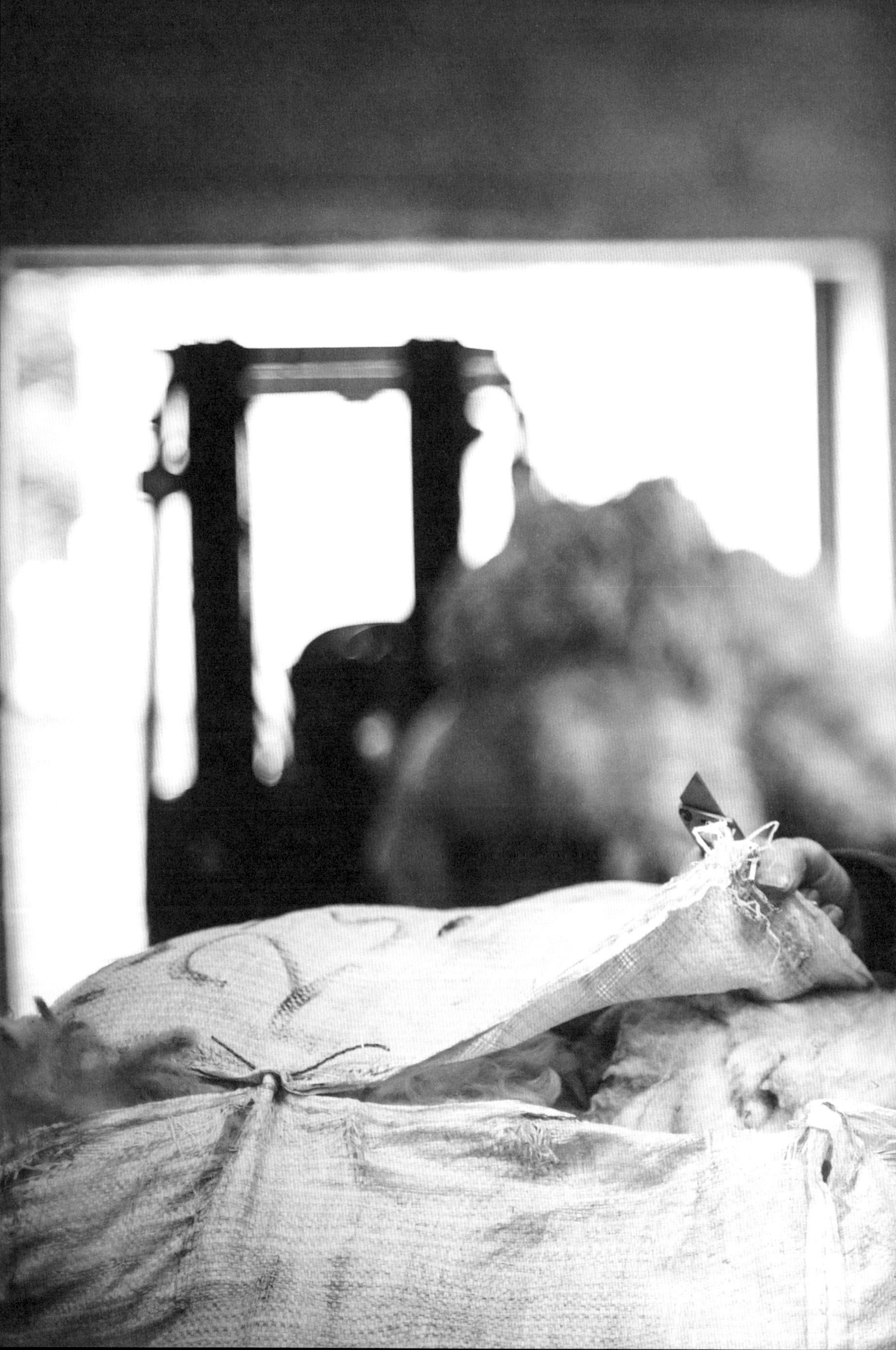

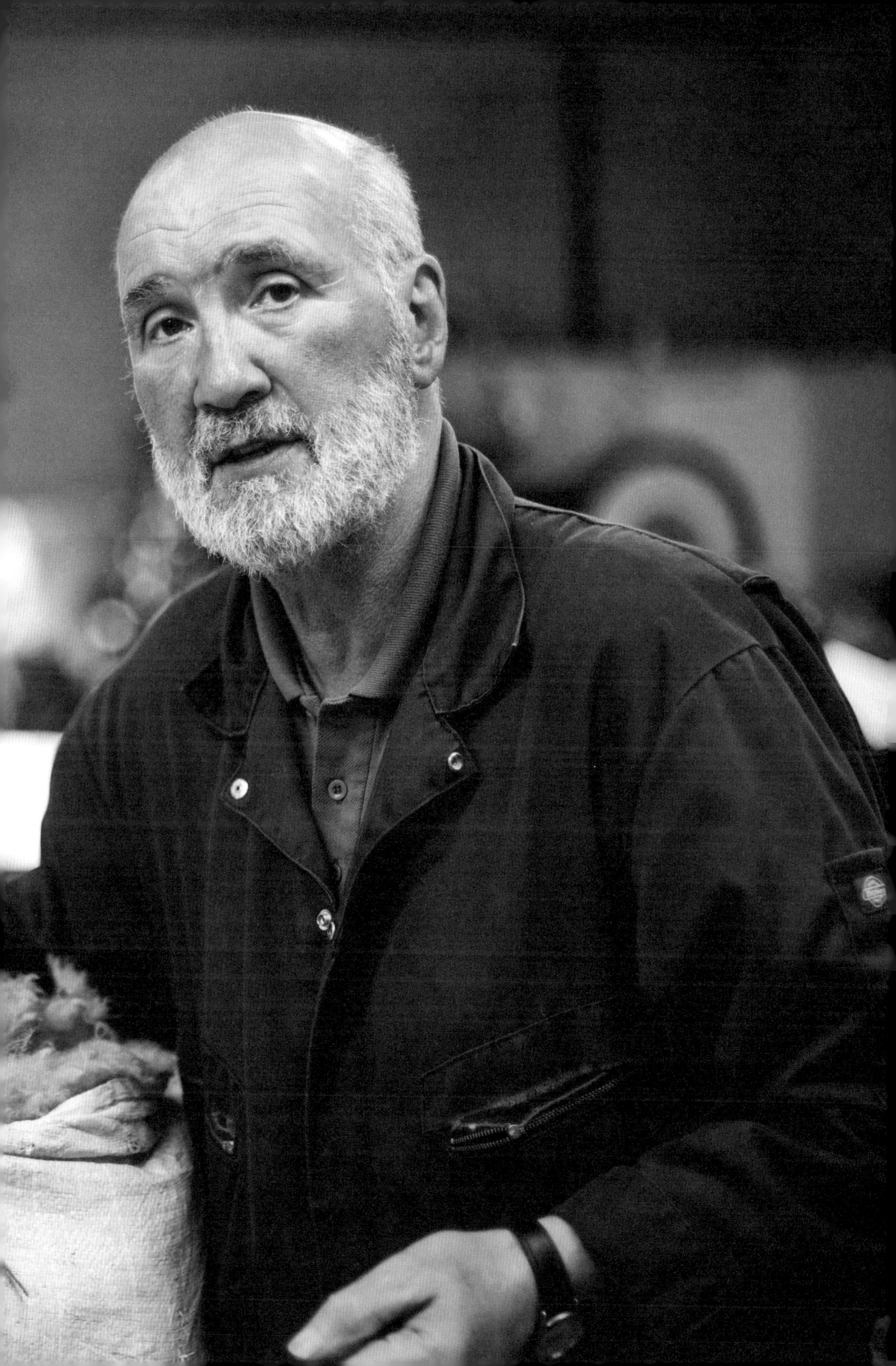

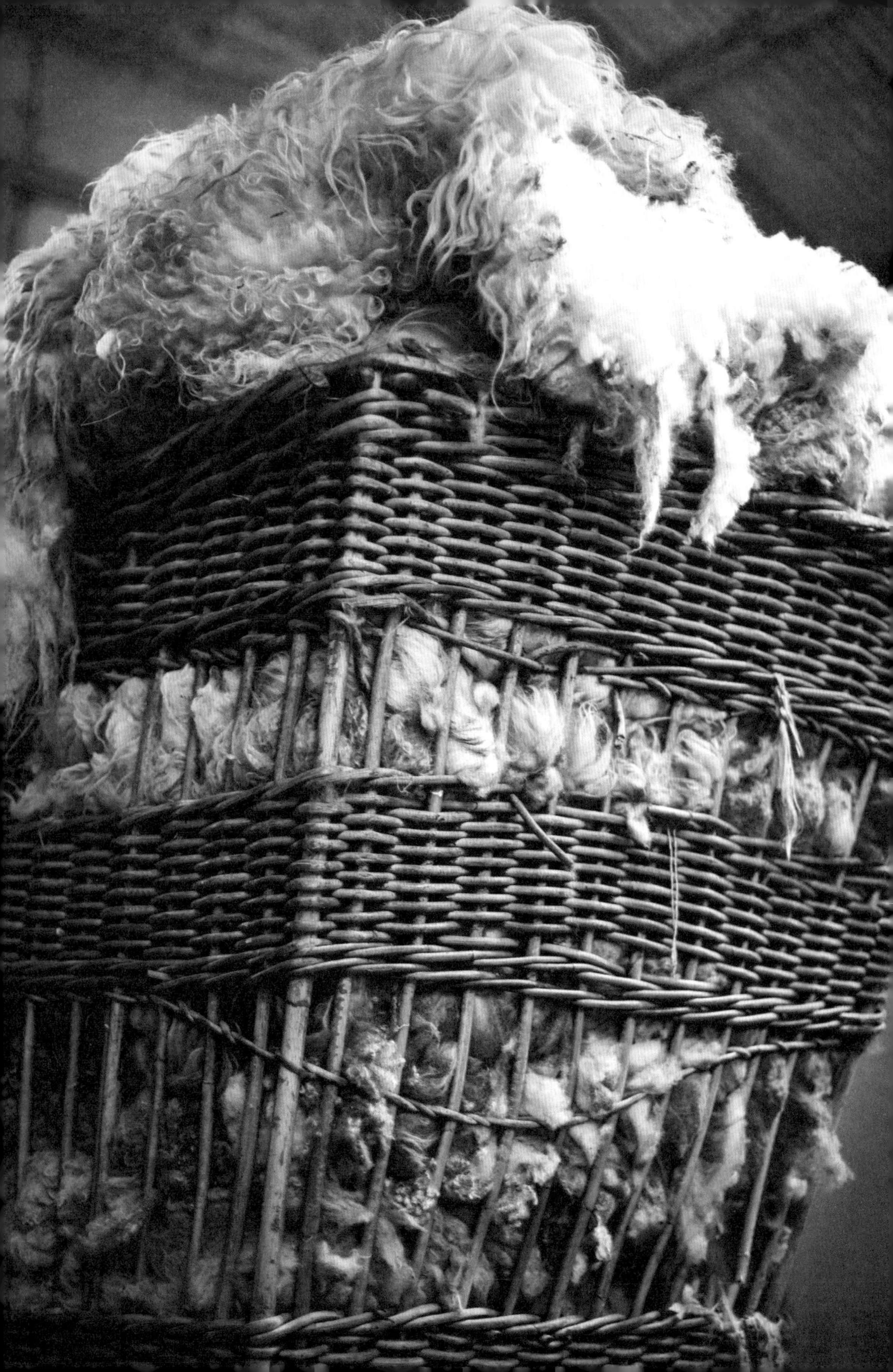

*"To achieve Shetland wool's famously soft handle, careful sorting of raw fleece is absolutely crucial. Through sorting we can separate fibres that are best suited for carpets and other homewares from the fine wool that is ideal for producing beautiful hand-knitting yarns. With our recreation of wirsit (worsted-spun) jumper weight and laceweight in association with the Shetland Museum, we have revived traditional styles of knitting and brought new life to this important aspect of Shetland's heritage and culture. I am proud to have played a role in this over the past 49 years."*

*Oliver Henry*

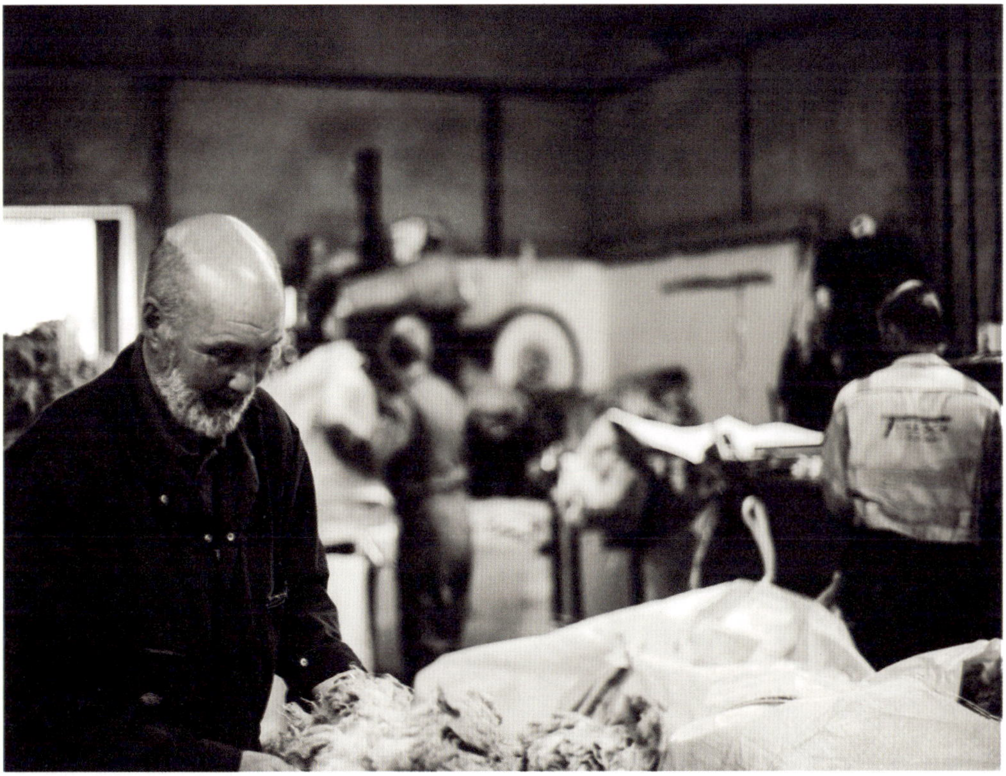

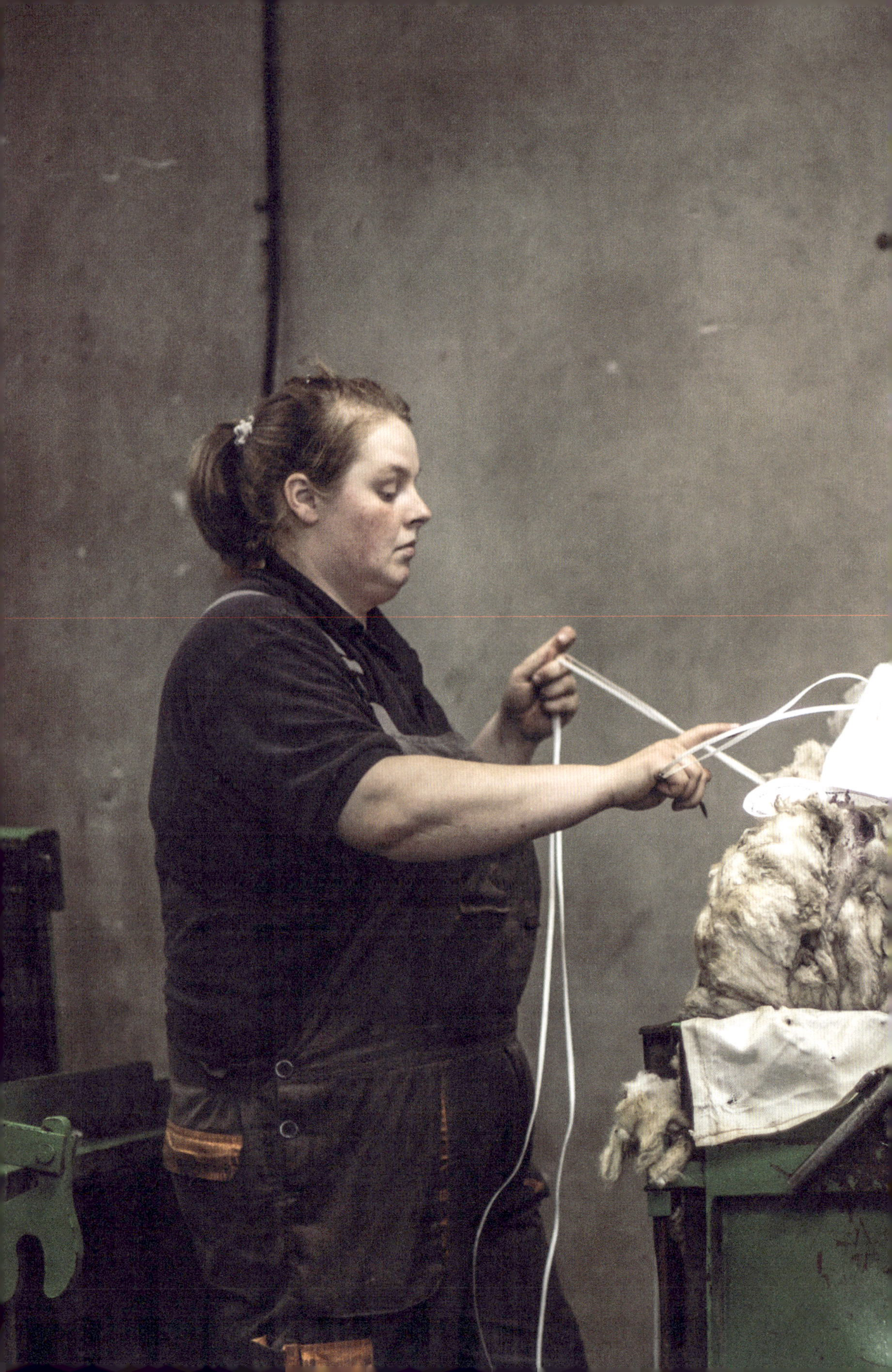

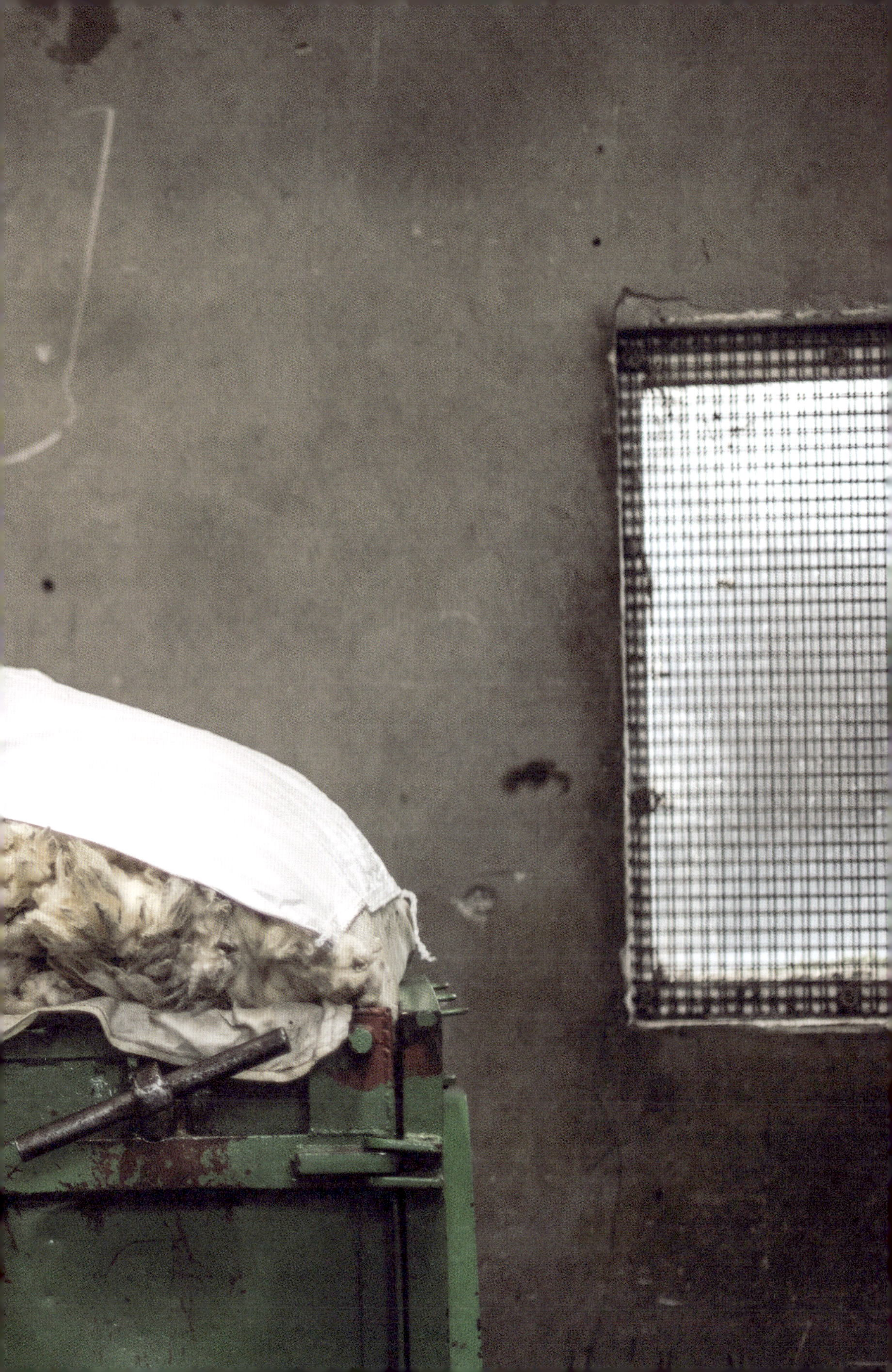

# Oliver Henry
## Woolman

Anyone who spends a few minutes around talented woolman, Oliver Henry, cannot fail to be inspired by his passion and expertise. No one has done more than Oliver to publicise and educate the world about the unique characteristics of Shetland wool. And no one has done more to highlight the importance of the skilled work of sorting and grading to the future of the Shetland wool industry. Oliver's matchless knowledge of Shetland wool—the story of the breed, the character of the fibre, the uses to which it has historically been put—makes him an important local resource, as much as a talented wool grader. He helped Dr Carol Christiansen and her team with their enquiries as they recreated the woollen garments of the peat-bog-preserved Shetland body known as Gunnister Man. Oliver has worked with the Shetland Museum on several other significant projects, including the development of a modern fine-lace yarn that approximates the characteristics of nineteenth-century handspun. He is always on hand to help with any woolly investigation, from Deb Robson's work on Shetland fleeces to Felicity Ford's exploration of the sounds of Shetland wool. His generous assistance has frequently proved invaluable to the present author in her own research. After 49 years sorting and grading, educating visitors from as far afield as Canada and Japan, judging wool on the hoof and handling many thousands of fine fleeces, Oliver has recently passed his management of Jamieson & Smith to another talented local woolman, Derek Goudie. The important legacy of Shetland wool is in good hands.

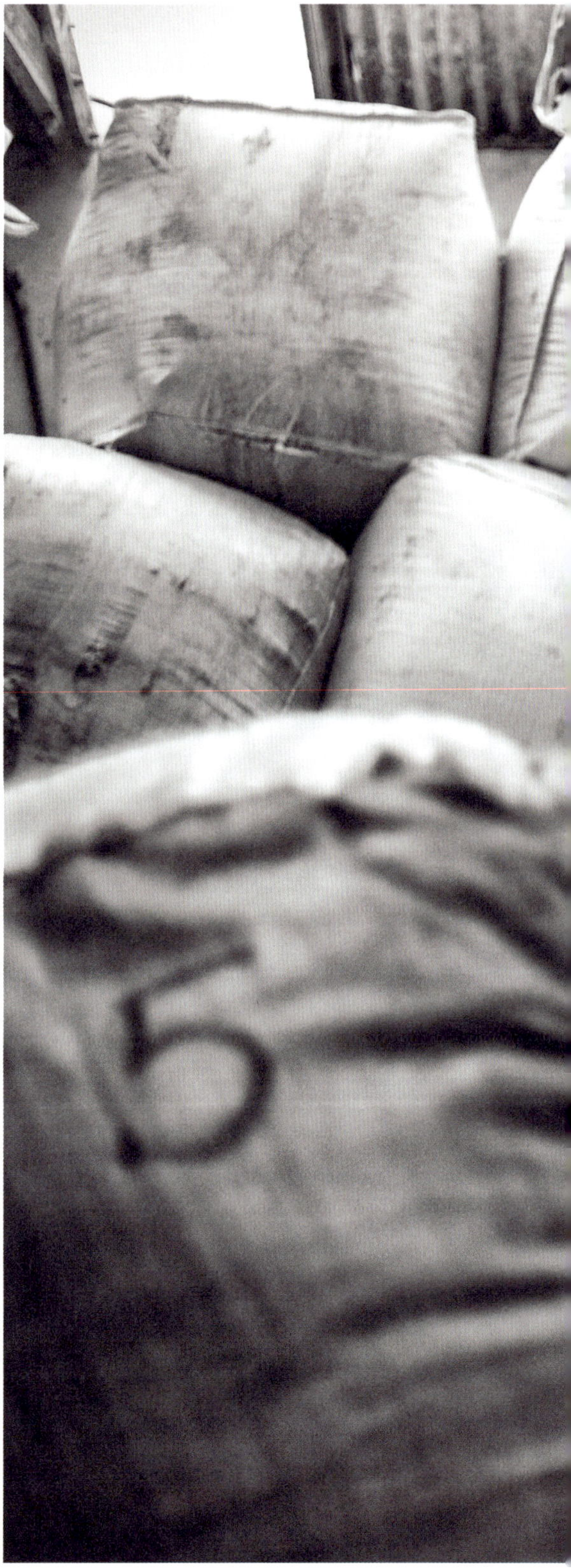

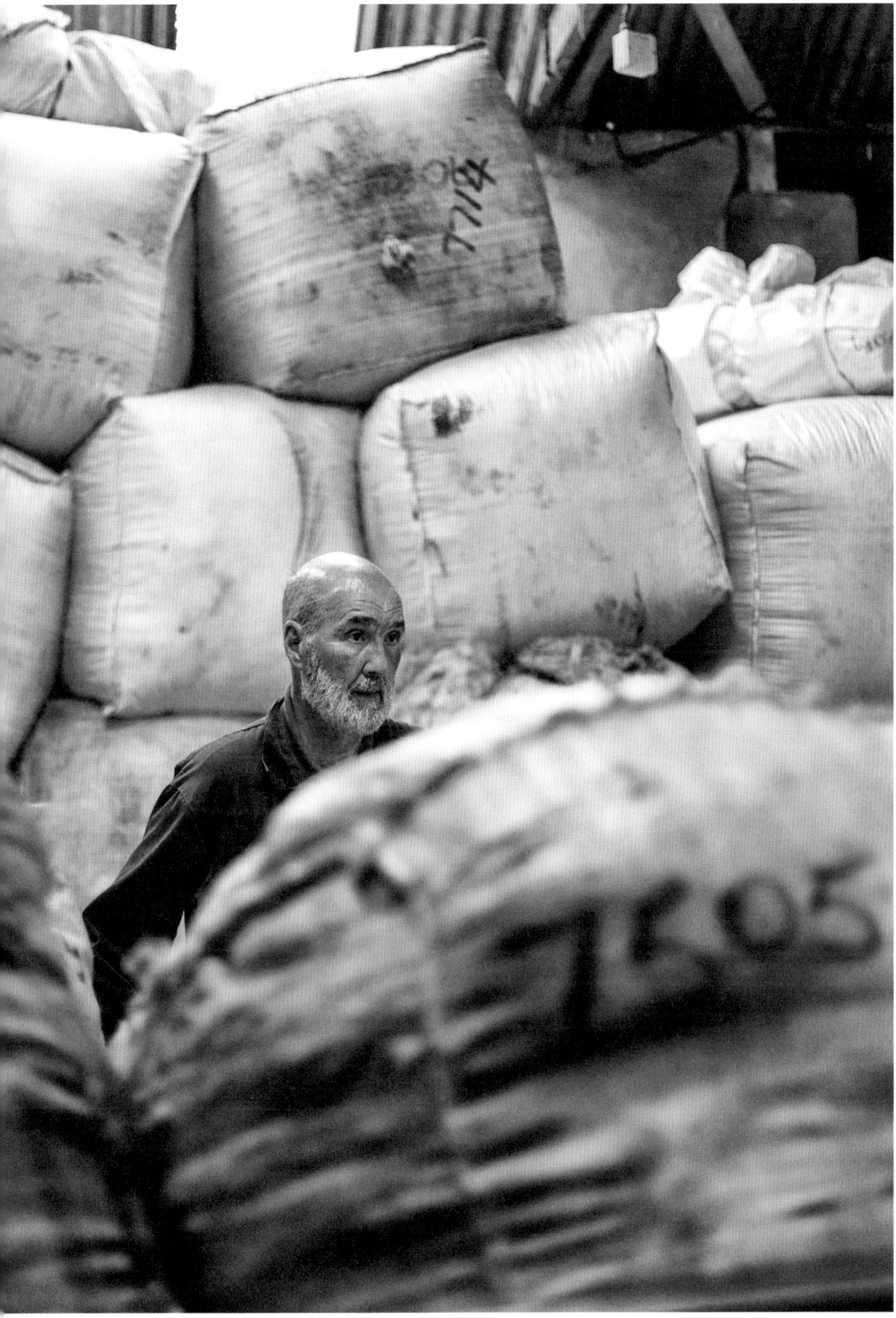

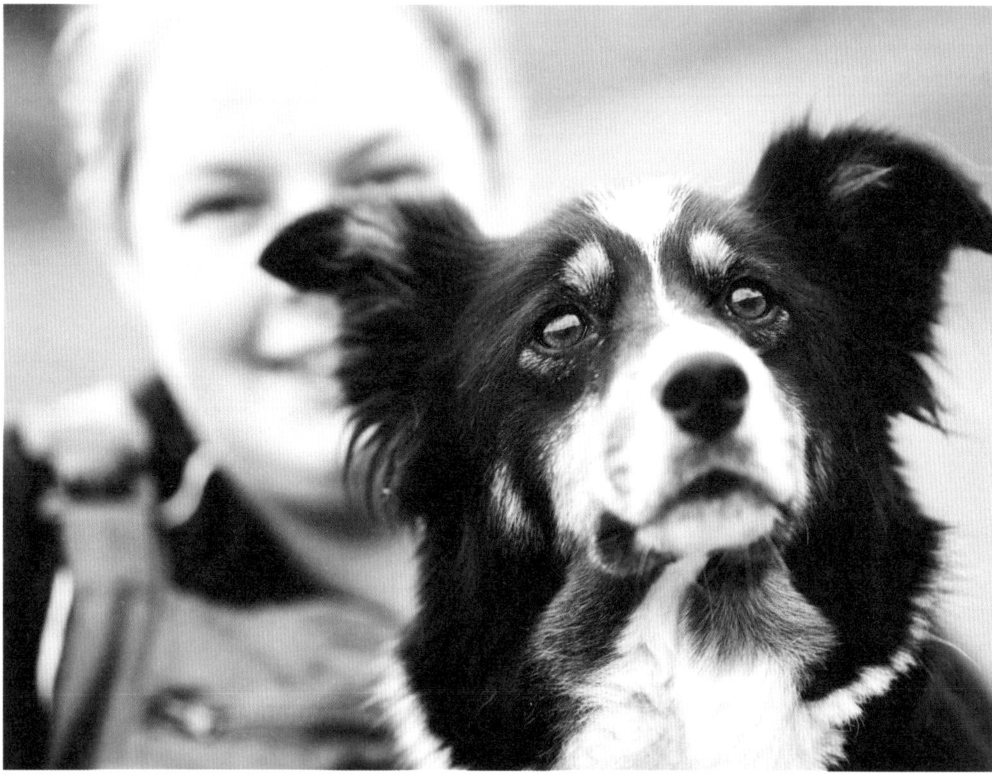

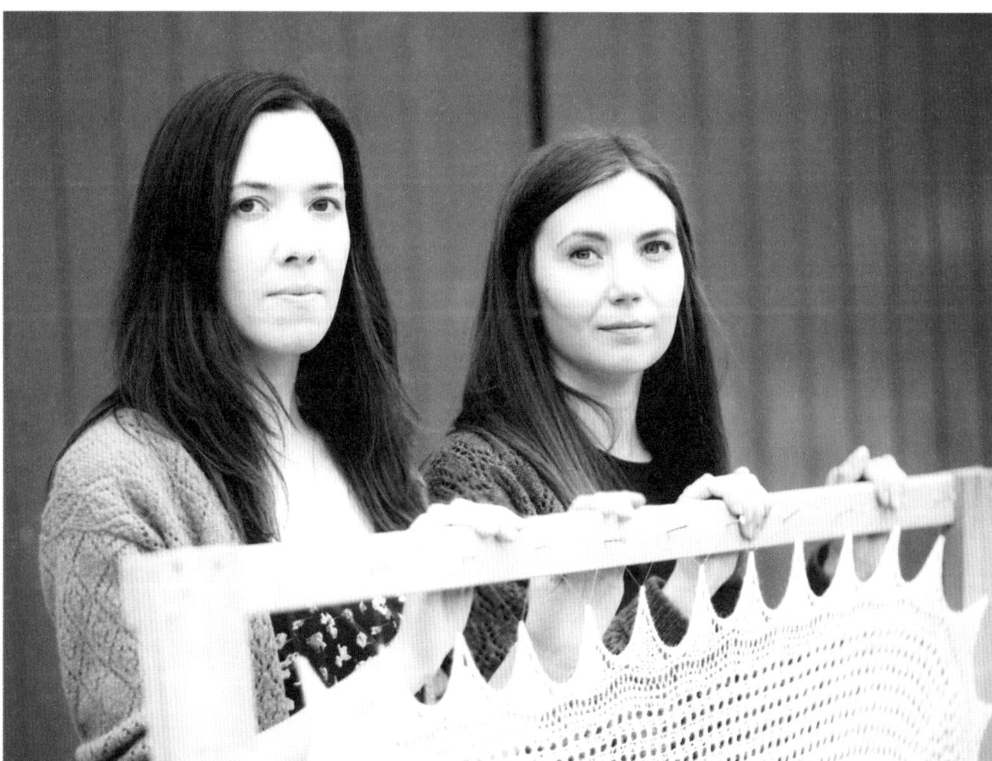

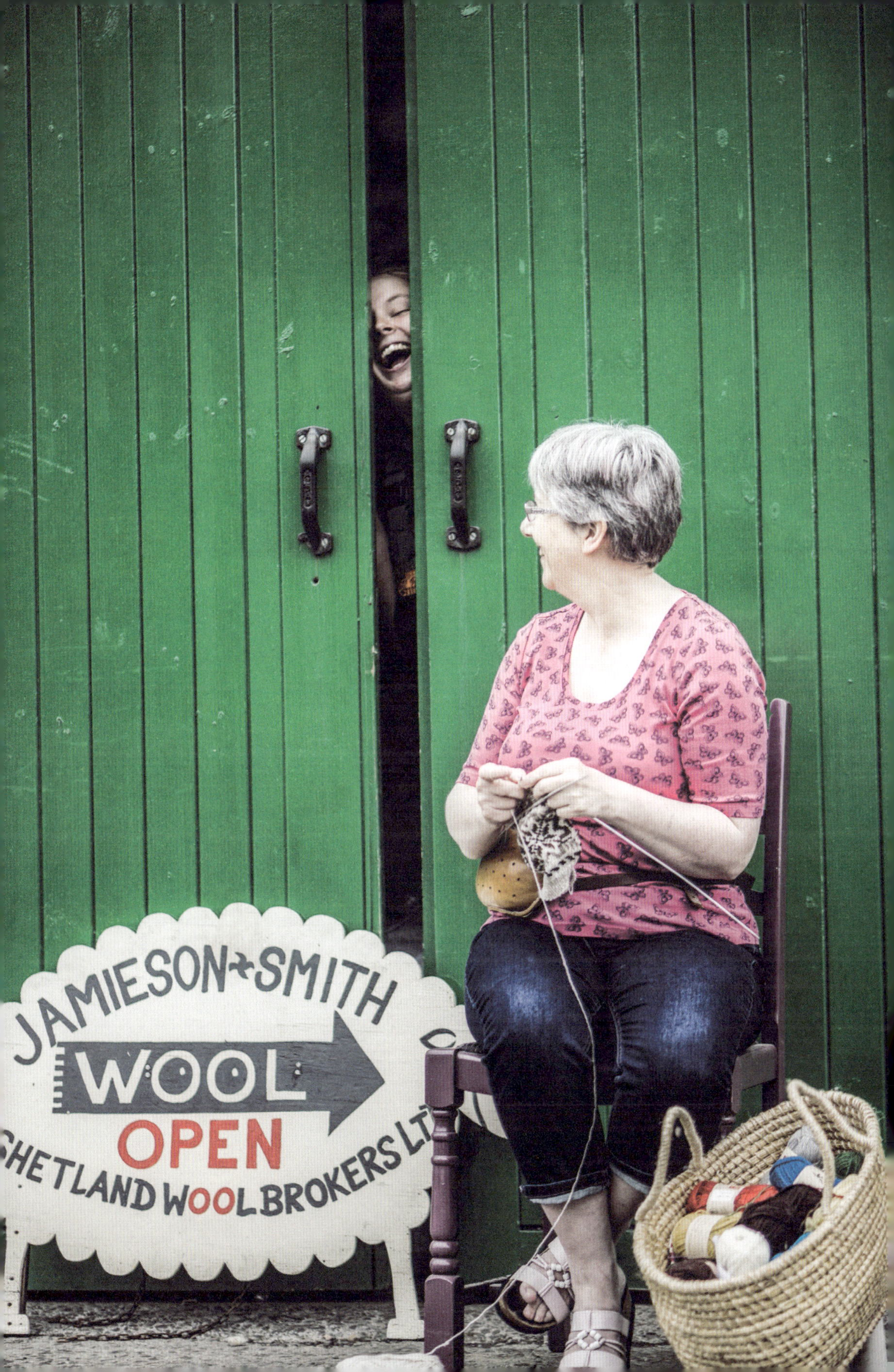
JAMIESON+SMITH
WOOL
OPEN
HETLAND WOOL BROKERS LT

# Donna Smith

## Donna Smith Designs

Donna Smith grew up on Burra Isle, where members of her family have lived since at least the 1800s. Having only spent her student years away from the island, she cannot imagine regarding anywhere else as home. "I love the sense of community, living among people I have known all my life. The memories. The continuity. Being surrounded by the sea." Donna and her husband, Trevor, built their home on her croft, where, amidst the demands of work, family, land and sheep, she creates beautiful hand-knit designs. "I am very interested in Shetland knitting and am keen to retain the methods that have been passed through the generations. I like traditional motifs, but, prefer to use them in a contemporary way." Often knitting with just two colours, Donna's patterns are characterised by their geometric restraint, strong lines and impressive lack of fuss: "I like clean shapes and am not keen on anything frilly." Donna is the creator of the world-famous baa-ble hat, and was the patron of Shetland Wool Week in 2015. "I often look at colours I have chosen and realise they are very much part of my environment," she says, "Burra finds its way into my work subconsciously."

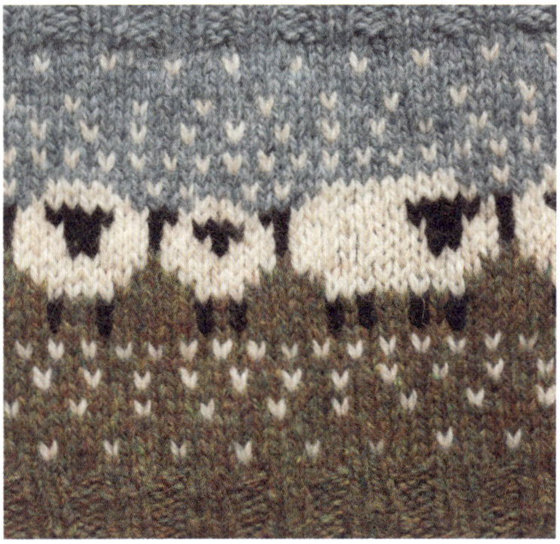

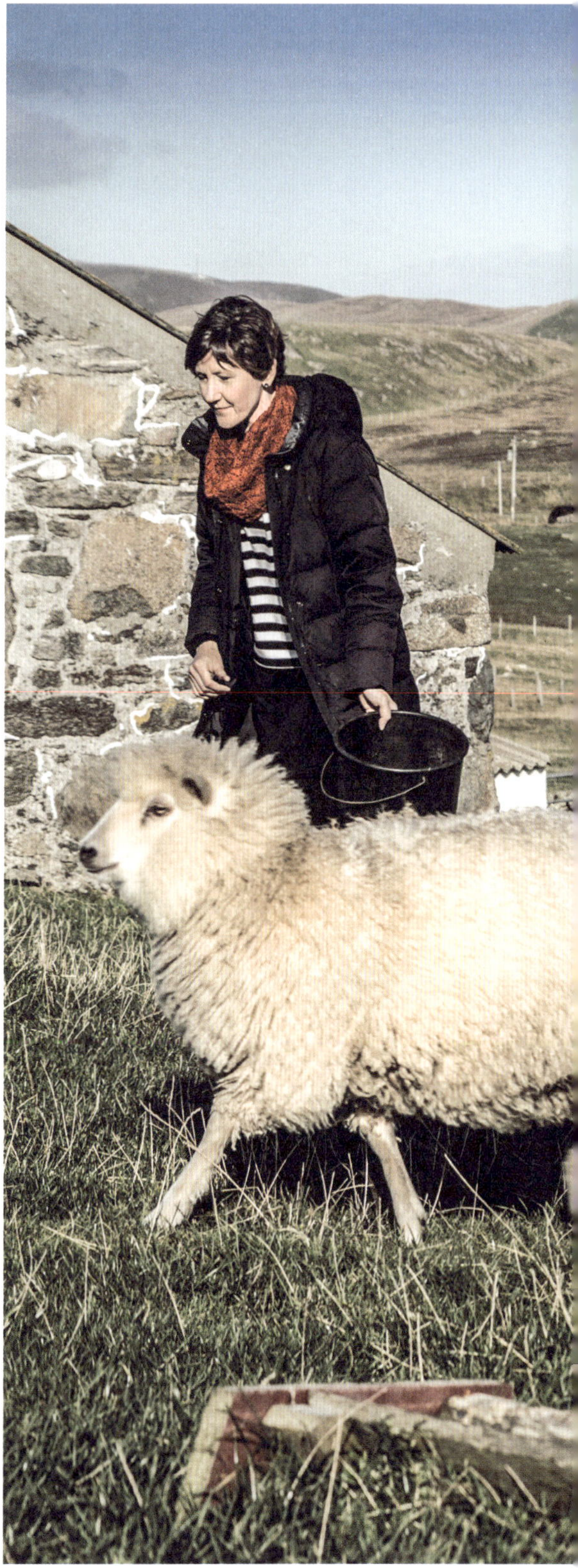

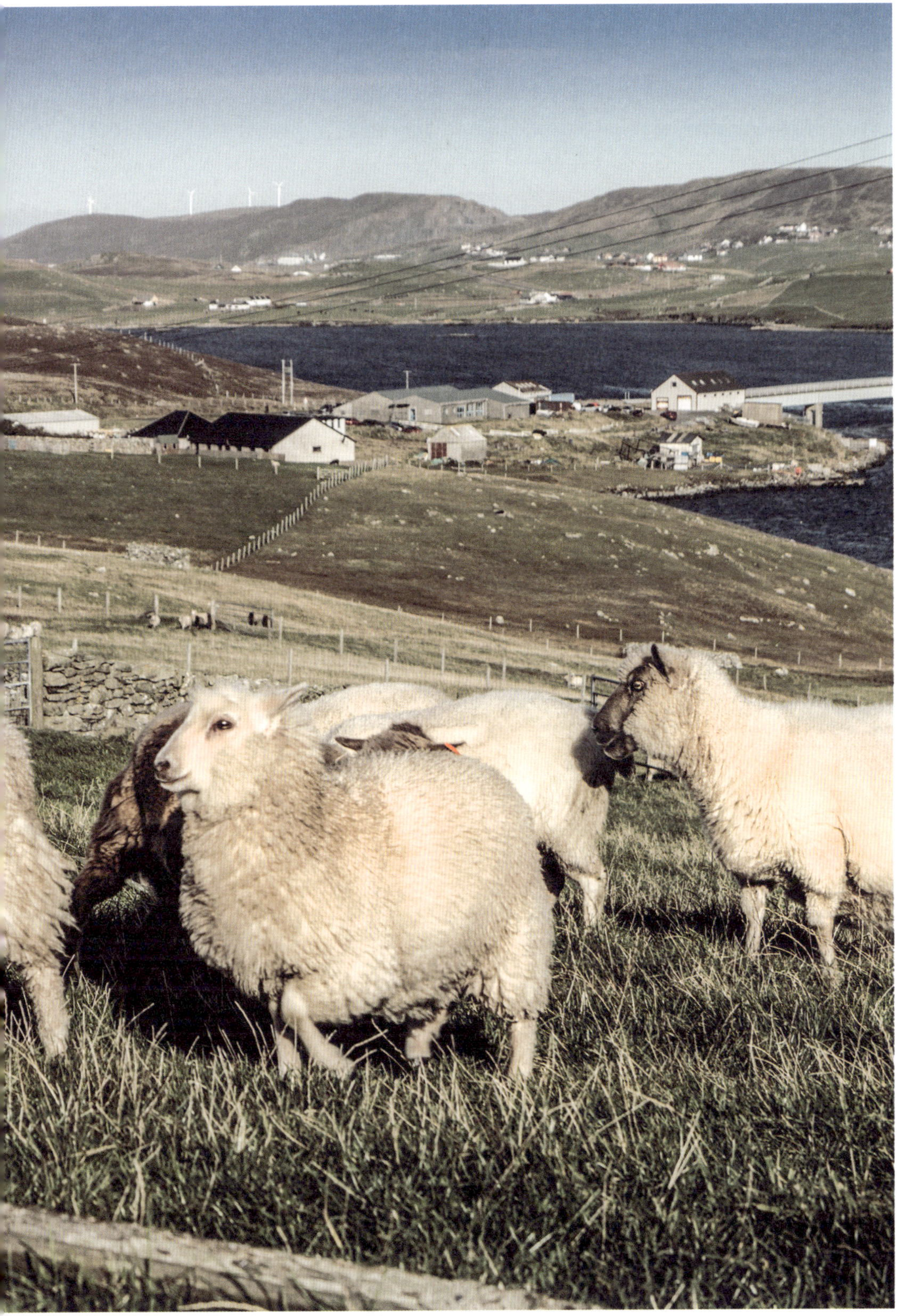

# Hazel Tindall

## Fairisle Designer & Knitter

Hazel Tindall has no memory of learning to knit and was able to do so before she could read and write. She grew up surrounded by the work of knitting, with the women in her family encouraged to tak de sock (knit) to earn some klink (cash). For Hazel's mother, knitting remained a chore, as she found herself endlessly kempin (toiling) to boost her family's income and satisfy buyers' requirements. But Hazel has made knitting her life's joy: the only time her craft seemed devoid of pleasure was when she knitted Fairisle yokes with pre-selected colours in the 1970s. Unable to exercise her unique skills of colour blending, Hazel found the demands of standardisation emptied the work of creativity. Hazel loves the infinitely colourful inventiveness of Fairisle knitting, and is a highly accomplished designer. She has an immediately recognisable and very distinctive style, in which large motifs and shade changes work vertically together, creating a true "allover" rather than a series of horizontal bands. She's published numerous popular patterns and produced the definitive video guide to creating a Fairisle allover. Hazel has twice won a competition to find the world's fastest knitter, with a record speed of 262 stitches in 3 minutes. She lives in Aith, on Shetland's beautiful west side. Across the voe, she looks out on the landscape that's been shaped by the lives of the women of former generations of her family. Hazel continues to reshape Shetland culture with her wonderful, colourful knitting.

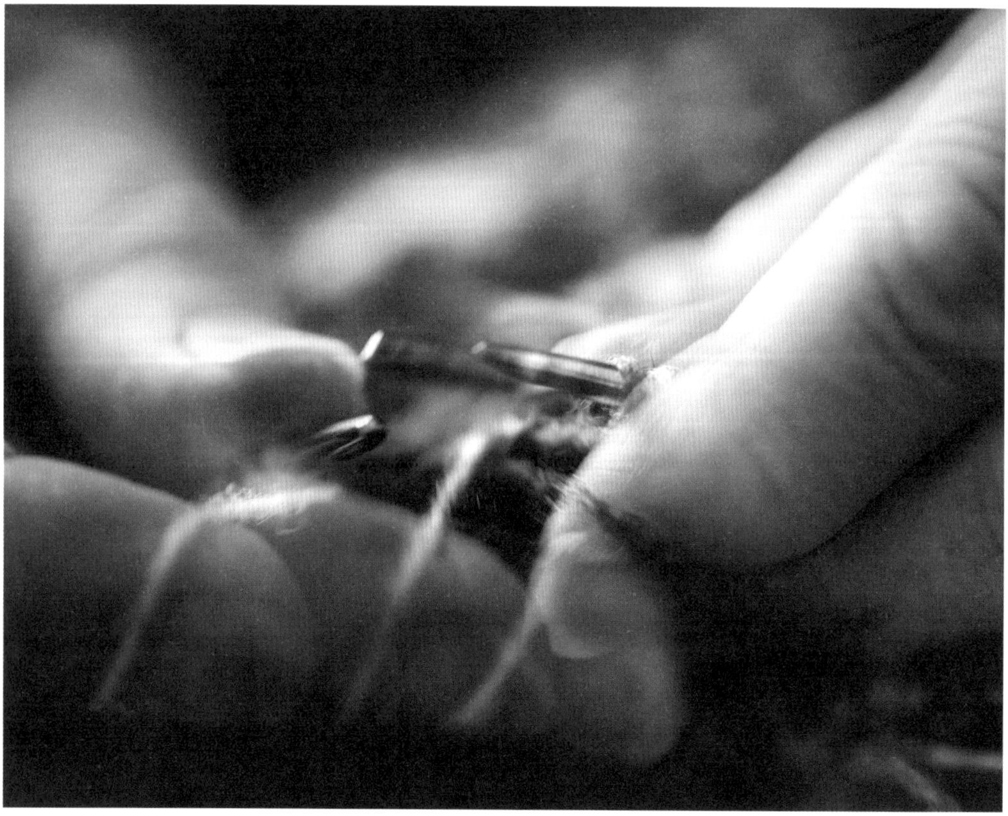

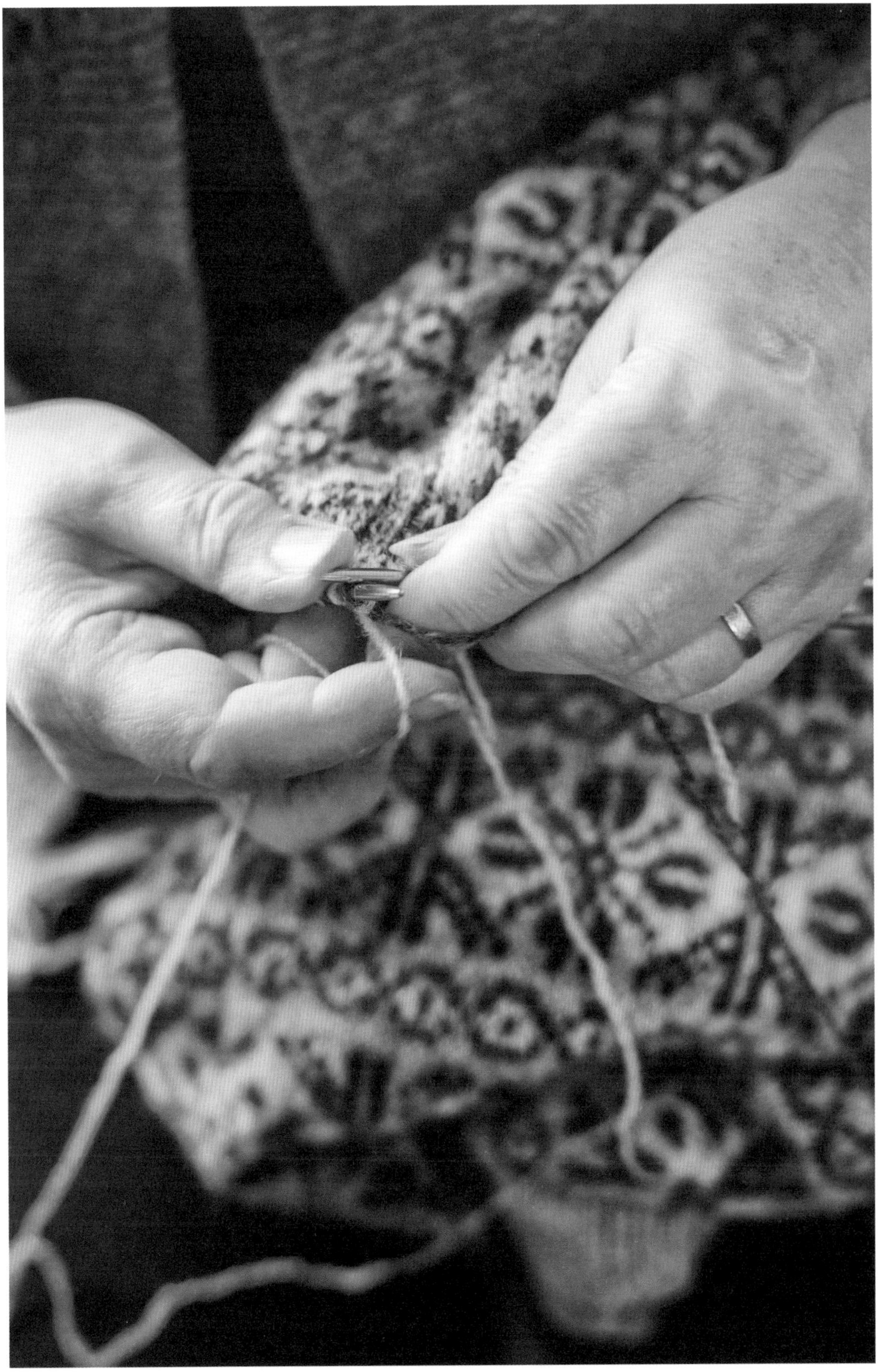

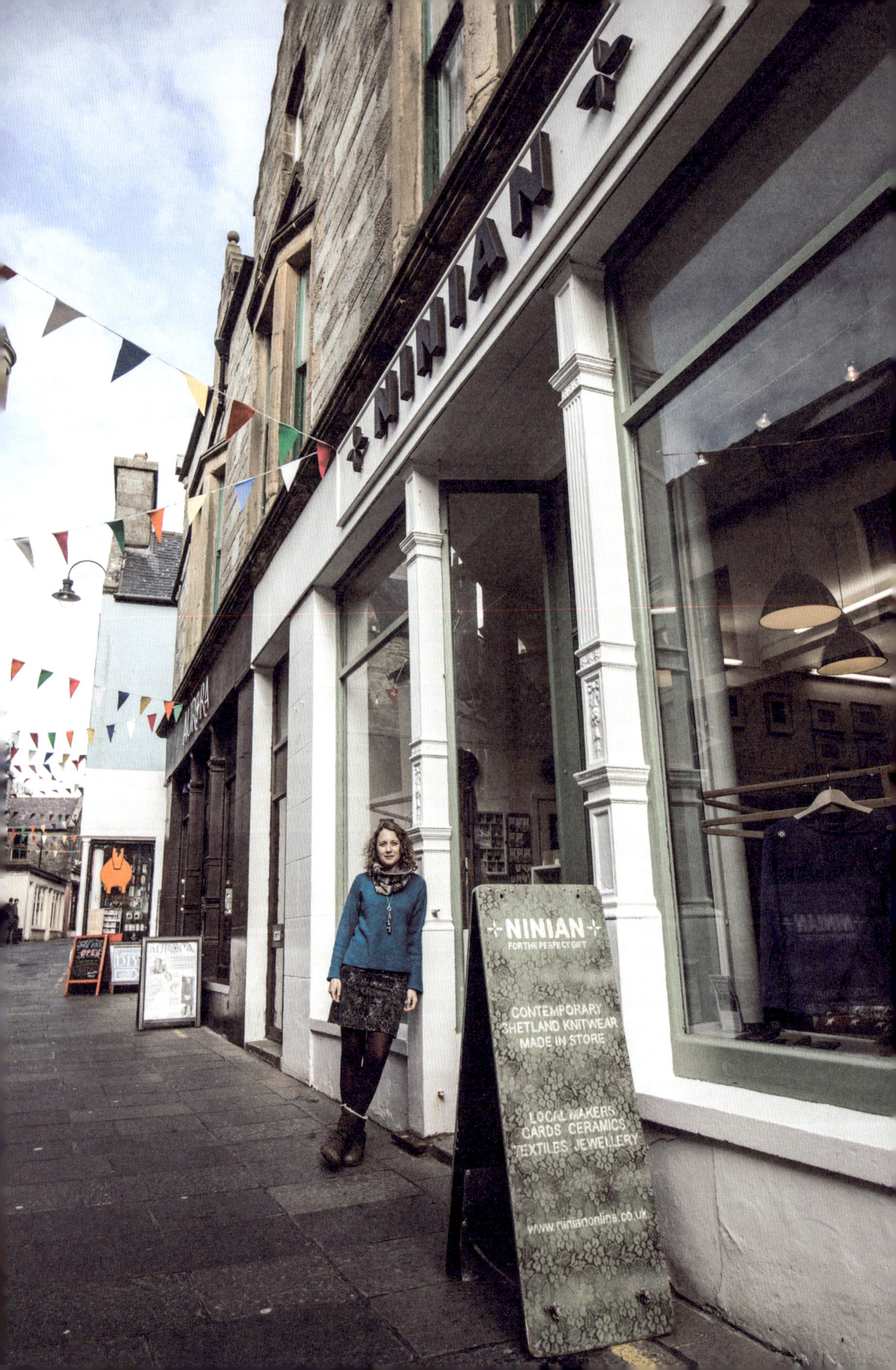
NINIAN
NINIAN
FOR THE PERFECT GIFT
CONTEMPORARY
SHETLAND KNITWEAR
MADE IN STORE
LOCAL MAKERS
CARDS CERAMICS
TEXTILES JEWELLERY
www.ninianonline.co.uk
AURORA

# Joanna Hunter

## Ninian

"Colours come to life here," says Joanna Hunter of the Shetland landscape—and her designs for her distinctive knitwear brand, Ninian, certainly bring life to colour too. With a bold and playful palette, coupled with classic simplicity of line, Joanna's textiles have been snapped up by Japanese and Scandinavian trade buyers, but the brand remains firmly rooted in her Shetland home. It's important to Joanna that Ninian has a central position for both its shop and studio on Lerwick's major thoroughfare, known simply as "the street". Everyone likes the fact that they can pop in for a nosey if they are in Shetland to see where and how our knitwear is made," Joanna says. "It makes such a difference to a customer's understanding of the hand-made quality of what we produce when they can trace it right out of the studio and onto the shelf." Two of the Lerwick buildings in which Ninian has found a home were previously knitwear outlets, and Joanna loves to hear local stories about the past lives of her premises. But such stories can also make her pause for thought. "Owning a shop in a building where my forebears went to sell their knitting—and were frequently treated with scant dignity—has made me determined to pay a fair price for all work, such as the hand-knitted gloves and hats we buy in to complement our own collections." Contemporary and forward-looking knitwear businesses like Ninian have brought a new vitality to Lerwick's retail landscape: "there's a great vibe on the street," Joanna says.

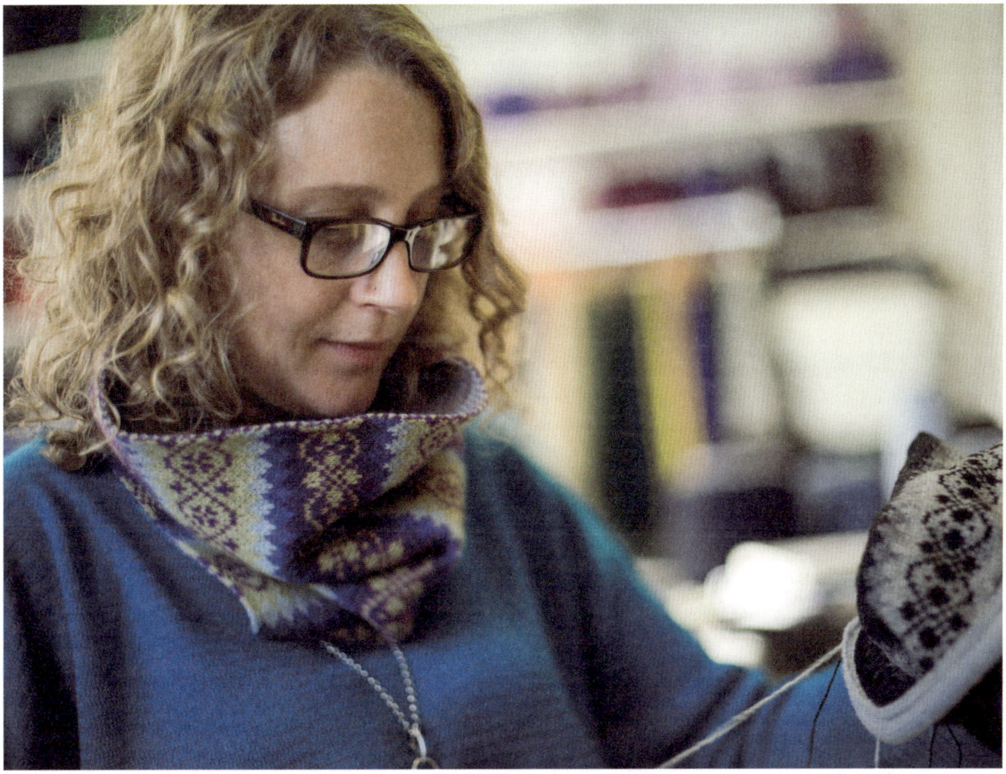

# Natalie Cairns-Ratter

## The Shetland Tannery

Working in Shetland during a busy lambing in 2010, Natalie Cairns-Ratter met her husband and did not look back. With a firm belief in diverse use as the best form of respect to domestic livestock, she was surprised to discover that Shetland sheepskins were treated as a by-product, and routinely discarded as waste. Learning the difficult and involved processes of tanning from scratch, Natalie established the Shetland Tannery on her Northmavine croft in 2012, from where she now produces sheepskins of extraordinary beauty. From shaela (grey) and eesit (white) through to Shetland black and moorit (brown), with their individual shades and markings, Natalie's skins reveal the wonderful aesthetic diversity of Shetland sheep. "Shetland sheepskins tell the living story of our rugged island landscape," she says, "our sheep live incredible lives, enjoying the lush heather hills of the summer months, and enduring long winters. The narrative of the seasons and environment is written right through their skins and fleeces. They are wonderful to work with." Natalie feels a deep connection to Shetland sheep as both crofter and craftswoman: "I always go back to the sheep, observing their behaviour, the way that they communicate. They give so much. I feel it is vitally important to celebrate these animals in their beautiful and useful skins." With admirable skill, knowledge and focus, Natalie's business is a showcase for the natural woolly beauty of the islands' native breed. "I hope in years to come that Shetland sheepskins will be as immediately recognisable as Fairisle knitting."

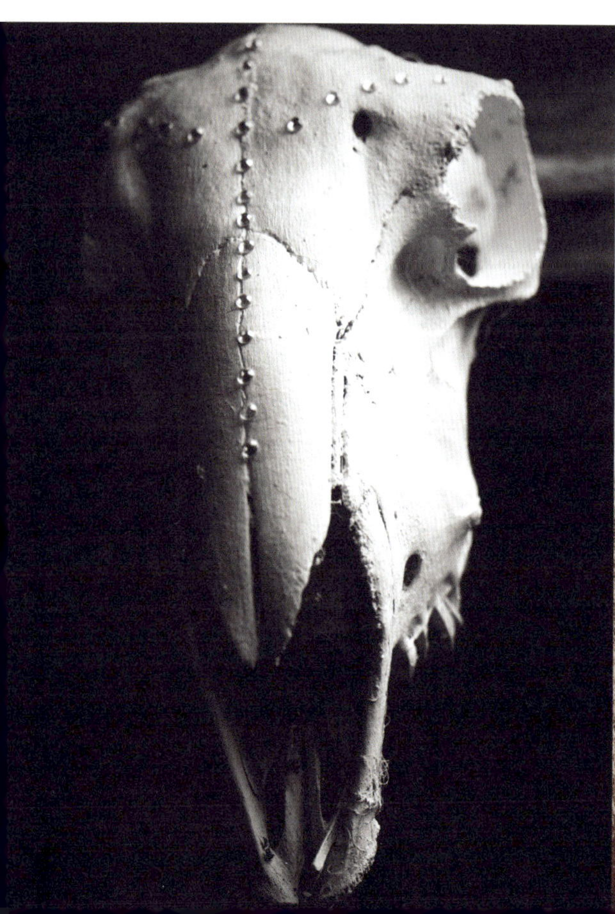

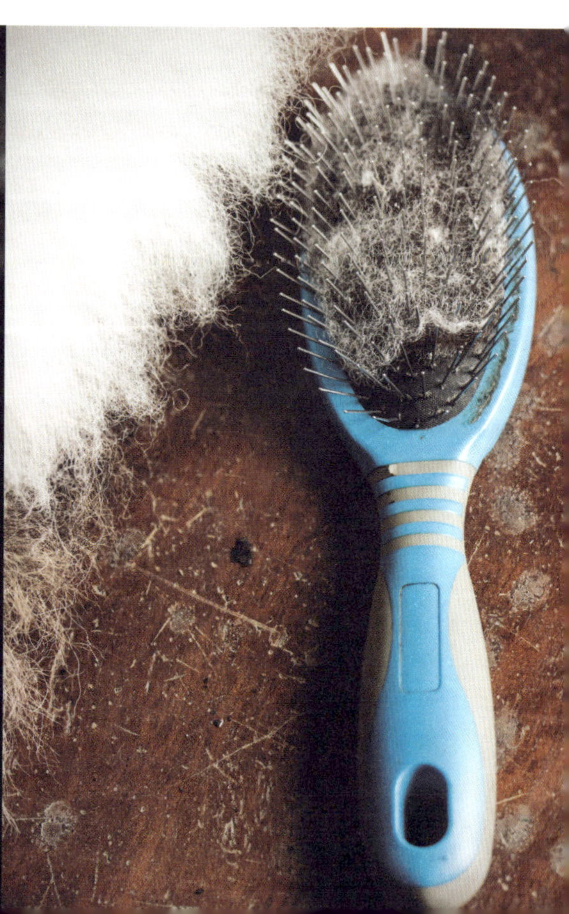

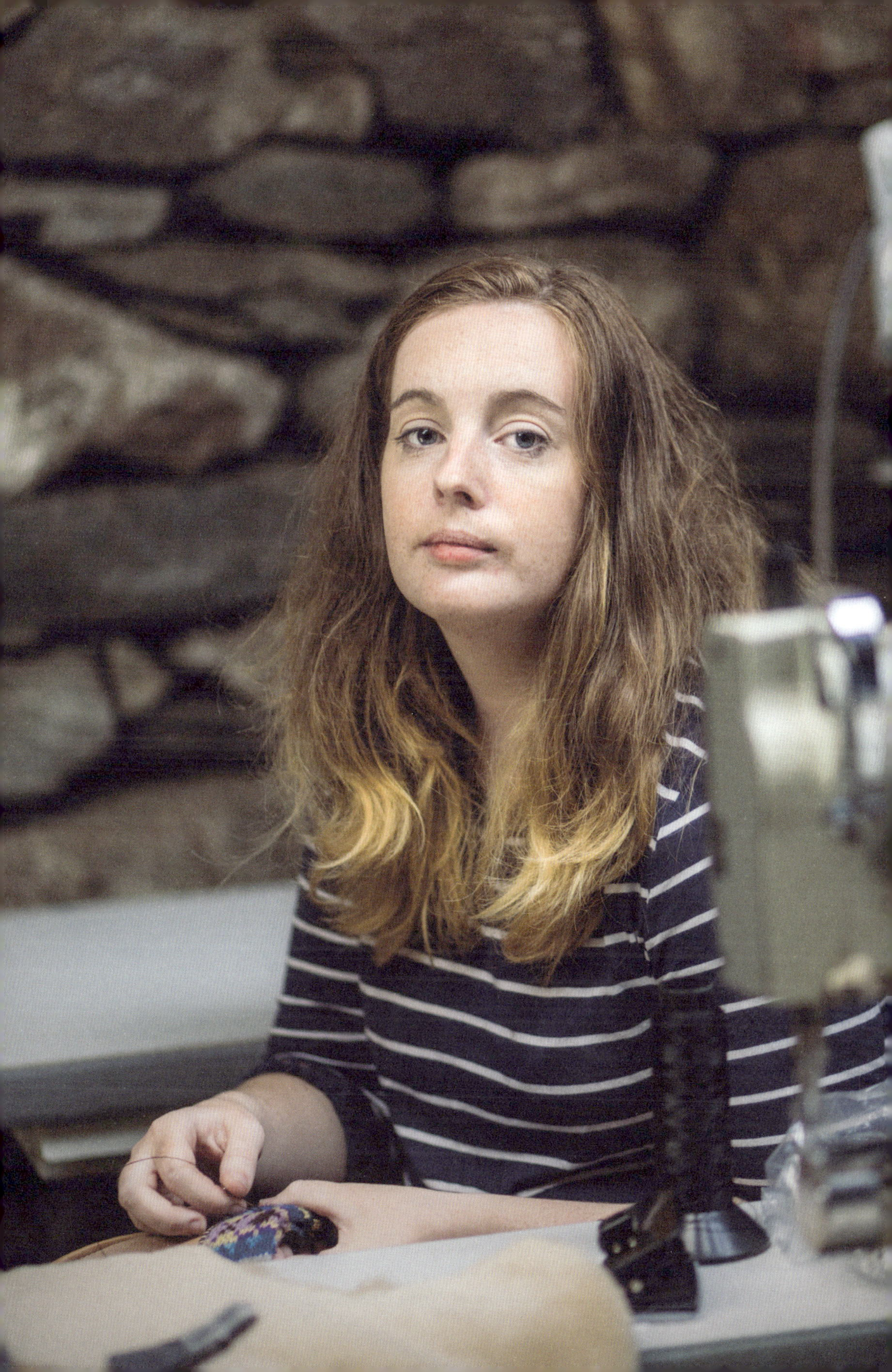

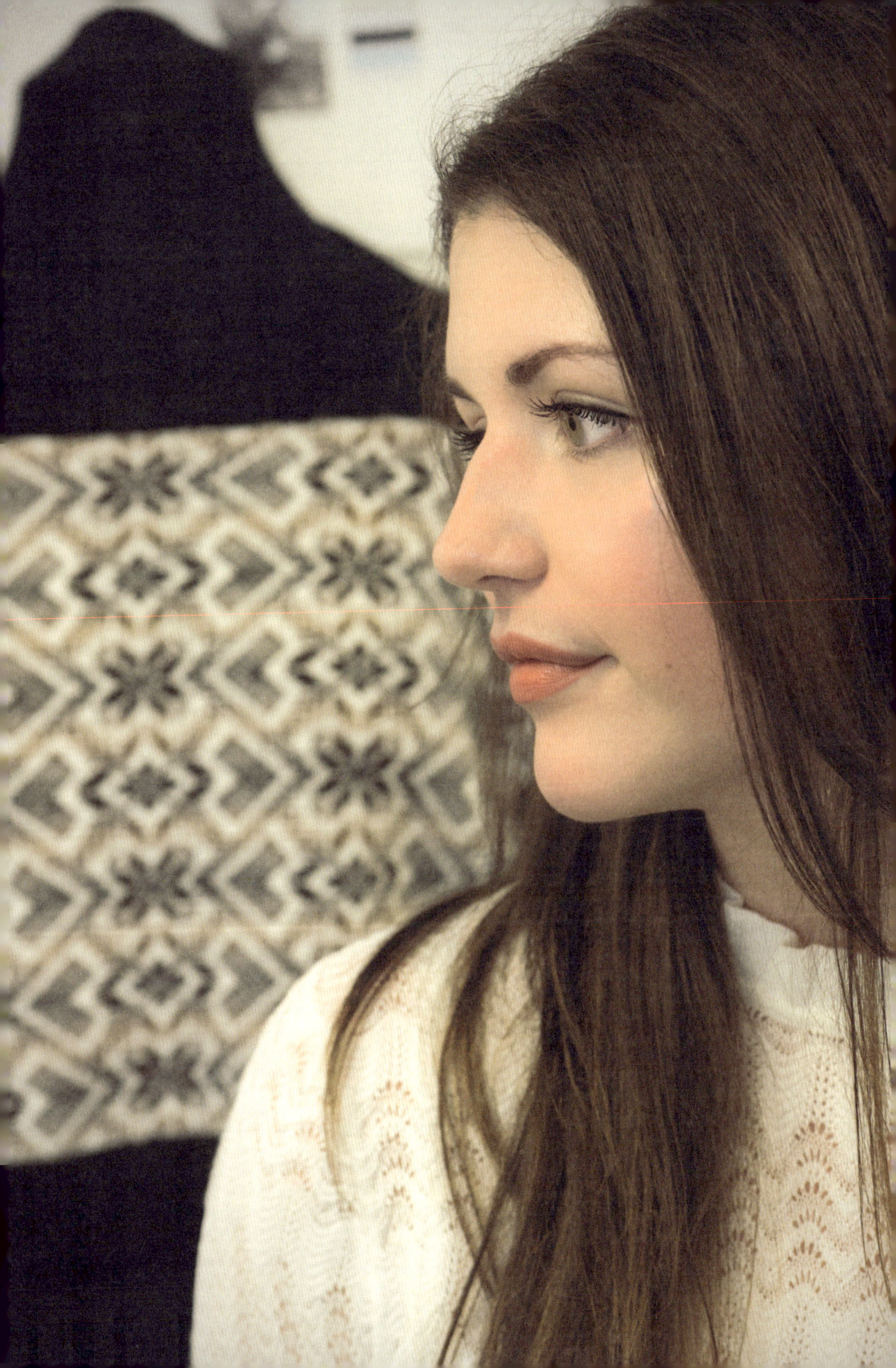

# Rhea Kay
## Student

Student Rhea Kay was always keenly interested in the creative arts. "I studied NC Art and Design for a year at Shetland College," says Rhea, "and saw the work that was being produced on the Textiles degree. It really opened my eyes to the level of experimentation and creativity that was achievable within the medium, and I continued to the BA Hons degree in Contemporary Textiles." Now in the second year of her degree, Rhea is already producing highly distinctive work characterised by beauty and balance. Fairisle motifs are translated into intriguing surface textures, and traditional Shetland colourwork is given new life with restrained palettes and contemporary shapes. "Part of me always knew I'd specialise in knit because of my connections to it in a personal, cultural and historical sense," she explains. Rhea has lived in the close-knit island community of Whalsay all her life. Growing up on a small croft, her memories have been continually shaped by the familial work of wool: clipping sheep, rearing lambs, and her grandmothers' and great-grandmothers' skilled knitting. "I see other students being inspired by their favourite artists and designers," says Rhea, "and this is the way my Whalsay heritage inspires me." Rhea intends to draw on this inspiration beyond her degree. "Developing a business seems daunting, but the supportive network I have around me and the unique resources of the College's Textile Facilitation Unit mean that I can explore these possibilities. Fingers crossed you'll see more of me one day!"

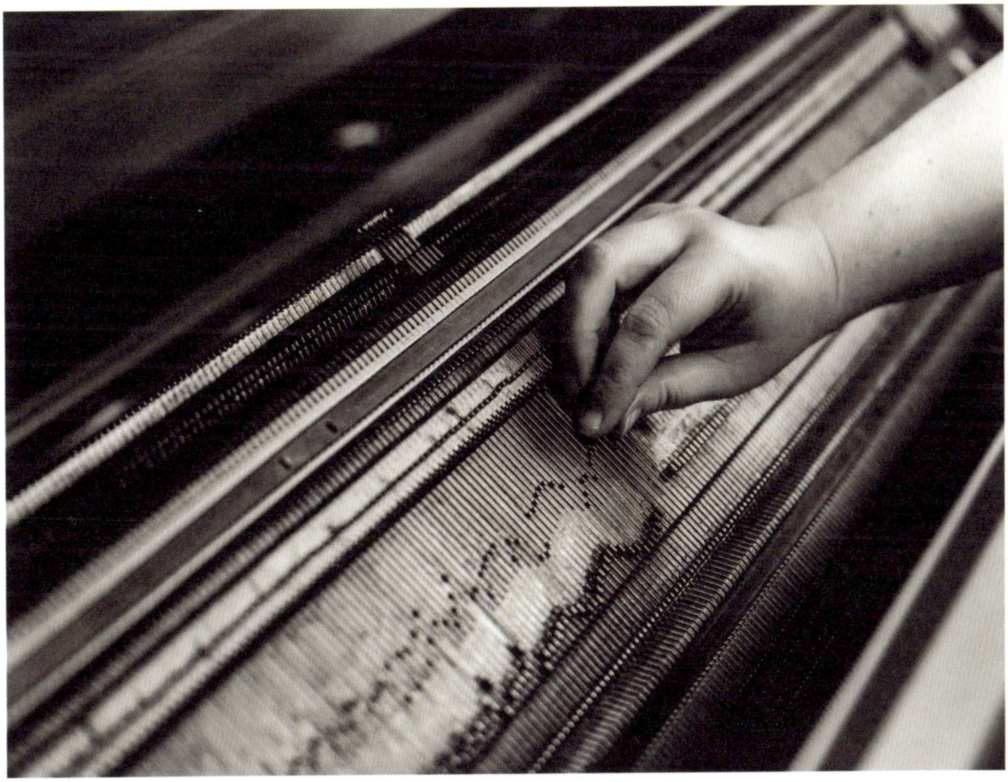

# Anne Eunson
## Lace Knitter & Designer

Anne Eunson grew up in Voe, in a family of fine knitters. Her mother produced beautiful lace scarves and haps for sale, and the first thing Anne remembers knitting is a vest for herself in plain riggies (garter stitch) to wear through the winter months. An extraordinarily skilled craftswoman, Anne has always loved the rhythms of fine lace, and spent her young life as a knitter absorbed in traditional patterns and techniques. Signing up for a degree in textiles at Shetland College in later adult life, Anne found her approach to her craft was completely transformed. "I realised I had certain ideas about what you could and couldn't do in knitting, and was quite set in my thinking," she says, "but suddenly I was able to see so many possibilities." Anne's degree not only enabled her to put her existing skills to great use, but also gave her the confidence to expand, and a context within which to do so. "My degree totally opened my eyes," she says. Anne has continued to work with lace, but in a manner that is refreshingly unconventional. Knitting with adapted curtain poles and strong fishing twine, she created for her front garden an incredible fence whose combination of scale with delicacy perhaps surprises most. The beautiful print o' the wave motifs surround the thriving garden, echoing the motion of the sea that's visible from every aspect of Anne's lovely home on Burra Isle. She's now working on another fence for her back garden.

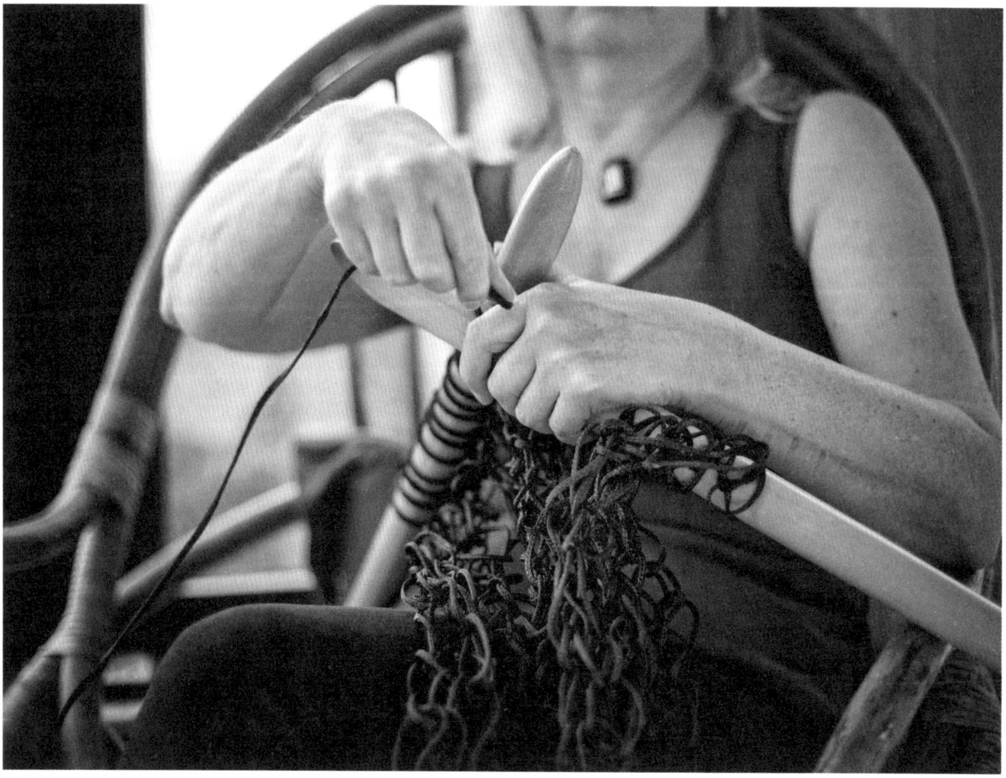

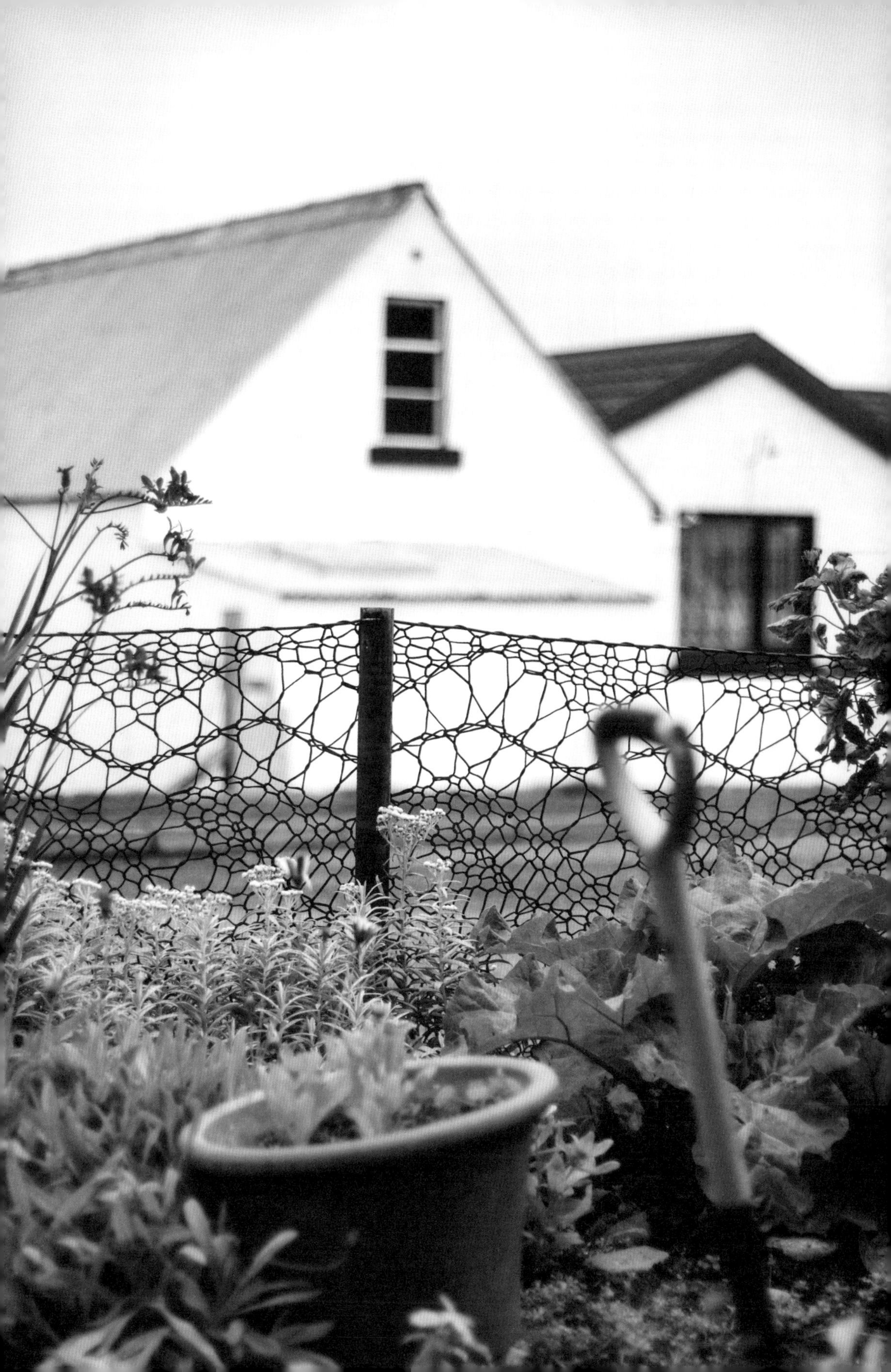

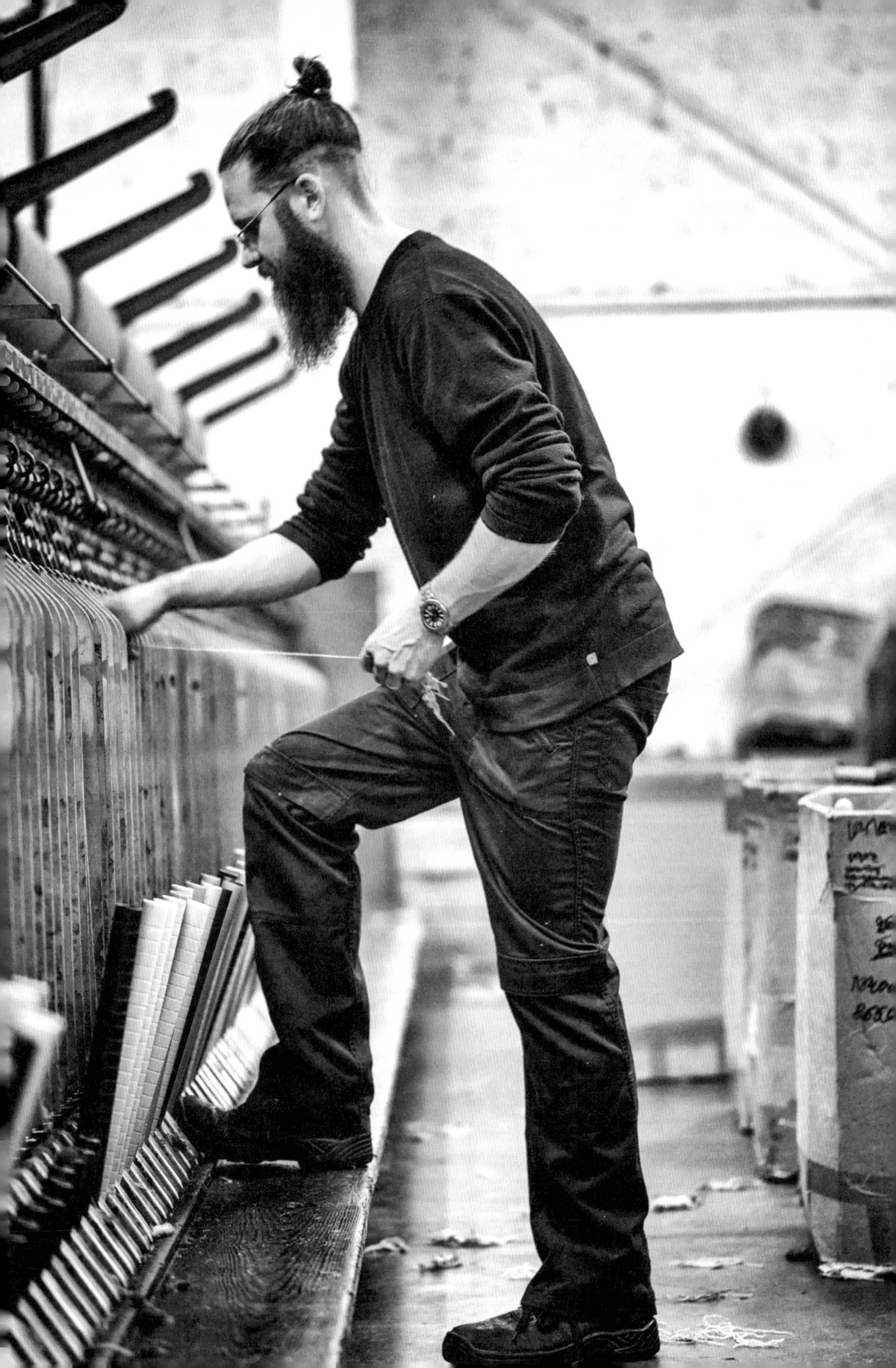

# Jamieson's of Shetland

## Mill & Manufacturer

Five generations of the Jamieson family have worked with Shetland wool. From Sandness, on Shetland's beautiful west side, late nineteenth-century Jamiesons first began developing their business combining wool brokerage with finished knitwear. Twentieth-century Jamiesons grew the company into a thriving retail operation and witnessed multiple changes in the islands' woolly landscape, including those brought by the coming of oil. Seeing traditional crafts and products threatened with decline, and wanting to ensure the local future of the industry, Peter Jamieson dreamt of developing Shetland's first commercial spinning mill. With the small beginnings of a single carder and spinning frame and the keen support of local bodies like the Shetland Knitwear Trades Association, his mill at Sandness went into operation in 1981. Jamieson's is unusual not only in the fact that it remains the only commercial mill in the islands, but also in the completely vertical nature of its operation. All processes of manufacture from fleece to finished garment are carried out in-house and the activities of carding, spinning, dyeing, blending, machine knitting, linking, weaving, marketing, and retail sales are performed by a dedicated team of over 40 employees. Peter's son, Garry, has inherited his father's energy and can-do attitude, and is just as happy fixing a blending machine as he is negotiating a new deal with a Japanese buyer. With a buoyant overseas market for both their hand-knitting yarn and Fairisle knitwear, Jamieson's is a local Shetland company with impressive international impact.

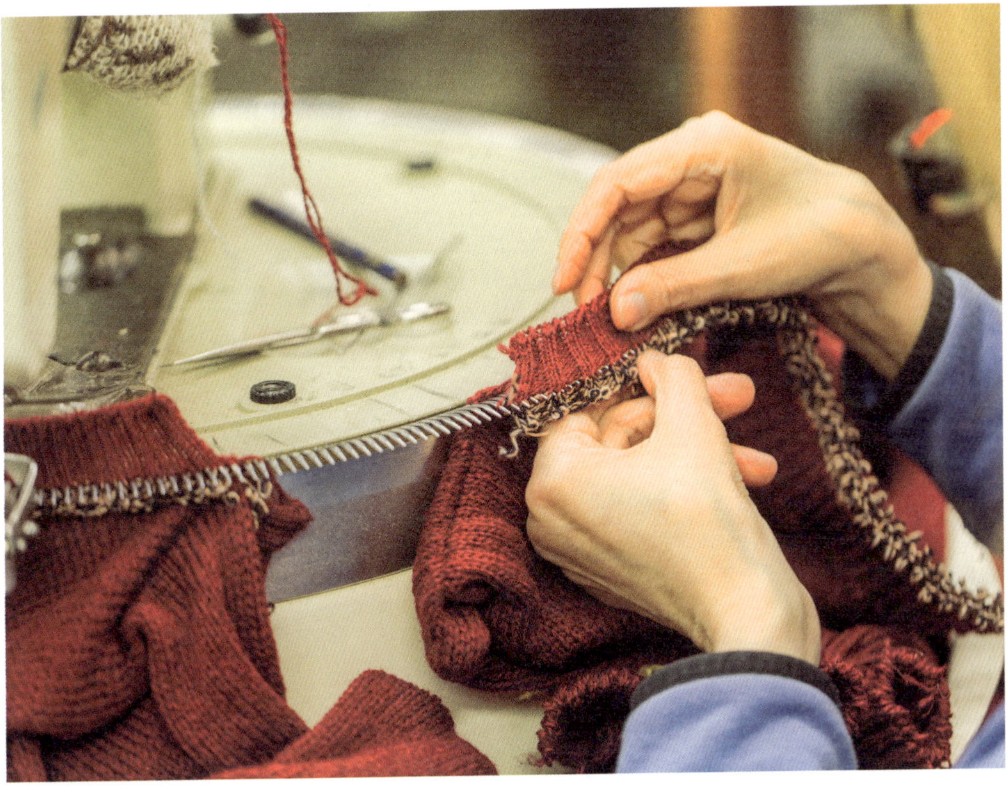

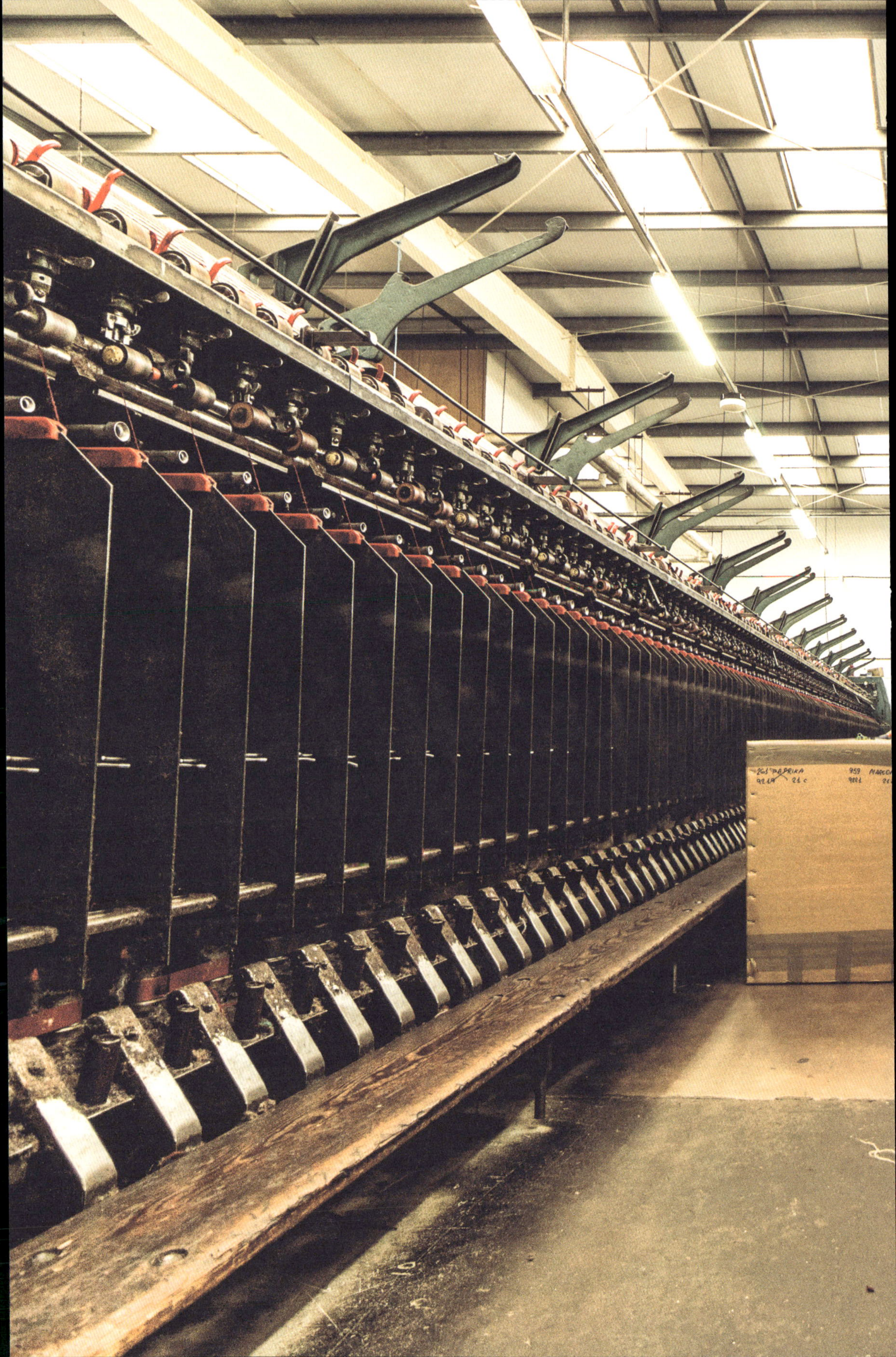

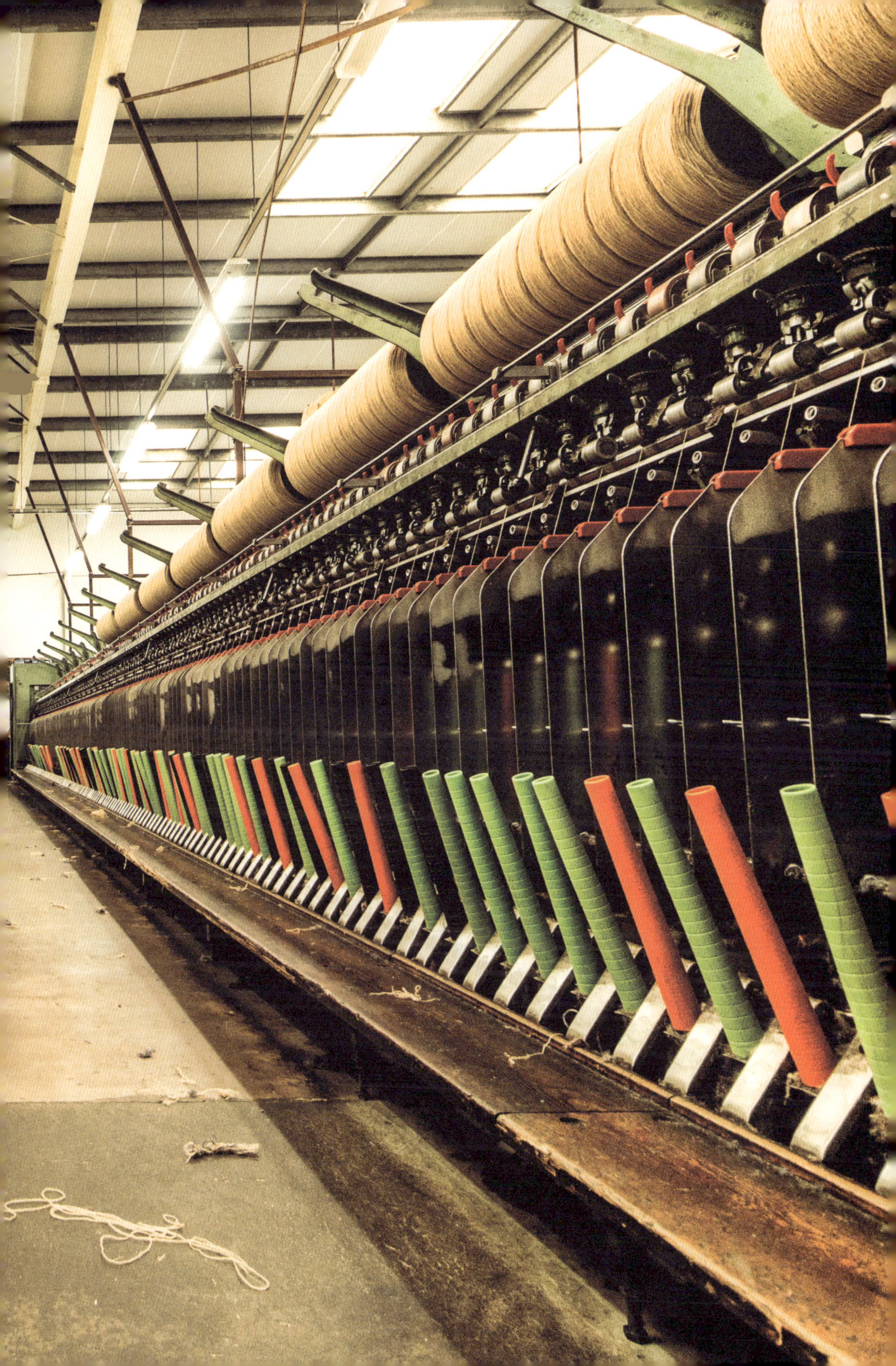

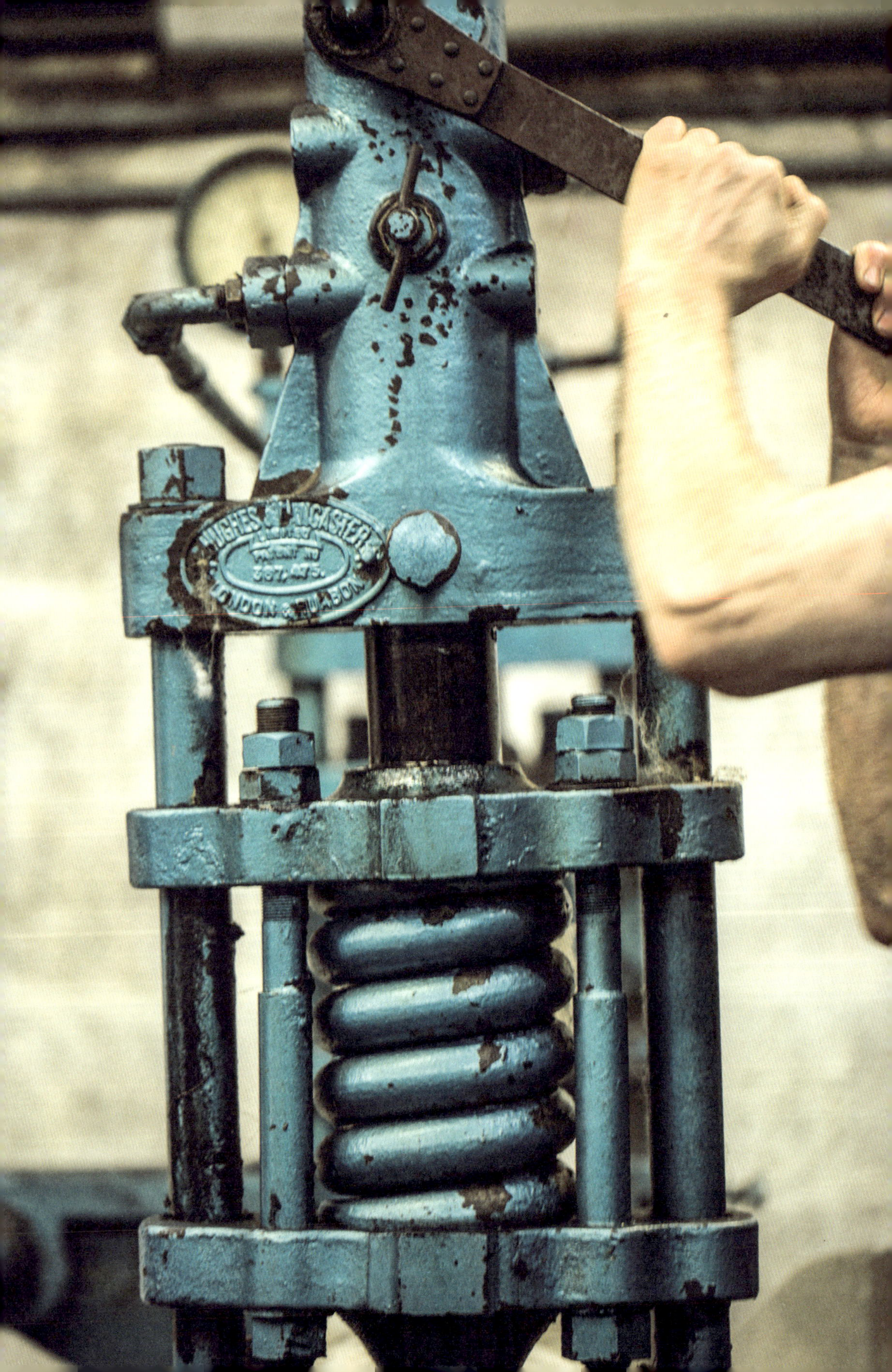
HUGHES
387,475.
LONDON

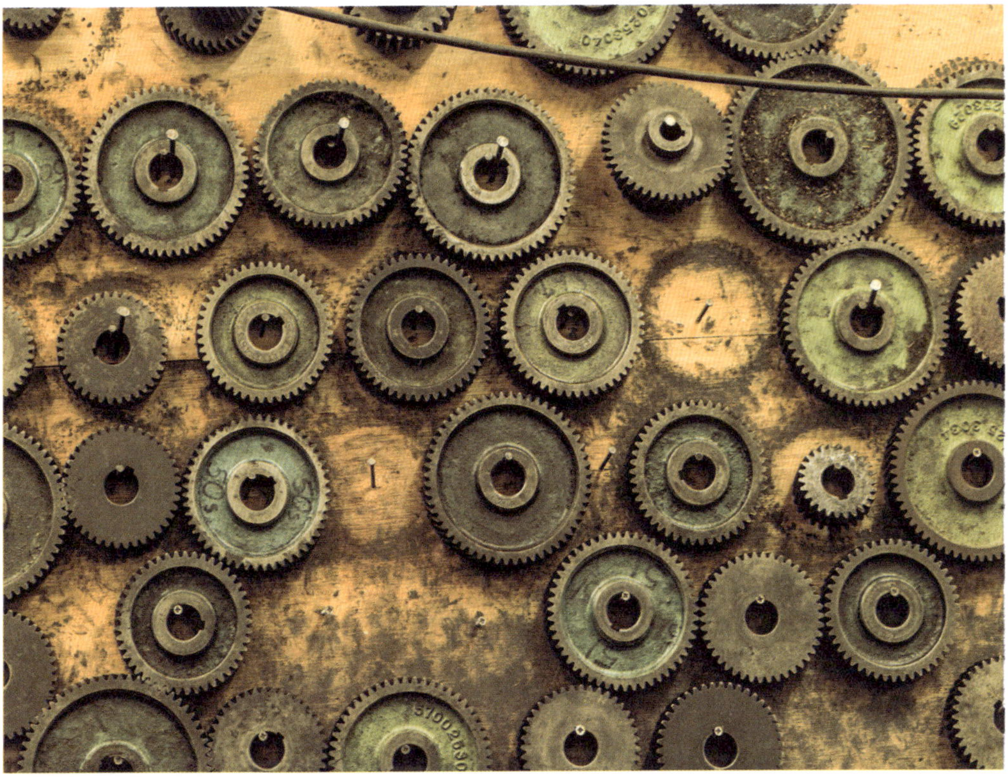

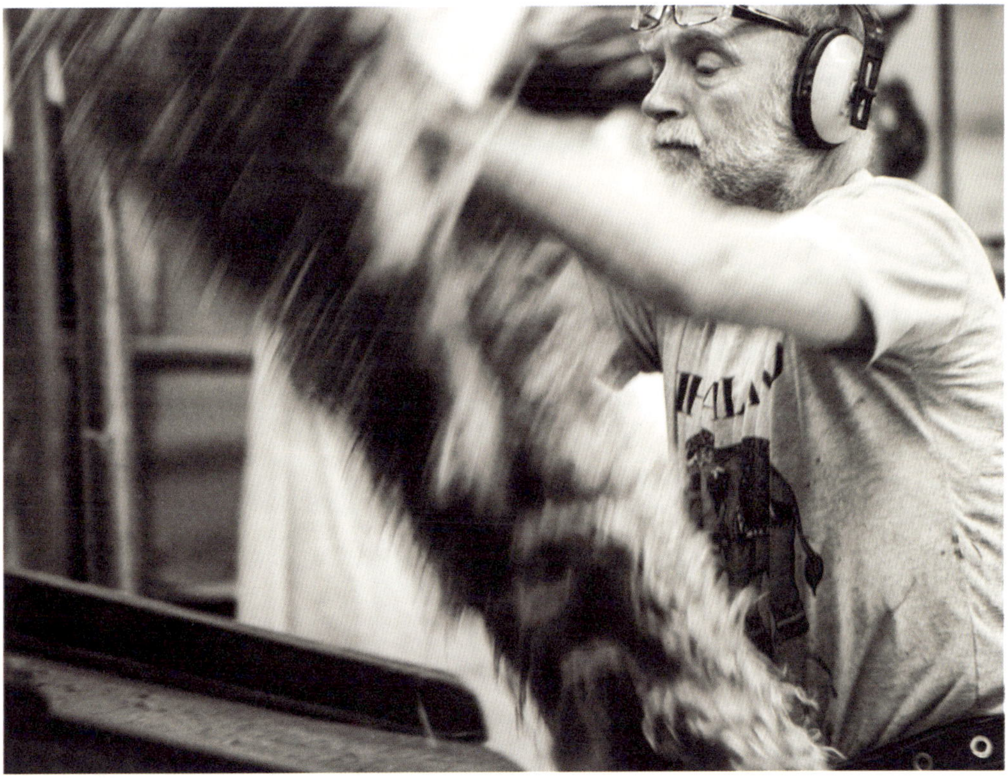

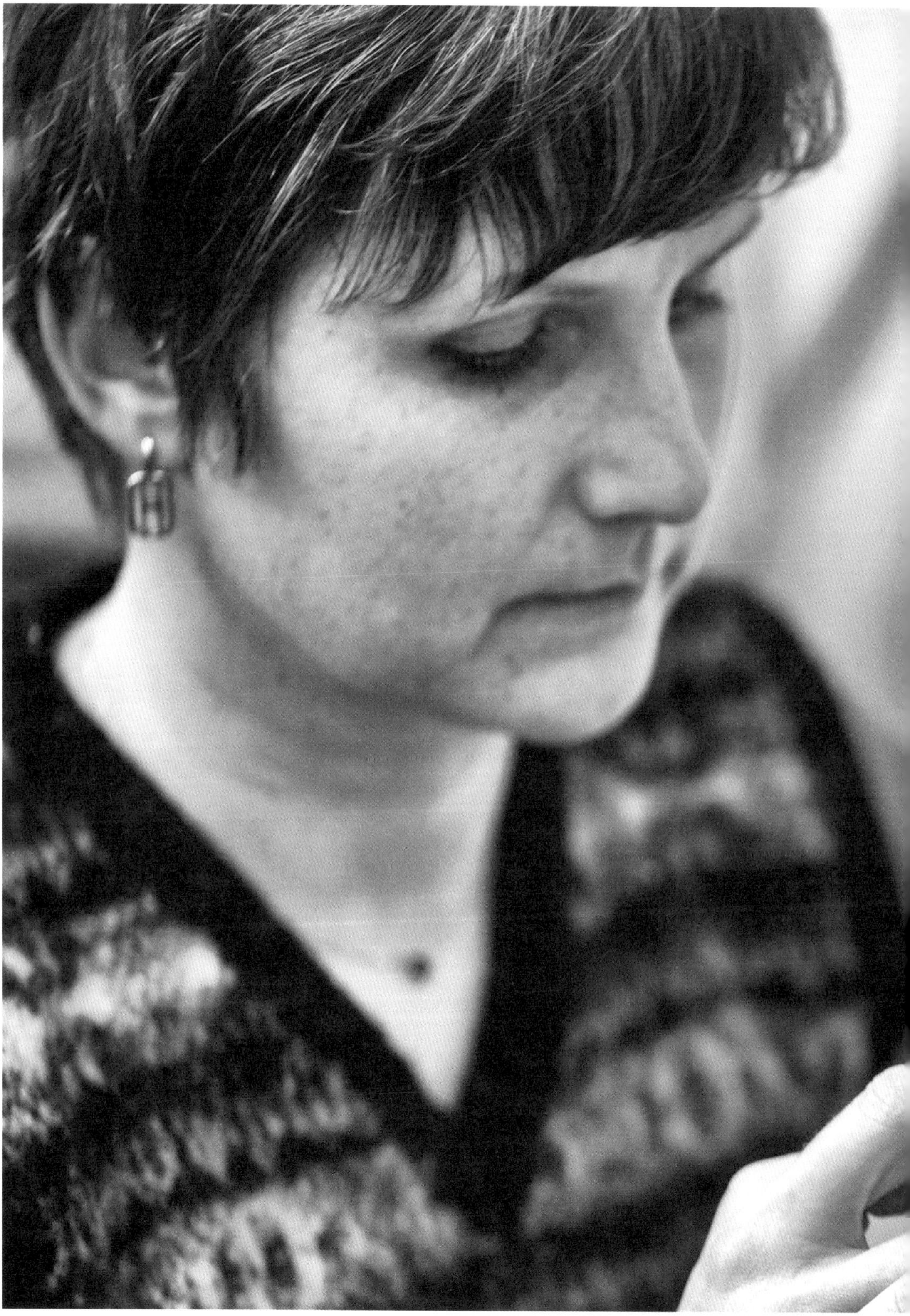

## Shades of Spindrift

Ivory, oyster, sand, salmon, sunset, paprika, flame, sunglow, peach, apricot, tangerine, pumpkin, amber, ginger, poppy, scarlet, crimson, madder, rust, cocoa, nutmeg, sandalwood, cinnamon, coral, spice, chestnut, copper, sunrise, ruby, peat, havana, moorland, thistledown, fog, osprey, leather, espresso, grouse, birch, mocha, coffee, oatmeal, cashew, camel, wren, tundra, burnt umber, burnt ochre, yellow ochre, scotch broom, gold, flax, buttermilk, buttercup, mustard, cornfield, mimosa, daffodil, lemon, chartreuse, granny smith, pistachio, marjoram, rye, lichen, thyme, artichoke, seaweed, earth, olive, tan green, autumn, old gold, bracken, spagnum, moss, ivy, laurel, moorgrass, turf, conifer, tartan, bottle, pine forest, pine, fern, leaf, prairie, leprechaun, lime, apple, celtic, emerald, jade, spruce, verdigris, mint, dewdrop, green mist, willow, eucalyptus, rosemary, sage, storm, woodgreen, rosewood, mirry dancers, black, charcoal, oxford, slate, granite, pebble, steel, heron, dove, stonehenge, stonewash, yell sound blue, blue lovat, titanic, peacock, nighthawk, mermaid, seabright, surf, aqua, caspian, splash, sapphire, petrol, lunar, lagoon, china blue, cloud, eggshell, sky, highland mist, lomond, atlantic, pacific, mirage, blue danube, teviot, bluebell, delph, clyde blue, royal, cobalt, prussian, cosmos, dark navy, admiral navy, eclipse, gentian, midnight, neptune, fjord, twilight, mist, lilac, hyacinth, purple, parma, lupin, aubretia, violet, anenome, lavender, wild violet, orchid, pot-pourri, cyclamen, clover, mulberry, dusk, purple haze, jupiter, zodiac, loganberry, port wine, purple heather, blueberry, bramble, foxglove, damask, old rose, rouge, mantilla, raspberry, peony, redcurrant, cardinal, maroon, cherry, plum, fuchsia, sherbet, lipstick, sorbet, blossom, rose, dog rose

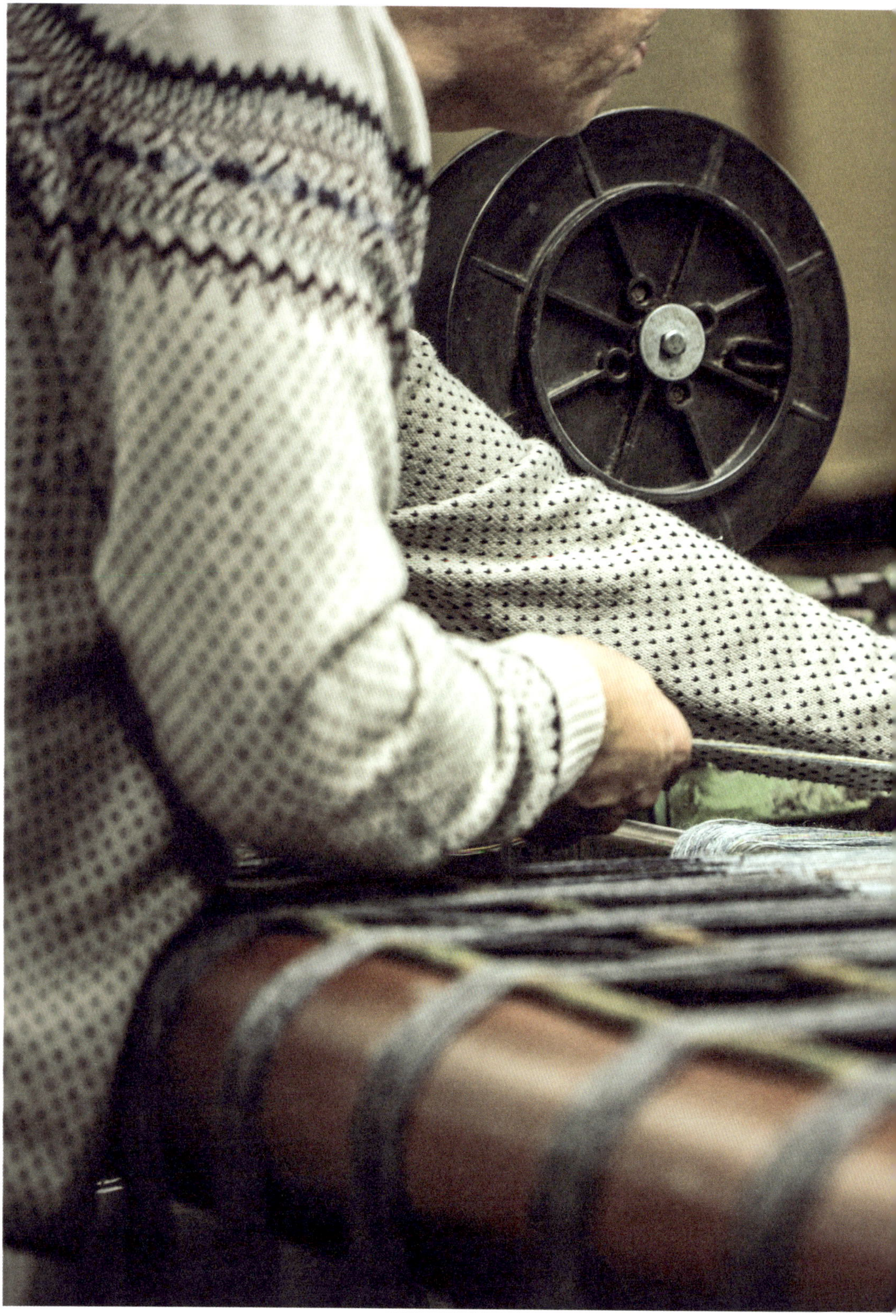

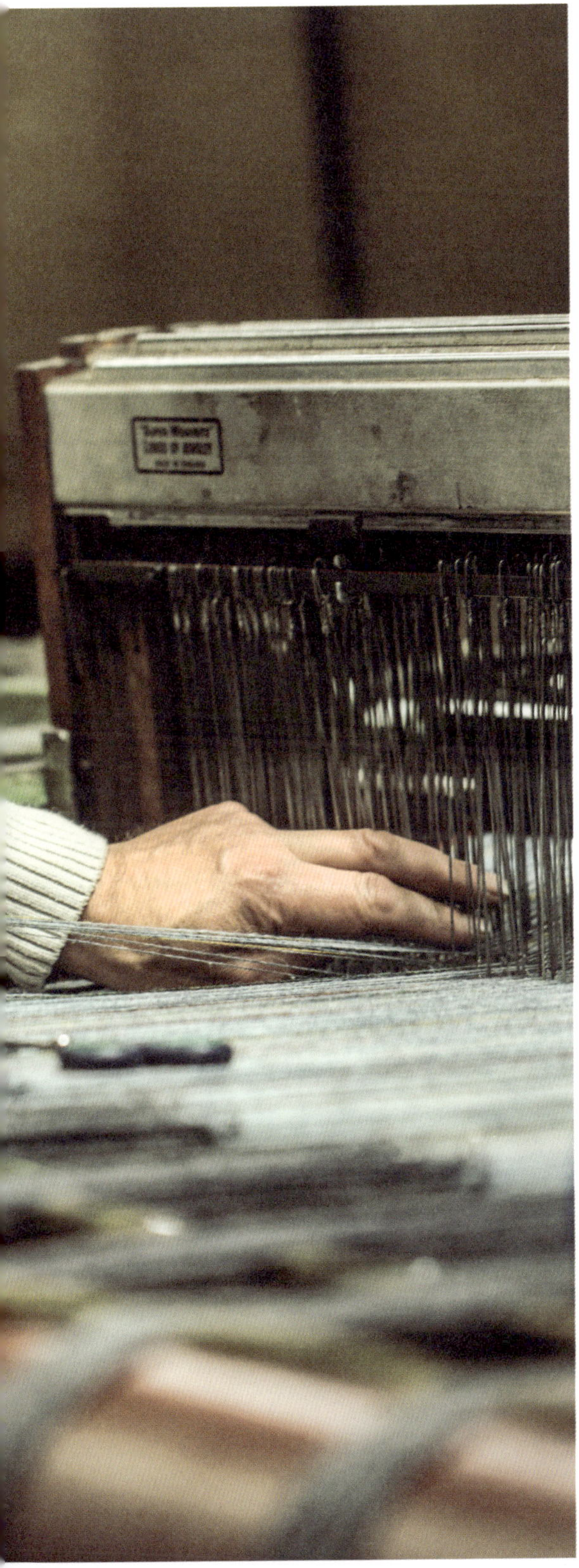

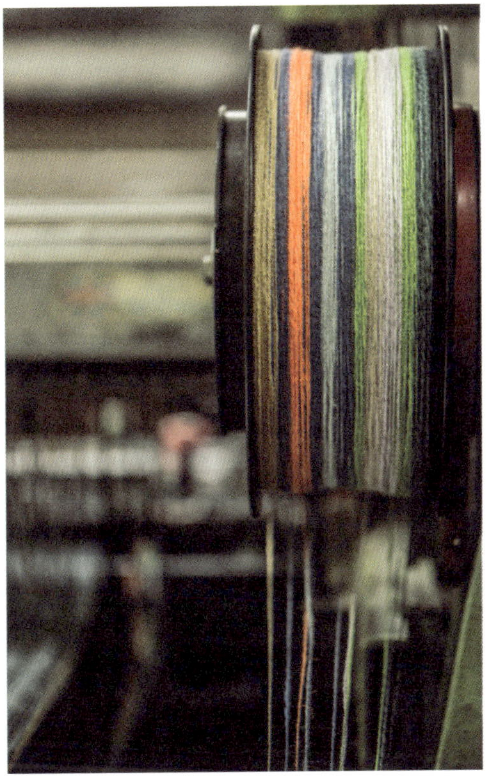

*"Some of our international clients think it is curious to find a company CEO fixing machinery on the factory floor. But that passionate connection to our product at all stages of its process is what makes us unique."*

*Garry Jamieson*

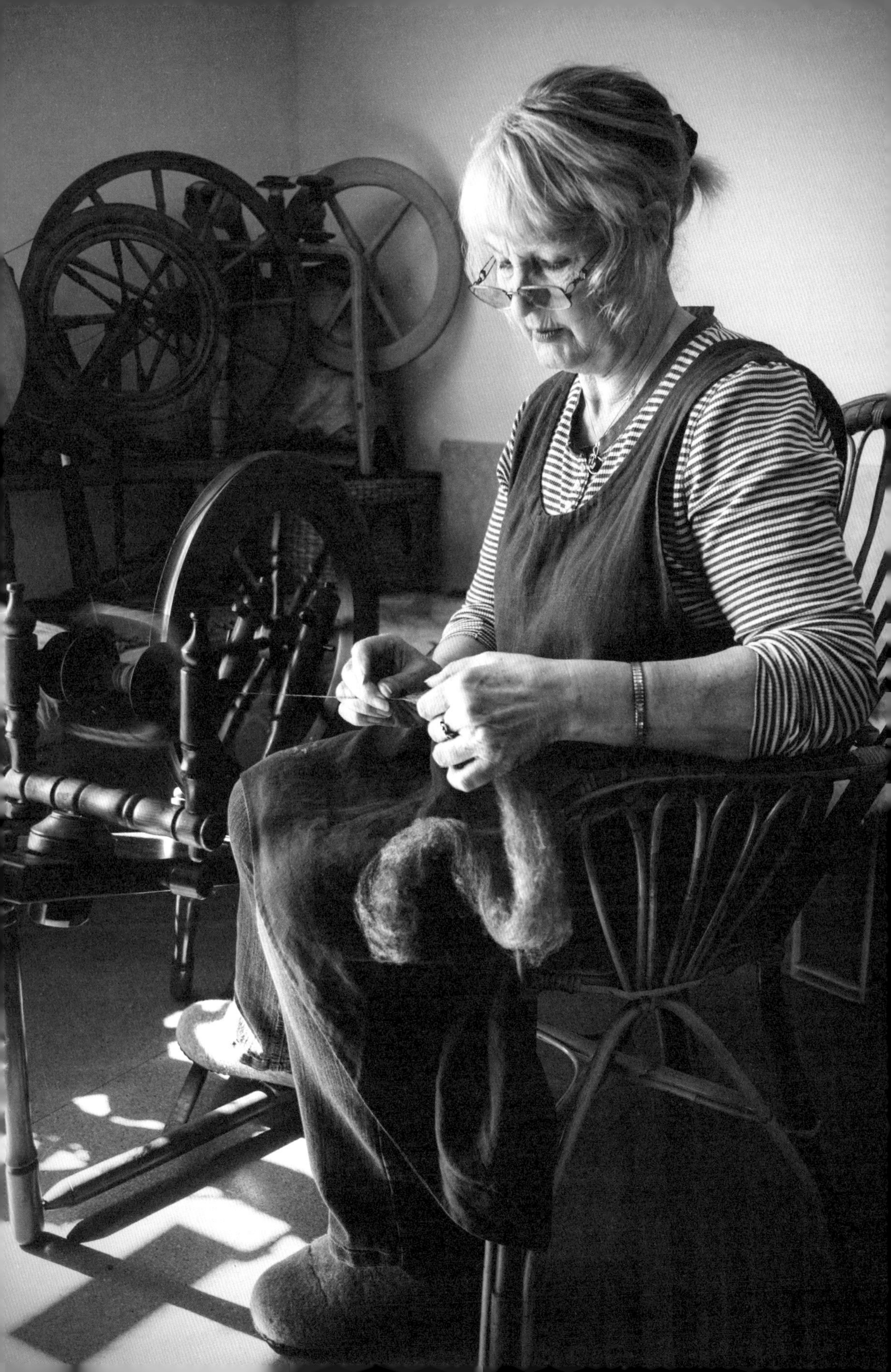

# Elizabeth Johnston
## Shetland Handspun

Talented craftswoman Elizabeth Johnston knows more about the character and qualities of a fine fleece than anyone in Shetland (with the notable exception of Oliver Henry). Hand spinning has a long history in the Shetland Islands, but it has long lacked a commercial context, and during the last century was a craft increasingly rarely practised by Shetland women (for whom it was much more profitable to knit than spin). But having long been fascinated by the spinning demonstrations at Shetland country shows, Elizabeth attended a night class and was immediately hooked. She went out and bought a wheel and did not look back. Determined to create yarn for production rather than just a hobby, over a six-month period she worked every day, spinning, plying and examining her work. As the speed, technique and quality of her output improved, she knew she could make hand spinning her business. From her tiny studio in Scousburgh, Elizabeth produces incredibly beautiful handspun yarns. For Elizabeth, the act of making is in itself a form of education, and through the insight of her crafts she's developed important knowledge of historic practices of textile production in the islands, sharing her skills through classes and workshops all over the world. A single Shetland fleece can possess an infinitely colourful variety, and Elizabeth speaks lyrically of grey-moorits, brown-moorits, blue tones, pink tones, gold tones, the sheer range of greys and blacks. "You just can't go wrong with the natural Shetland shades," she says.

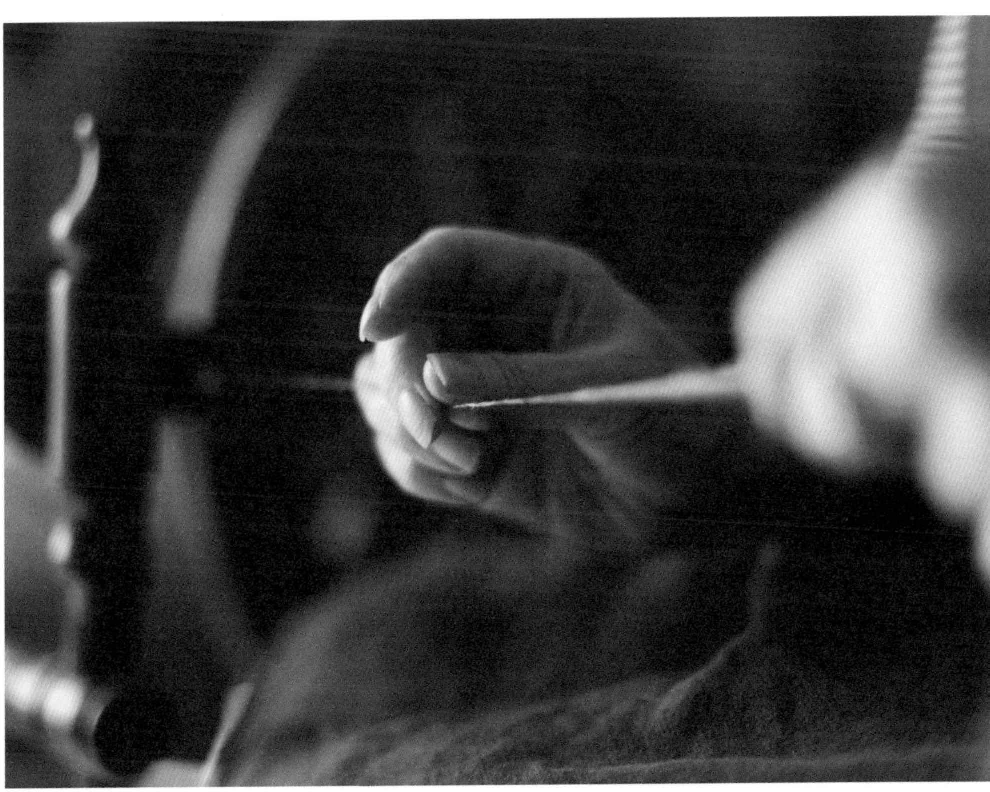

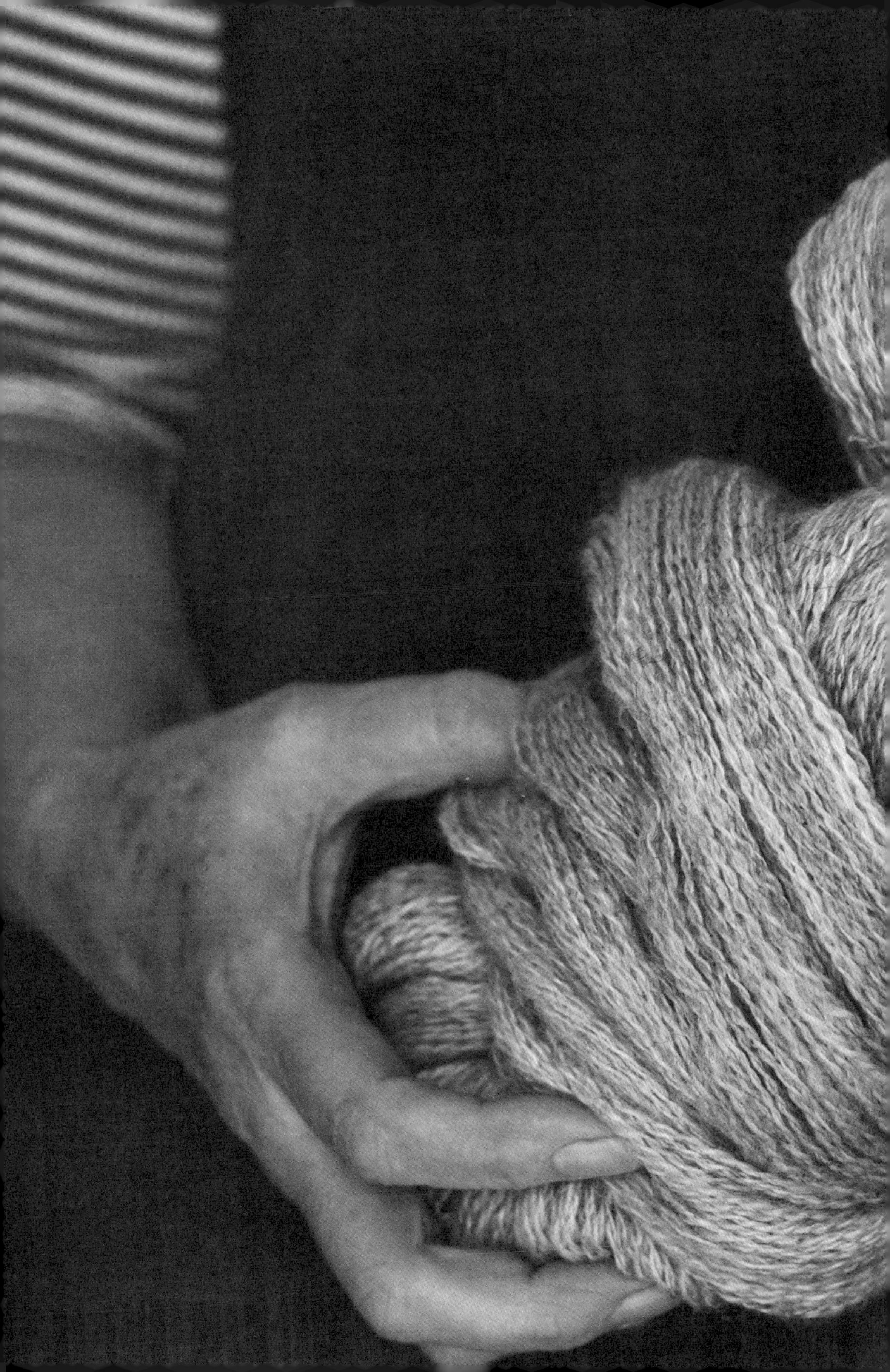

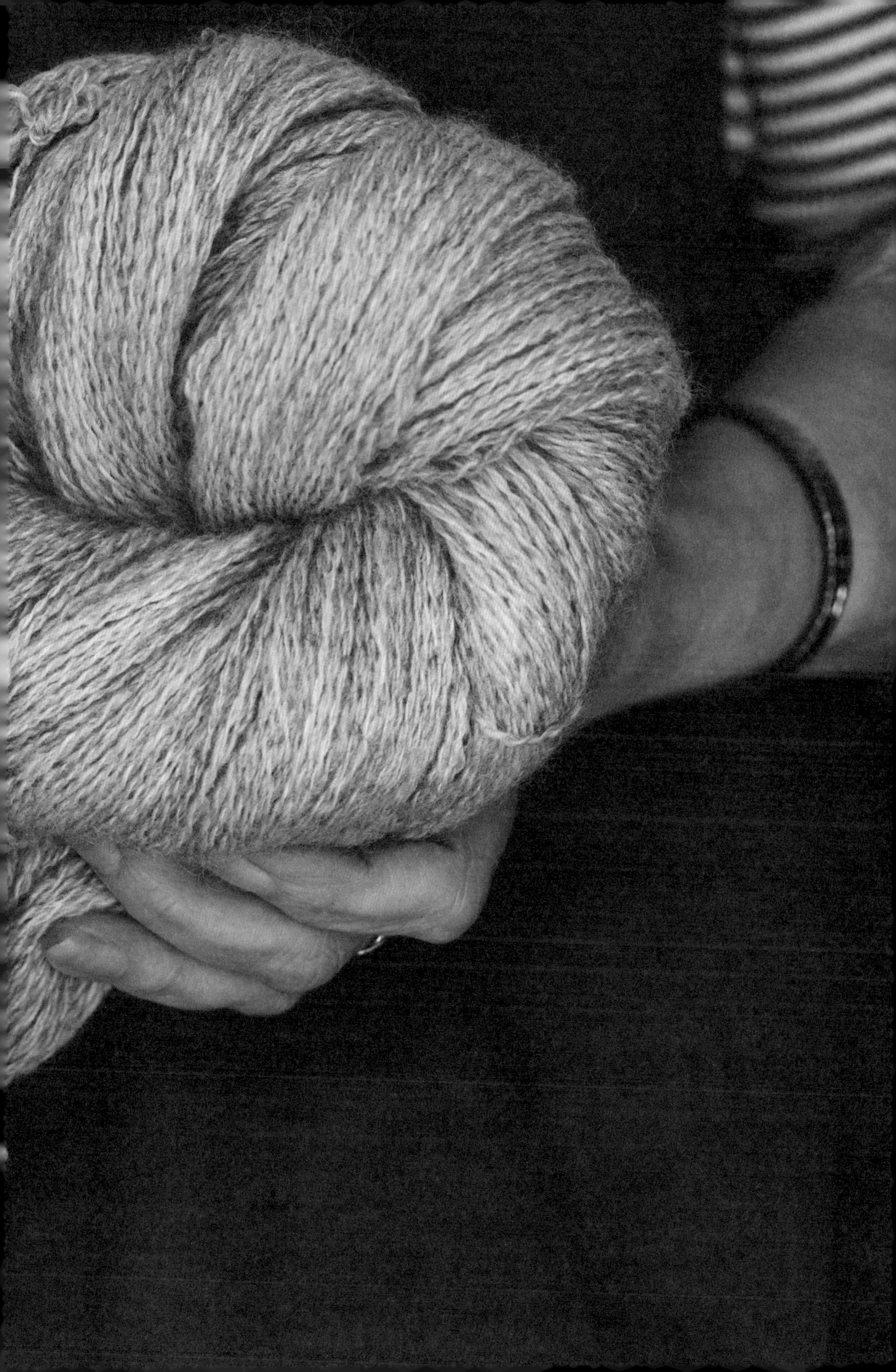

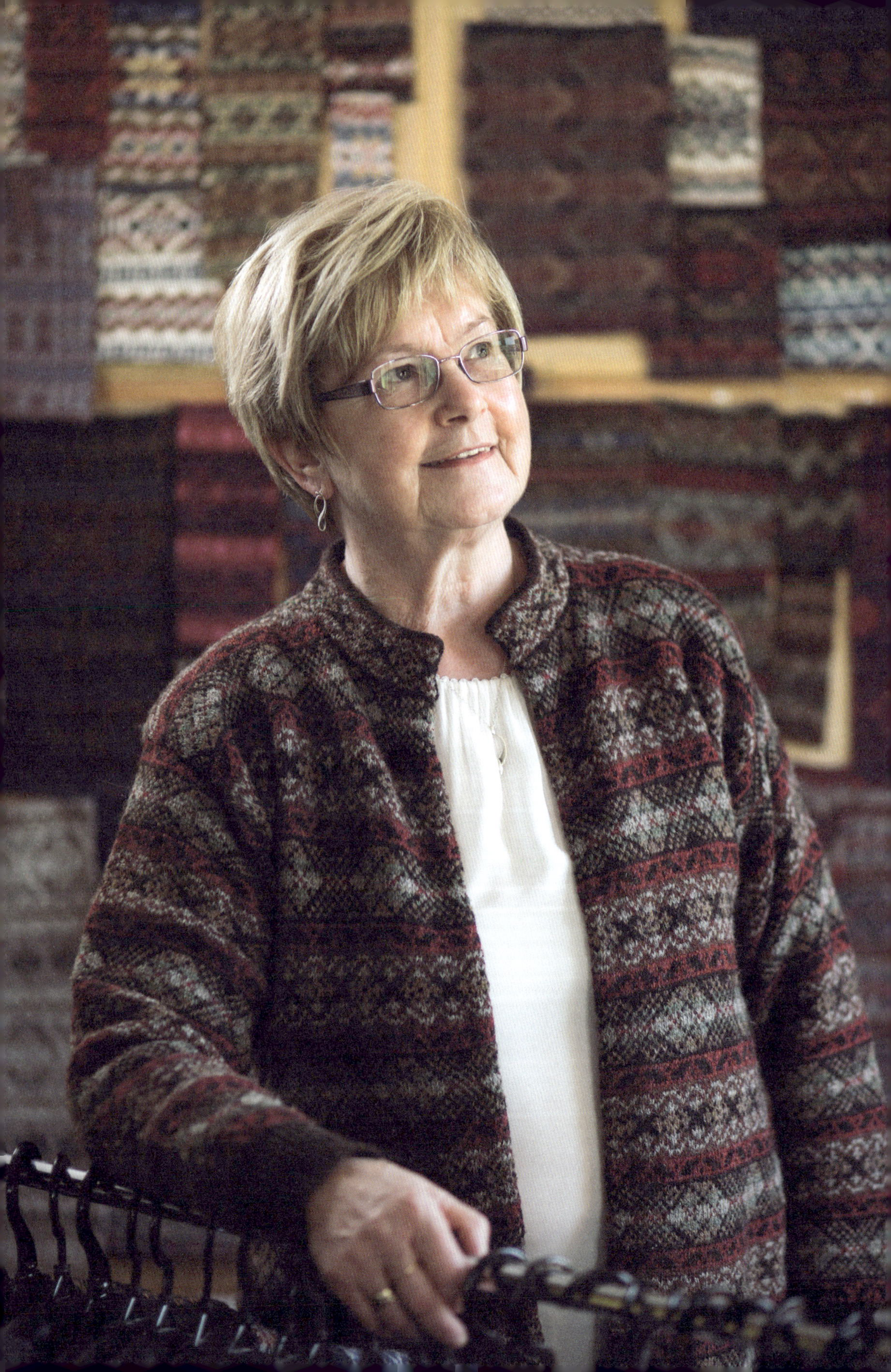

# Wilma Malcolmson
## Shetland Designer

Born in Garderhouse, on the west mainland of Shetland, Wilma Malcolmson grew up with an immediate and instinctive love of pattern and colour. By her teenage years, she was knitting allover Fairisle to order, and, after her marriage, produced plain garments on her machine at home, a form of work which, like many Shetland women, she could fit in around the demands of her young family. But Wilma was still gripped by colour's creative potential, and when she heard of a machine that could produce Fairisle fabric she knew she had to have one. With the support of the Shetland Knitwear Trades Association and the constant encouragement of her husband Leonard, Wilma developed a thriving business, first from home, and later from the Shetland Designer studio and workshop that Leonard built for her in Cunningsburgh in 1988. "One pair of hands can do so little," says Wilma, conscious of the fact that her business has always been the collective work of the hands of many women. The hub of a whole community, some of whom have been knitting for Shetland Designer for over thirty years, Wilma says that one of the best things about her work is the sense of sociable connection that exists among this group of women. Featuring rich jewel tones, careful gradients and surprising juxtapositions, Wilma's Fairisle patterns are frequently breathtaking and always recognisable. With her inspiring creative energy, she is without doubt one of the most important designers working in Shetland today.

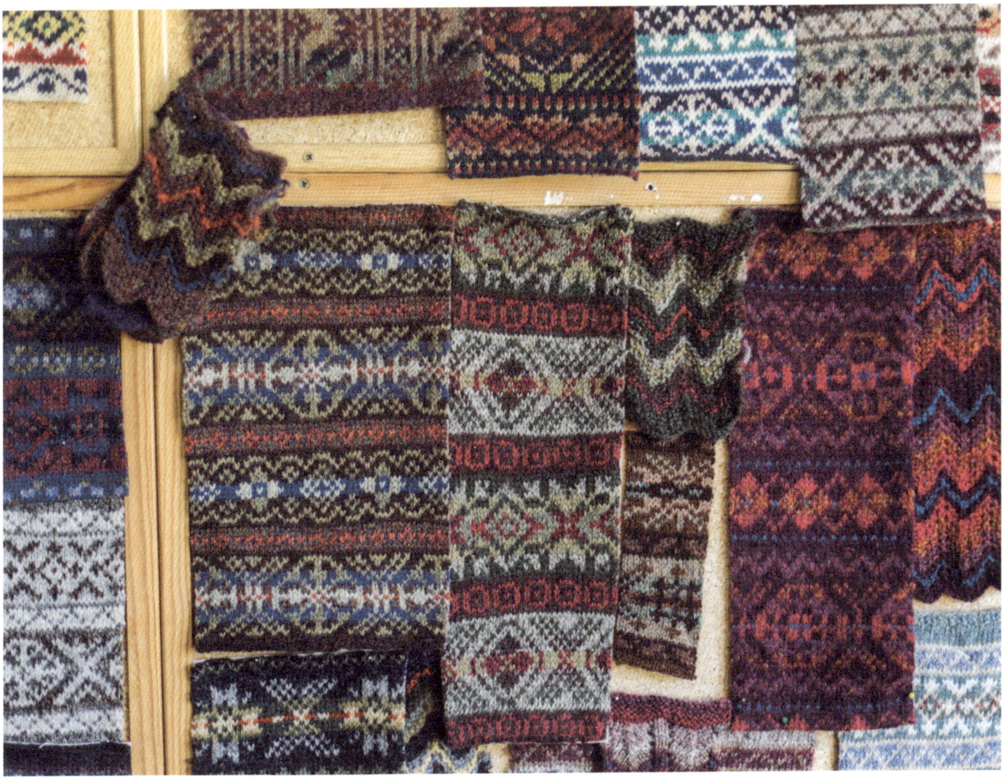

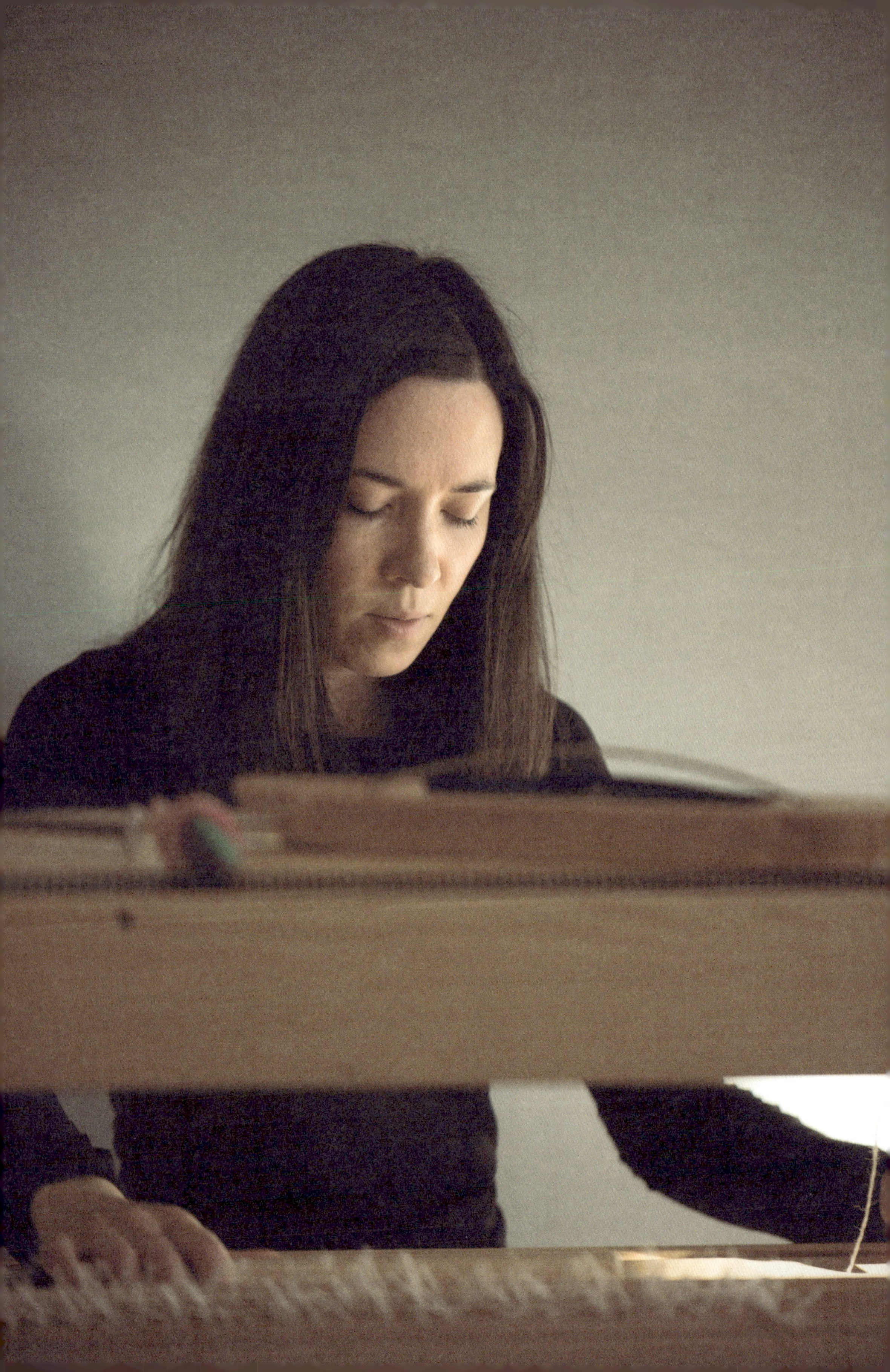

# Kharis Leggate

## Home is an Island

Weaver Kharis Leggate creates beautiful textiles and upholstery from her Shetland home. Shetland's changeable environment is a constant source of inspiration. "I love it when it is stormy, the noise of the wind and the sea whipped up wild, and that contrast with the eerie quiet of the hills when the weather is still. I like to get feelings like these into my weaving." Like the Shetland weather, Kharis's textiles have a mutable quality, appearing as if they might change into something else at any moment. "I have a very instinctive connection with what I make," says Kharis. "If I create a sample and immediately sense the coastline, or the feel of the air, or the atmosphere of a particular old crofthouse, I immediately know it is right to take forward to completion." Subtle symphonies of blues and browns and greys, her textiles are certainly suggestive of an island mood. For Kharis, the act of weaving is deeply reflective and creative. "Weaving is a like a meditation for my whole body. My hands touch every inch of the warp as I measure it to thread the loom. Both feet are moving on the pedals, and both hands work with the weft throwing the shuttle. As I'm weaving I'll pause to run my fingers over the emerging pattern and fabric. It is completely absorbing." Surely a Shetland weaver to watch, Kharis was awarded the title of "best emerging talent" for her work with British wool by *Country Homes and Interiors* magazine in 2015.

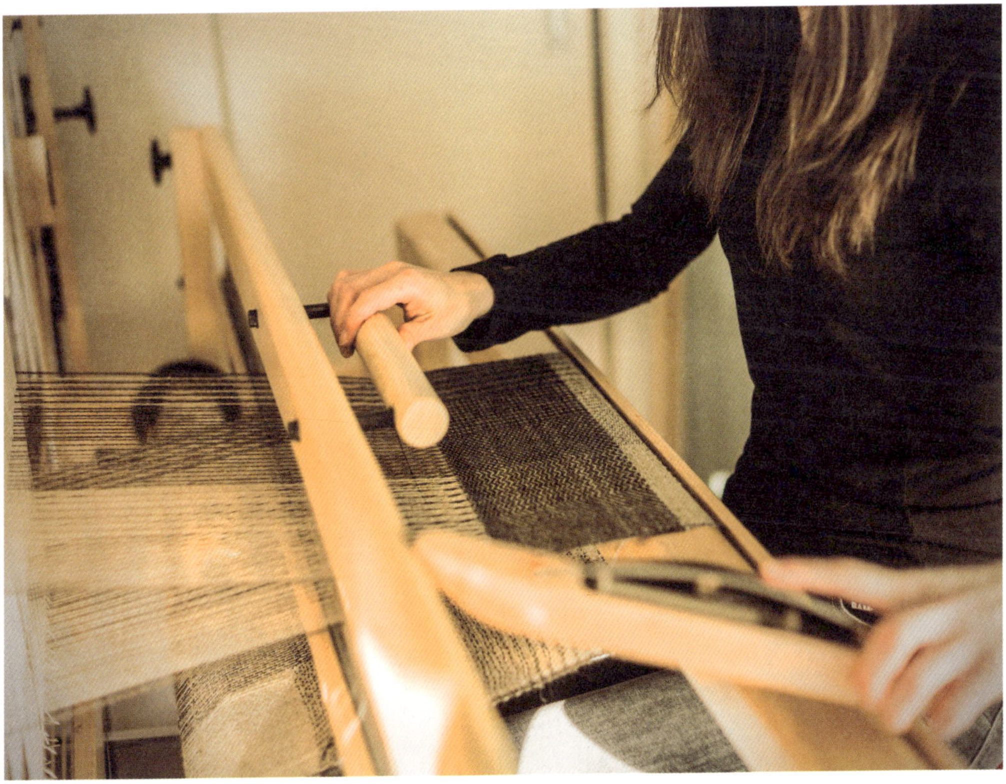

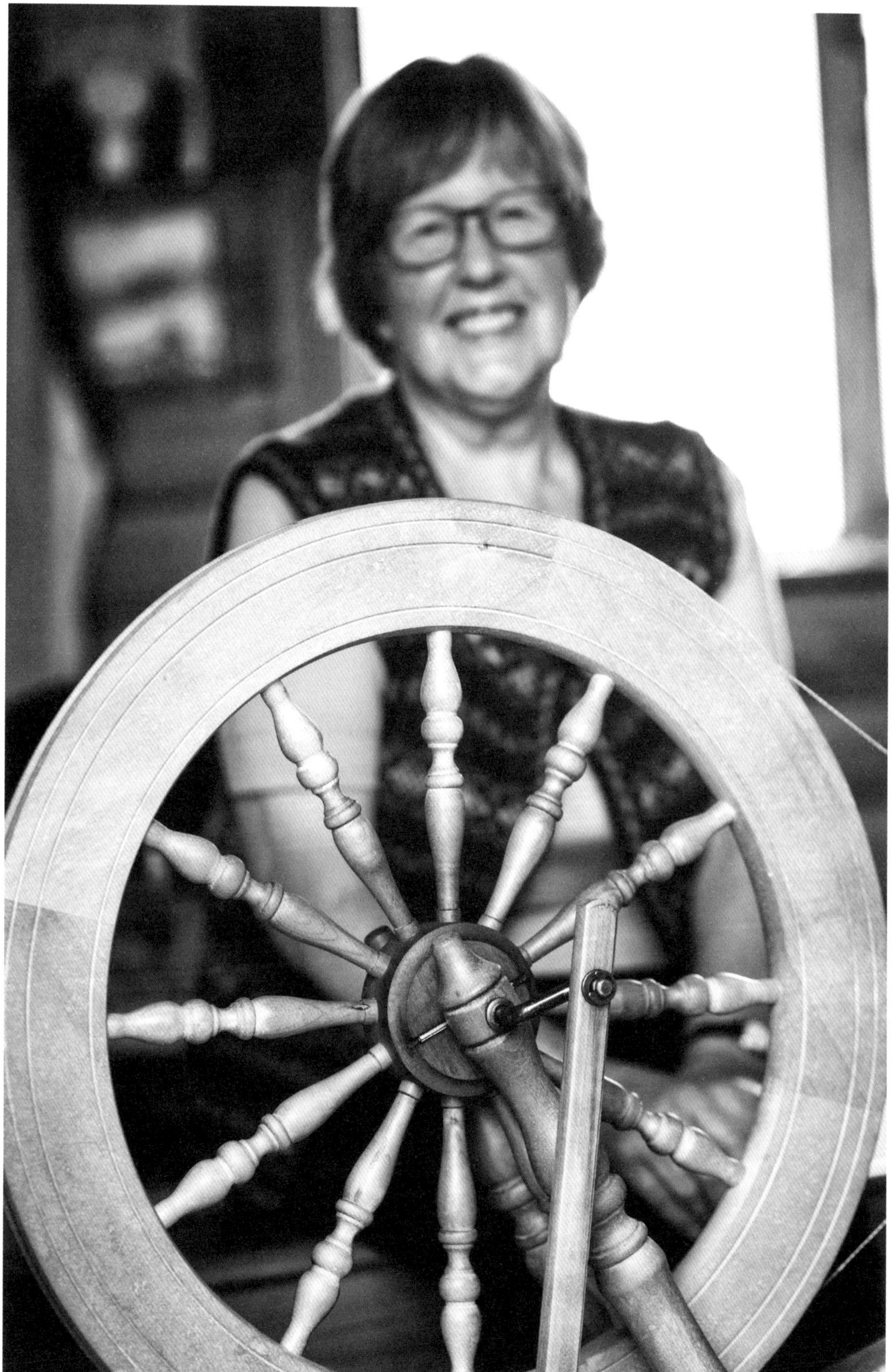

# Ina Irvine

## Handspinner & Fine Lace Knitter

Growing up on the bonnie isle of Whalsay, Ina Irvine was surrounded by knitting and knitters, and does not recall a time when she, her mother or three sisters didn't have wires and wirsit (yarn) in their hands. "It was a way of life," she says. Whalsay is well known for its distinctive Fairisle style, and, as a girl, Ina knitted colourful mitts for sale, moving on to work children's border jumpers and yokes. As a young woman, Ina gutted fish over summer and then knitted through the long winters to supplement her income. Later, Ina worked to order for several knitwear businesses, and her samples came to form the basis of commercial patterns popularly produced by Debbie Bliss and Margaret Stuart. Unusually for a Shetland knitter (who tend to stick with one style or the other), Ina creates beautiful lace as well as Fairisle, and taught herself to spin in 1983. Beginning by producing jumper weight, she and her wheel were soon capable of transforming a good Shetland fleece into light, cobwebby laceweight, and the shawls and stoles Ina creates from her own handspun are among Shetland's finest. Ina is both an extraordinary craftswoman and an ordinary Shetland knitter: someone who has spent her lifetime quietly producing textiles of world-class quality. From her garden shed studio in Symbister emerge stoles, scarves and shawls of incredible fineness which have been commissioned as official gifts to members of the Norwegian and British royal families. She's an artisan to aspire to.

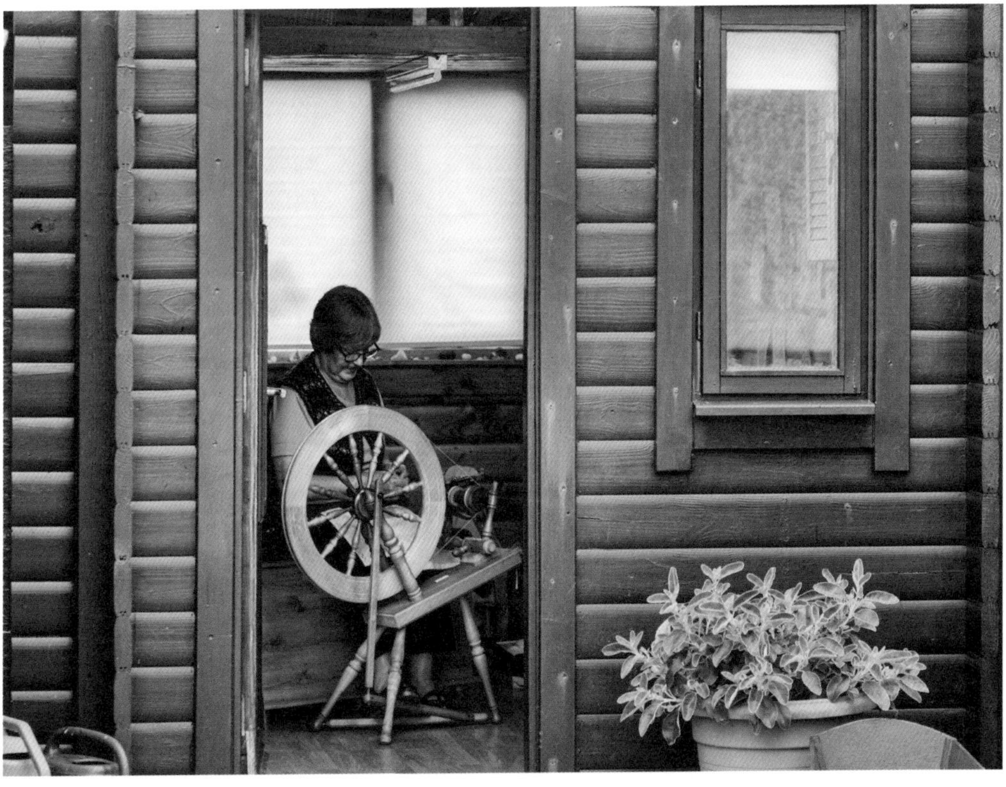

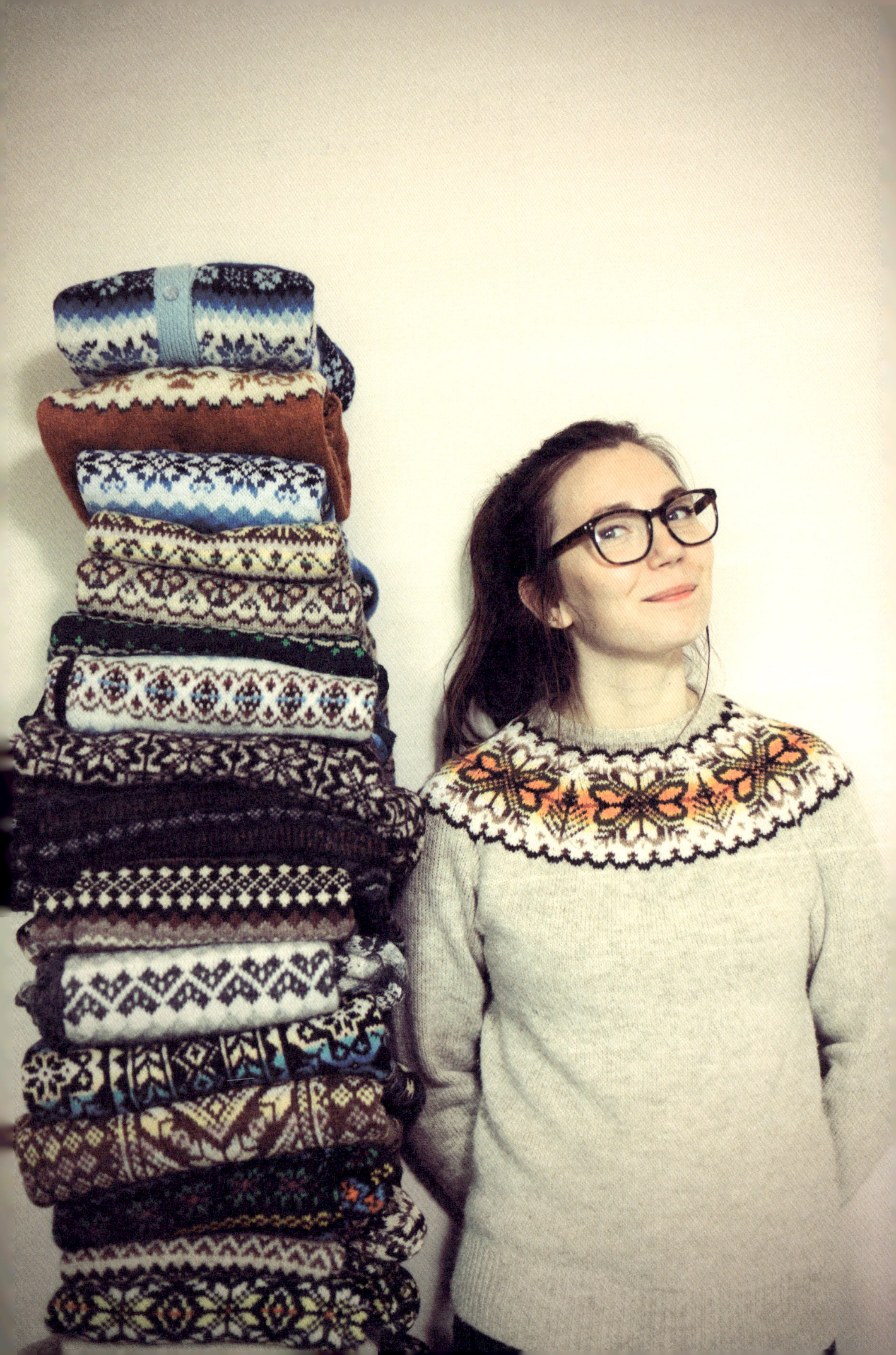

# Ella Gordon

## Ella Gordon Designs

Ella Gordon was born and raised in Lerwick and the life of the toon (town) defines her work, from the youthful sensibility of her handknits to the saleroom and charity-shop finds she adds to her vintage knitwear collection. Reflecting on the meanings of local moments of transition has led Ella to draw much of her inspiration from the 1970s, when Shetland's landscape was completely transformed by the discovery of North Sea oil. In Shetland, the 1970s were a decade in which novelty clashed with tradition, new opportunities modified old ways, and the islands embraced their own version of modernity. Ella's designs emerge from a place that's looking back while looking forward: her iconic crofthoose cushions might incorporate a traditional peat stack and shovel, but are revivified by their fresh and unexpected colour palette.

Ella studied textiles at Shetland College, and with her precise and recognisable sense of colour, her work in both machine and handknitting immediately stands out from the crowd. Her business has grown from creating ready-made homewares to producing highly popular patterns, and she brings a keen intelligence and sense of humour to everything she does.

Ella's work speaks of her deep pride in her local textile heritage even as she reinvents tradition. She was patron of Shetland Wool Week in 2016, and her popular crofthoose hat has been made in hundreds of different colourways by enthusiastic knitters all over the world.

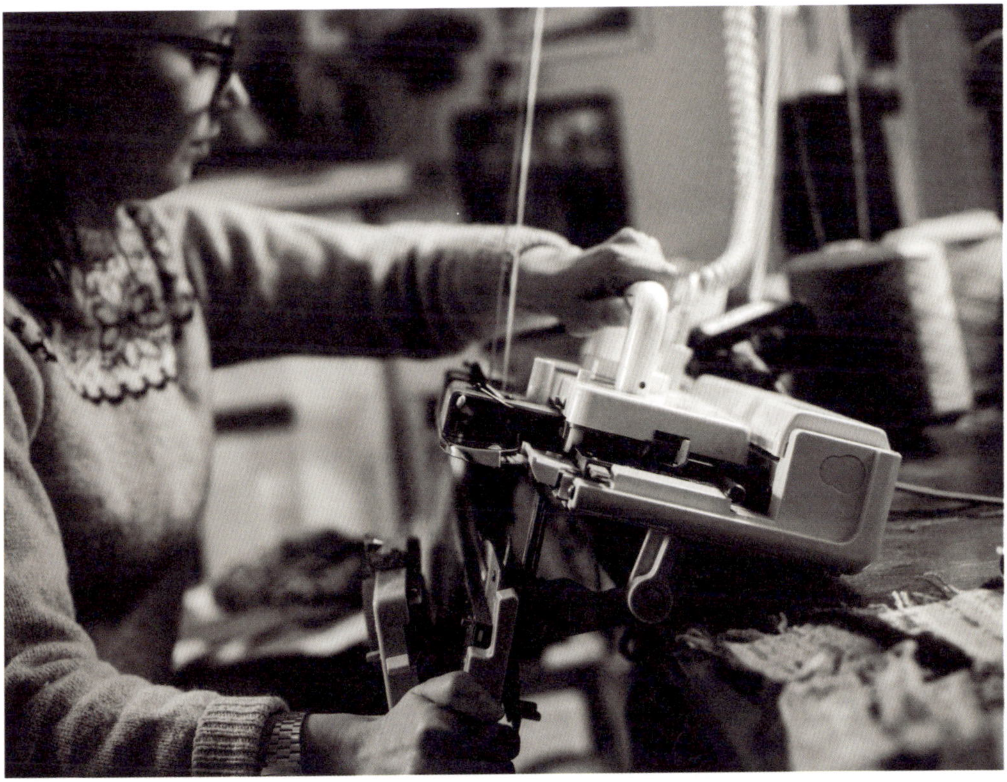

# Misa Hay

## Shetland Wool Week & Shetland Wool Adventures

Misa Hay visited Shetland in 1999 on a school exchange and fell in love with the beauty of the isles. She decided she was going to move to Shetland, and, after graduating from university, did just that. "It is a real privilege to be able to live, work and raise a family in such a creative and inspiring place," says Misa. "I love Shetland's open landscape, the wonderful light, the local architecture, and the fact that old traditions retain such a vibrant contemporary life here." Misa has worked in marketing for Visit Scotland and Promote Shetland and, for the past six years, has organised Shetland Wool Week. "I feel inspired by the Shetland wool industry every single day," says Misa, "In a world of mass-produced fast fashion, I think it is absolutely amazing that wool can be grown, spun into yarn and made into garments, all in one small place, using local expertise and skills." Attracting thousands of visitors from locations as far afield as Brazil and Japan, Shetland Wool Week has certainly spread the international word about the unique nature of Shetland wool, and has had significant local impact too: "the event has really boosted the self-confidence of local designers, and sparked interest in the young generation of Shetland knitters." Misa has recently formed her own tour company to share her passion for Shetland wool and the isles. Fuelled by her creative energy and talent, there's surely no better way to learn more about the islands' textiles than by embarking on a Shetland Wool Adventure.

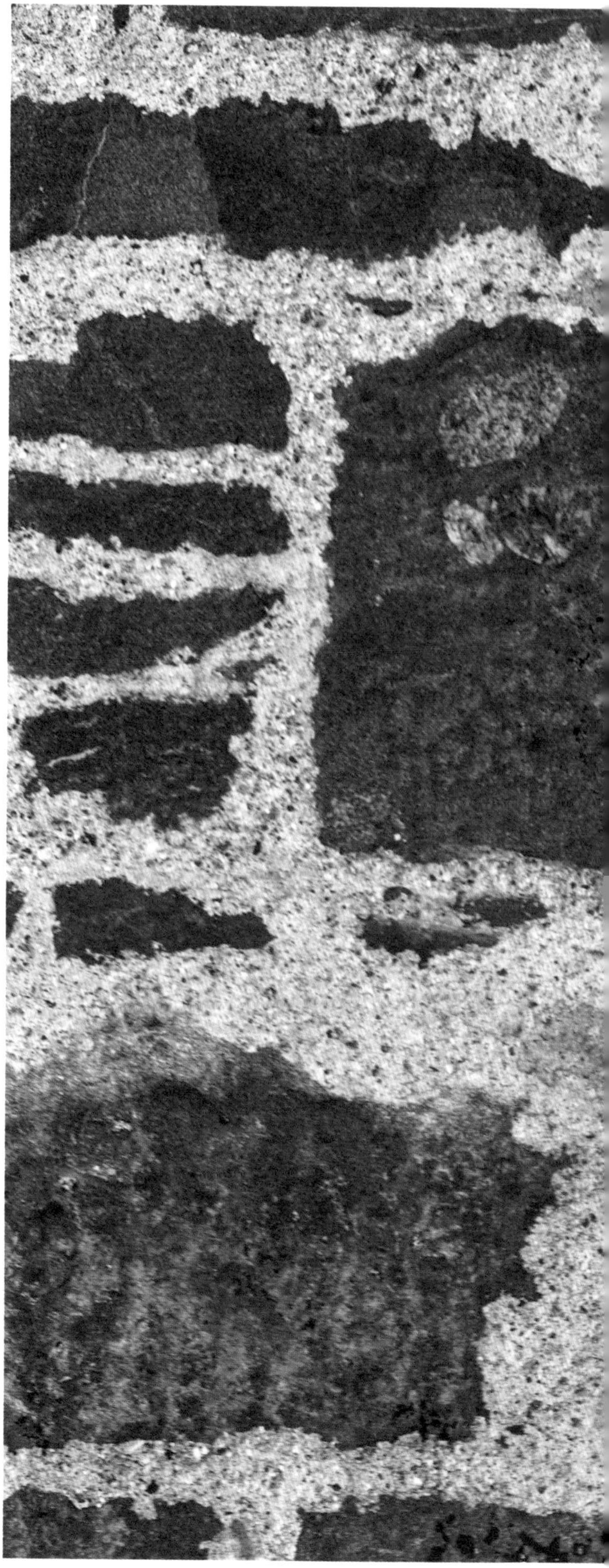

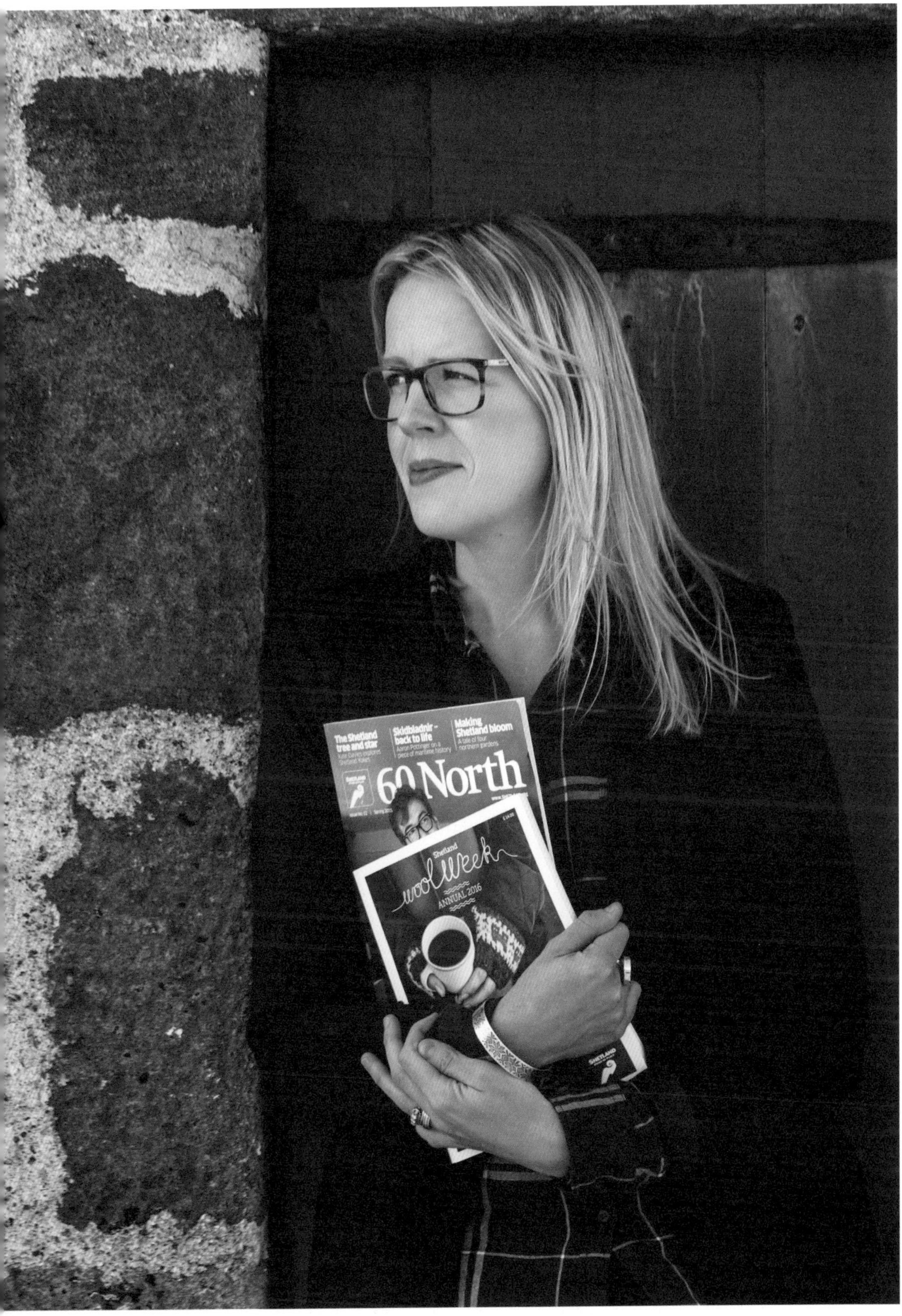
The Shetland tree and star
Skidbladnir – back to life
Making Shetland bloom
60 North
Shetland
wool week
ANNUAL 2016

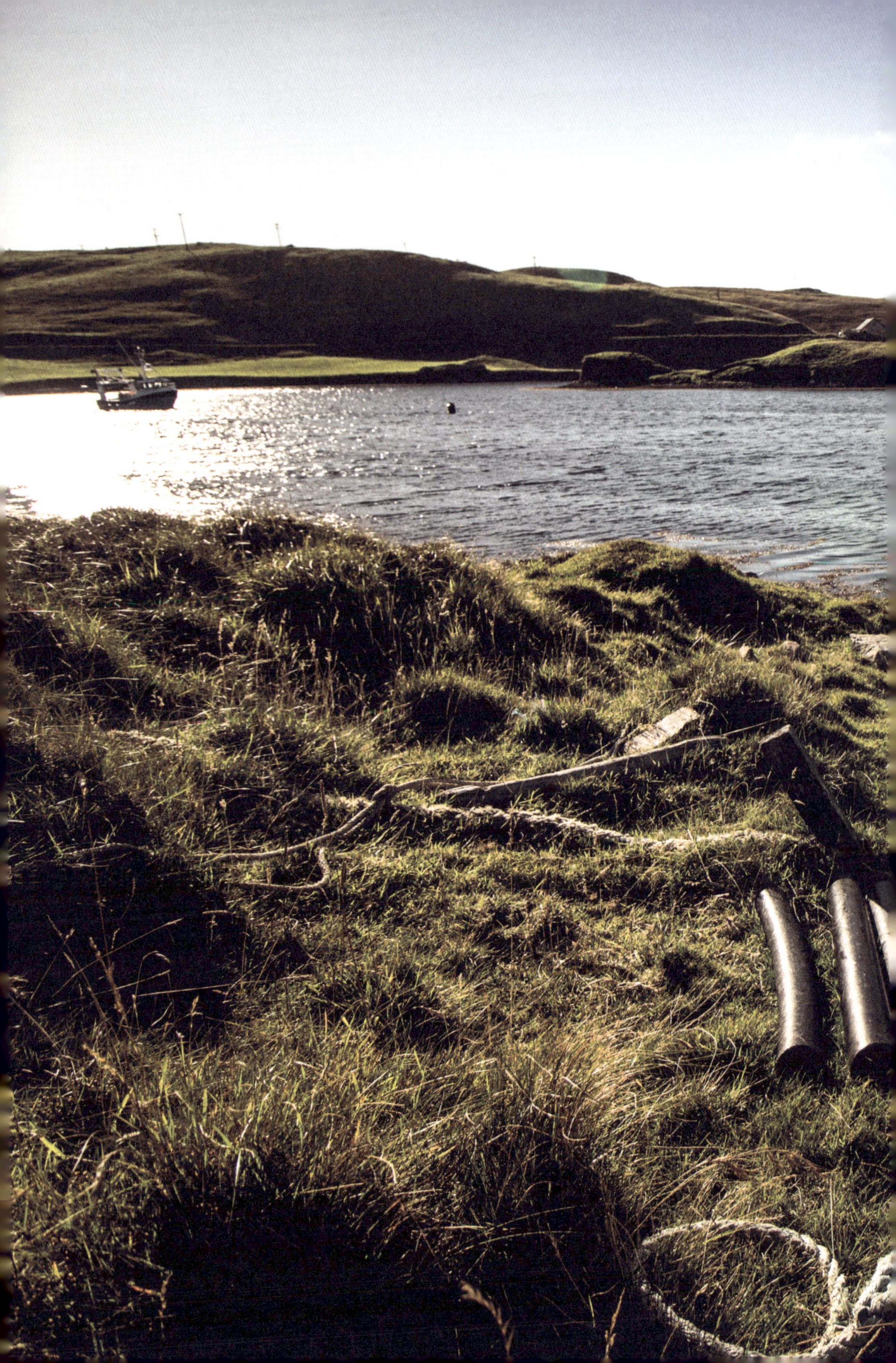

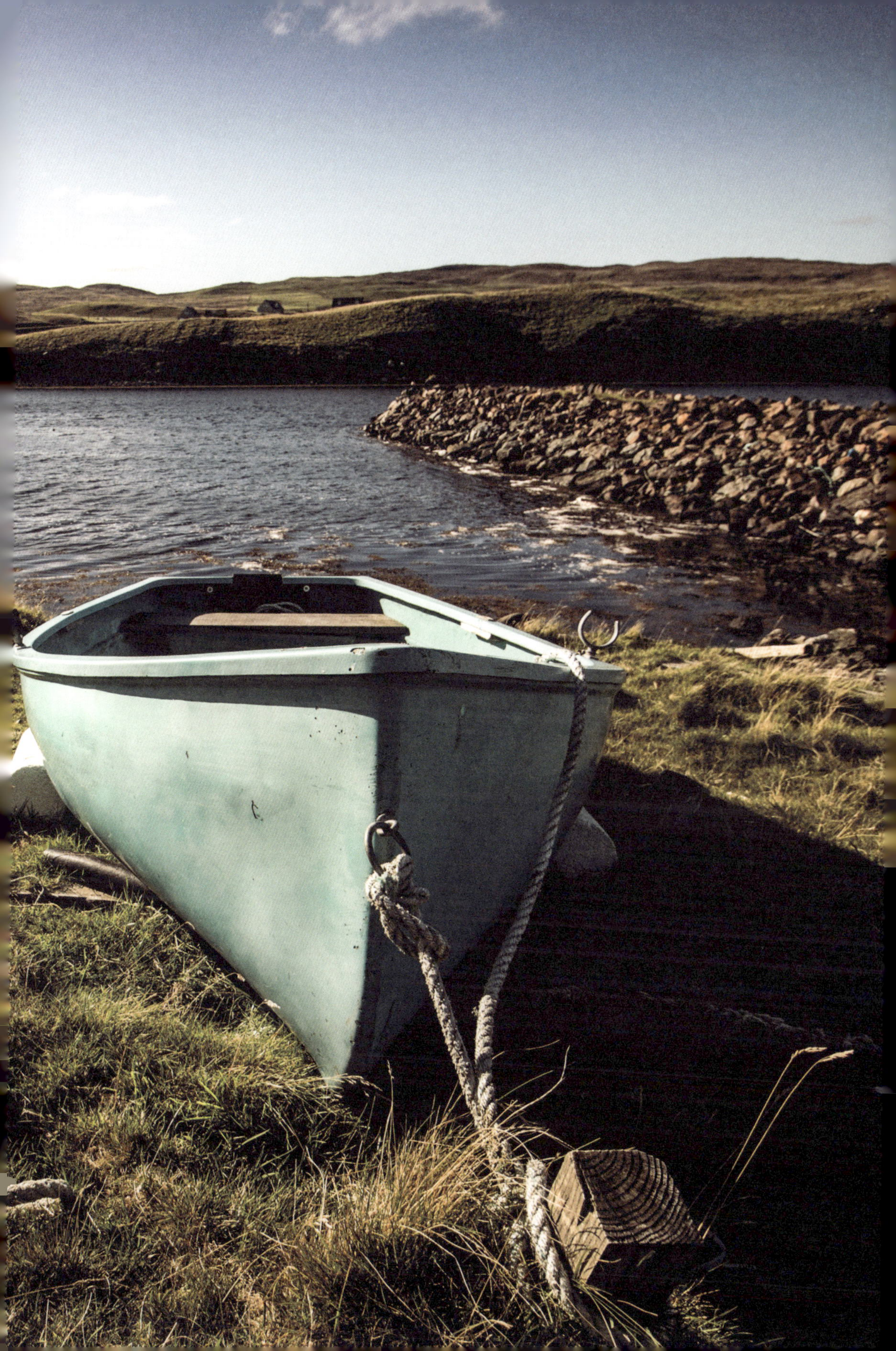

# Helen Robertson
## Artist & Craftswoman

Helen Robertson is an impressively thoughtful Shetland maker, whose work crosses the fields of art and craft. "I find I need to have both in my life to achieve creative balance," she says. "Too much art would exhaust me, while too much craft might prove frustrating." A commission to create a bride's tiara in 2001 allowed Helen to discover "a new way of wearing Shetland lace that might lead a new audience to appreciate the skill and ingenuity of the knitters of Shetland past." Inspired by Shetland's knitters, many of her pieces convey a deep, commemorative respect for the hard work of the women of the islands, and the difficult lives they led. "I try to express an appreciation of their struggle in my work, and to tell that story to a wider audience." A recent piece inspired by the Gloup fishing disaster of 1881 suggests the interminable but unutterably beautiful skill of Shetland lace. Working their way through grief, pain and eviction, the work of their hands their only resource against economic destitution, Shetland women knitted on, even as their husbands, sons and brothers were lost in the print o' the wave. Many of Helen's art pieces immortalise the details of ordinary Shetland life as precious: a scrap of silver knitted lace hung in a window, a piece of birch driftwood discovered on the shoreline. Continually exploring new paths of connection between Shetland wool and other media, Helen is currently researching and testing vitreous enamels in colours that speak to the jewel-like shades of Shetland yarns.

On 20th July 1881, fishermen from the North Isles of Shetland and Havera put to sea in their sixareens. A storm blew in from Iceland: 10 boats were lost and 58 local fishermen drowned. Coastal communities were devastated and many families were left completely destitute, with 34 widows and 85 orphans created by the disaster. Unable to pay for the loss of the boats as their lairds requested, some families faced eviction. It was a black day indeed. All of the widows and some of the children would have been knitters. The print o' the wave pattern suggests the wake of a boat through water. The six men represent a sixareen crew. The knitting goes on.

Materials: marine whipping twine, creosote, driftwood, painted figures (bought), wire (knitting needle).

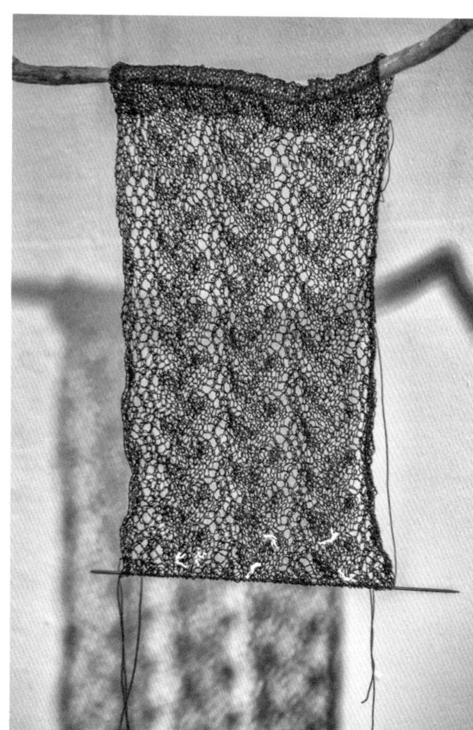

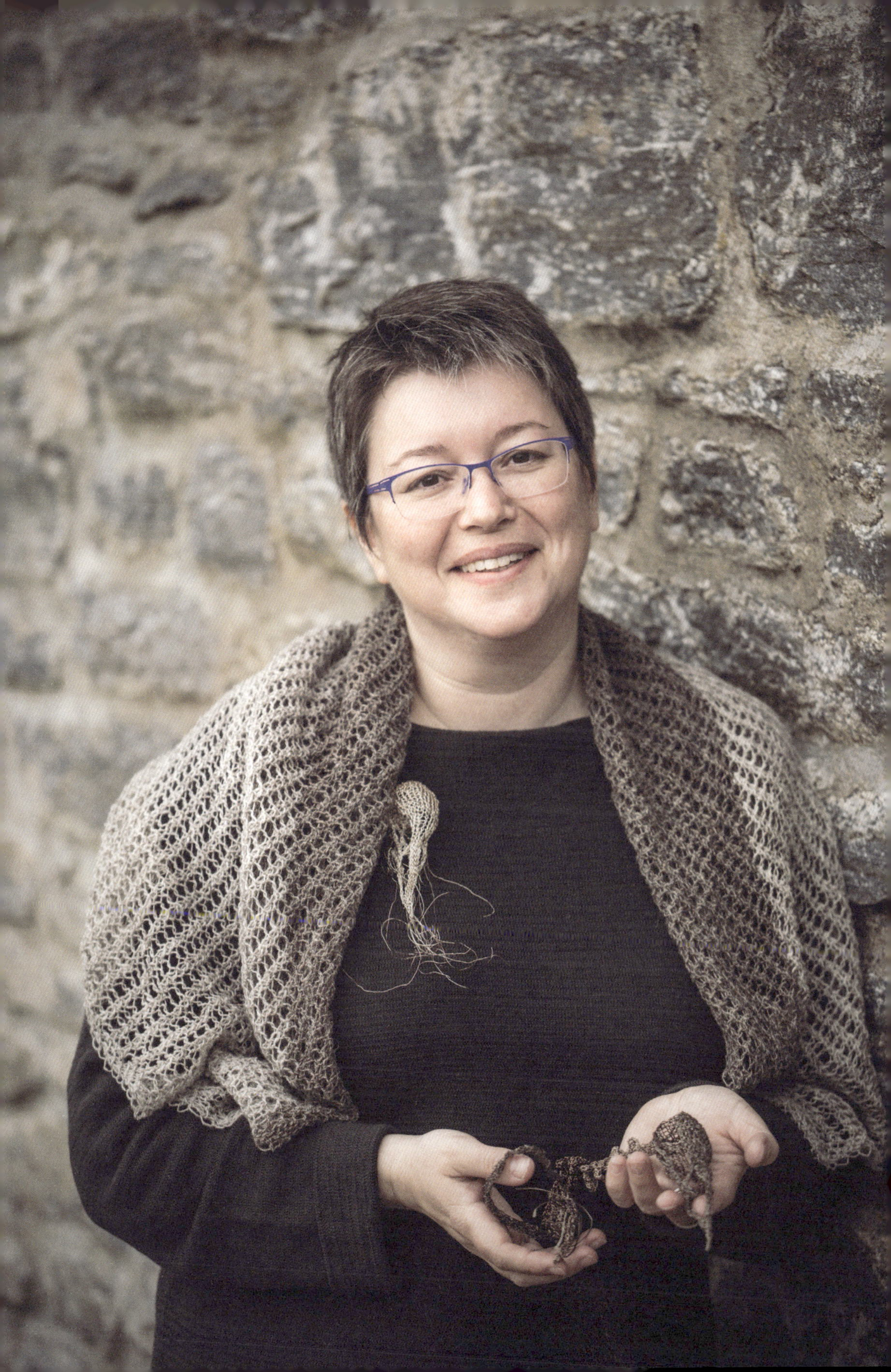

# Tommy Mouat
## Craftsman

Joiner Tommy Mouat has always had an inventive streak. He built his family home from scratch, and, over the past 50 years, the landscape around his Northmavine croft has continually been reshaped by the work of his industrious hands. With nothing but tools and his own labour, he's changed barns into glasshouses, brought green energy to his croft, and transformed an unproductive field into a thriving woodland with his singlehanded planting of 3000 trees. With the encouragement of his daughter Emily (a talented designer), Tommy's craft has supported knitters all over the world, from as far afield as New Zealand and the Netherlands, with the beautiful wooden boards he creates for them to dress their work. He's pictured here with glove boards that he's made from reclaimed hardwood.

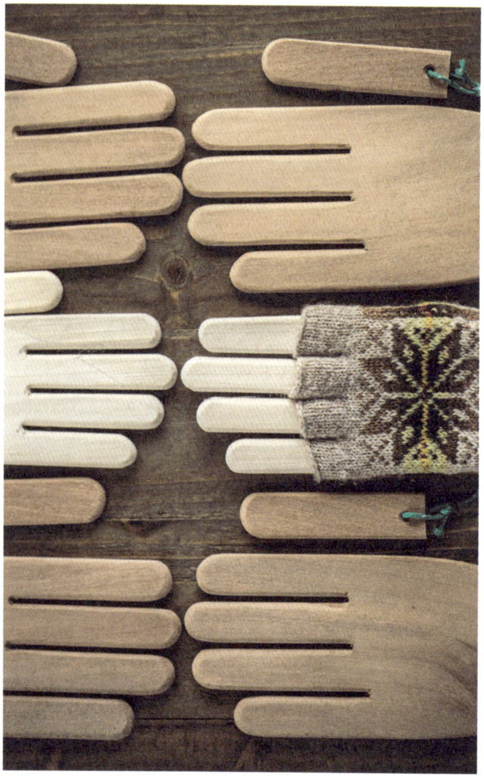

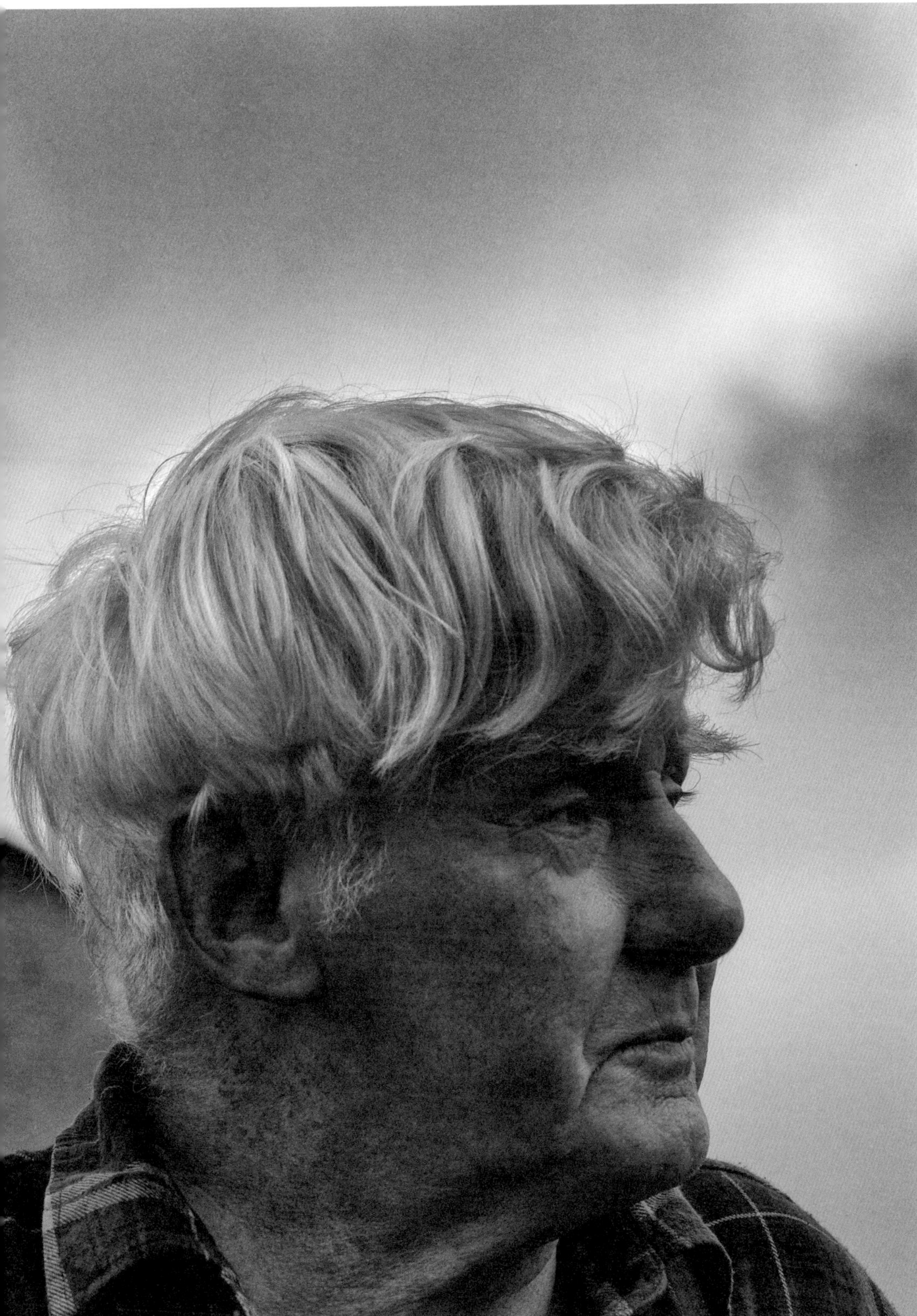

# Andy Ross & Kirsty Jean Brabin

## GlobalYell/Shetland Tweed Company

Andy: "GlobalYell is a charity, offering space, time and equipment to a wide range of craftspeople to develop individual and collaborative projects. From our island studio, we encourage people to walk and see the landscape differently, to use our reference library, to play and to experiment. Shetland repays patience and those who take time to explore. The stunning scenery, the space and light, the colours of the seasons and the drama of the islands all bring me great joy. The fact that I have made my own creative place here which others can enjoy gives me a sense of pride, while also being quite humbling. I am very lucky to live here."

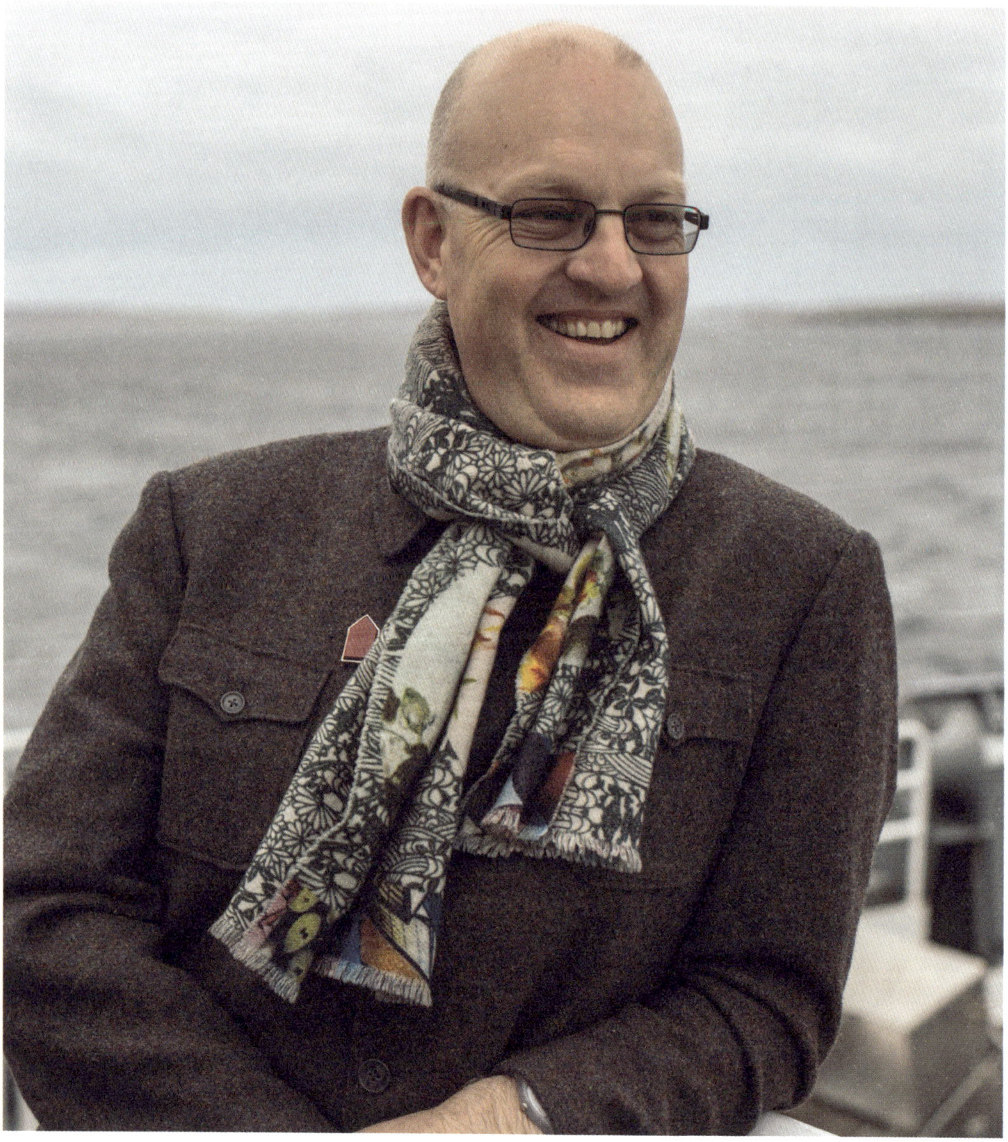

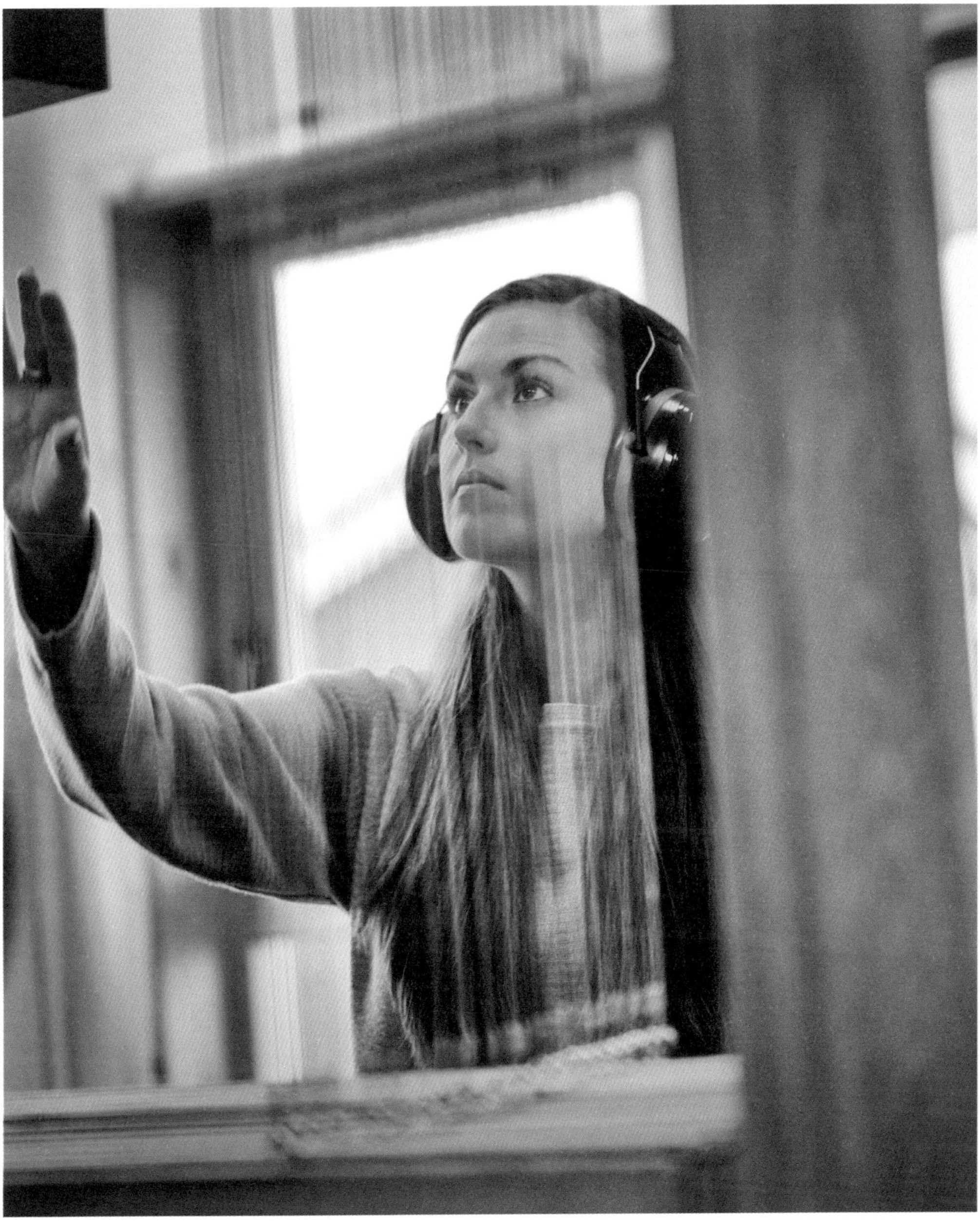

Kirsty: "I was weaver in residence at GlobalYell in 2013, and Shetland crept into my heart, quickly becoming the place I felt closest to as a weaver. Shetland is a fantastic creative hub, and I am surrounded here by talented and inspiring craftspeople. Running the Shetland Tweed Company in partnership with Andy, we explore our shared passion for Shetland's landscape, people, and the important local heritage of weaving in our designs. With a long history of cloth production in the area, I'm proud that Yell once again has weavers working here creating Shetland tweed with Shetland wool. We've recently gone into production, with our longest-ever warp woven at 60 metres. Our new Lammas and Blen collections will soon be available for sale by the metre."

# Niela Nell Kalra

## nielanell

Working as a defence lawyer in northern Scotland, Niela Kalra found her creative impulses unfulfilled. Gripped with the desire to *simply make* familiar to so many talented craftspeople, she studied textiles at Shetland College, found that she thrived on the challenges of design, and quickly established a new life and thriving business in Shetland's south mainland. With characteristic élan, Niela transformed a run-down garage on Hoswick's main thoroughfare into an extraordinarily inviting workshop and retail space. Filled with cosy nooks, rich colours and gorgeous textures, Niela's studio sings of its creator's unique aesthetic. In machine knits composed of fine, luxurious yarns, Niela has discovered a medium connecting complex and thoughtful creative concepts to eminently wearable design. Inspired by the idea of clothing as skin or camouflage, or by the notion of a garment as a liminal object defining the boundaries of the self, Niela's designs can be worn in multiple ways, creating a comfortable cocoon or spectacular showpiece to suit the shifting temperament of its wearer. Bold and graphic, sculptural and tactile, Niela's work is definitively outward-looking and eclectic. "It's not just one thing, one tradition," Niela says of Shetland design. "Things move forward by embracing difference and establishing new perspectives." As a proud promoter of the south mainland's local community and economy, and with prominent commissions, such as creating the Shetland fiddlers' costumes for the 2014 and 2015 Edinburgh Military Tattoo, Niela brings her distinctive vital flavour to the contemporary world of Shetland textiles.

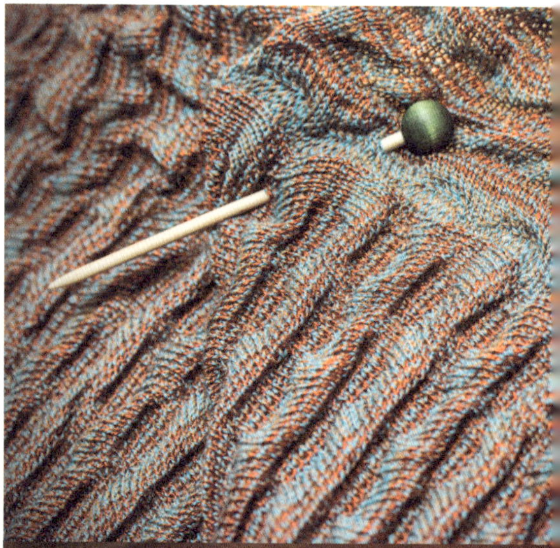

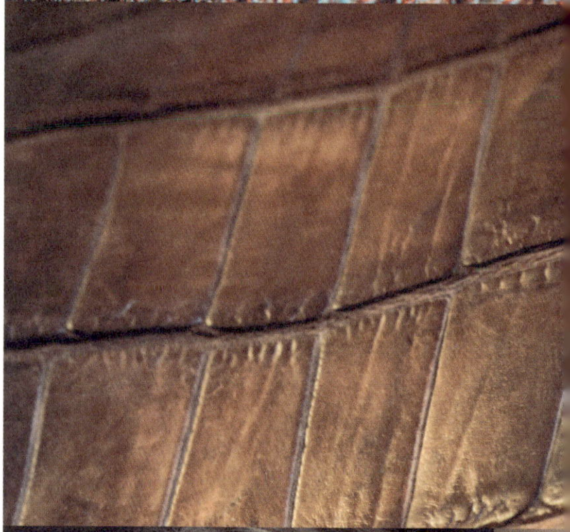

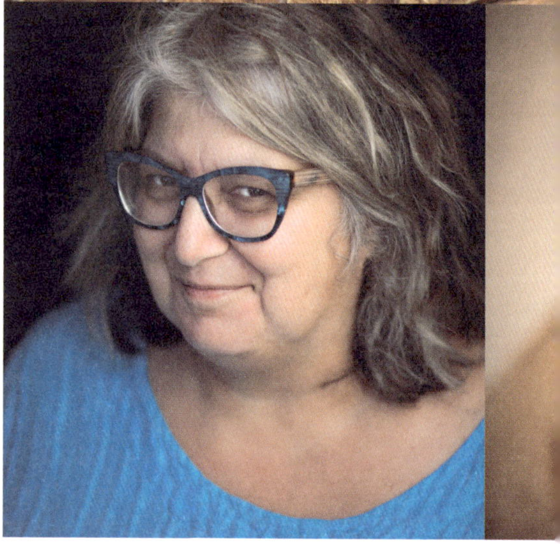

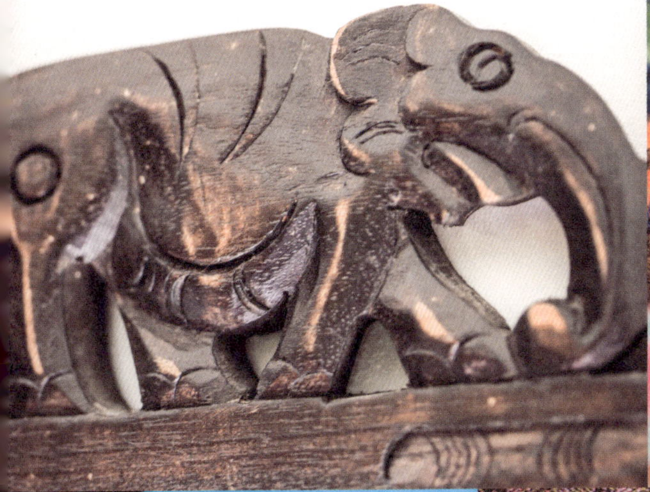

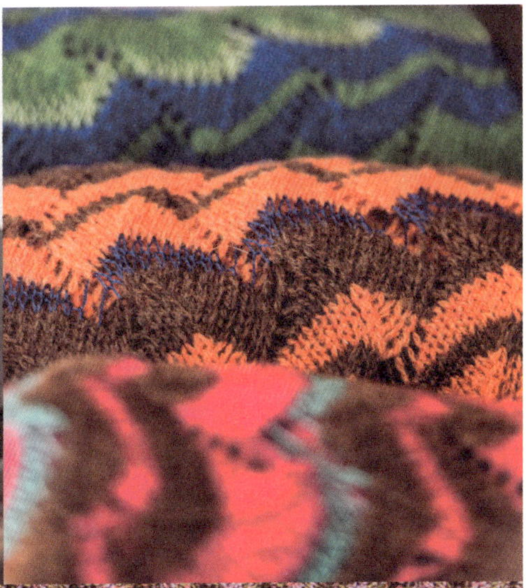

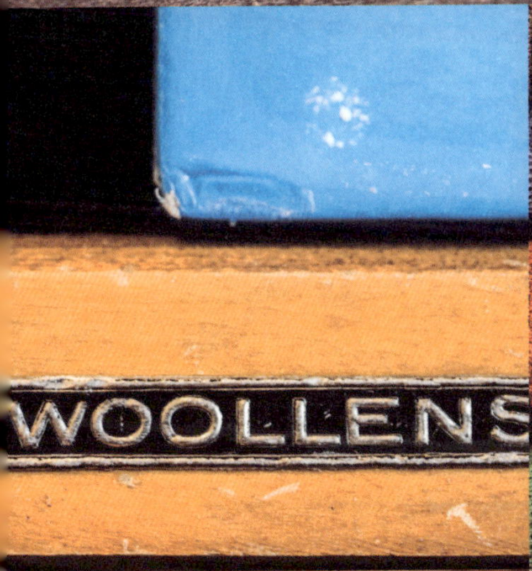
WOOLLENS

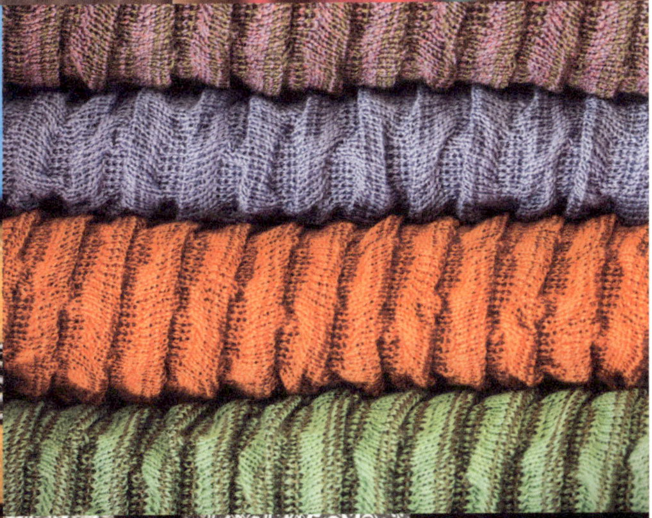

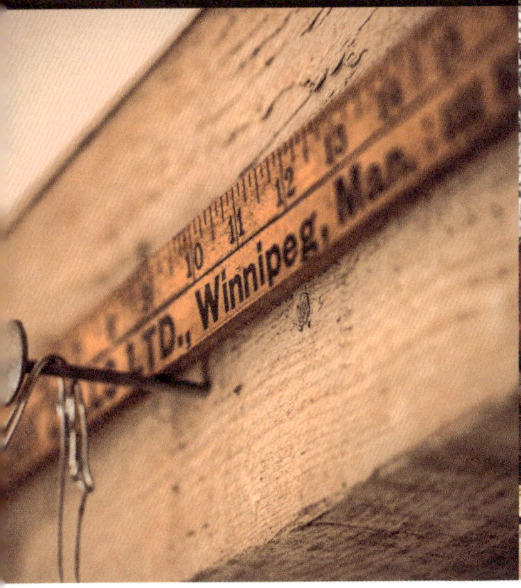
LTD., Winnipeg, Man.

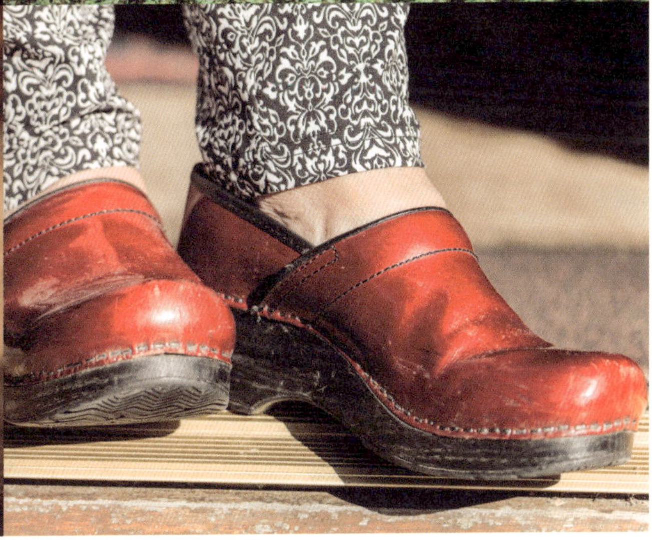

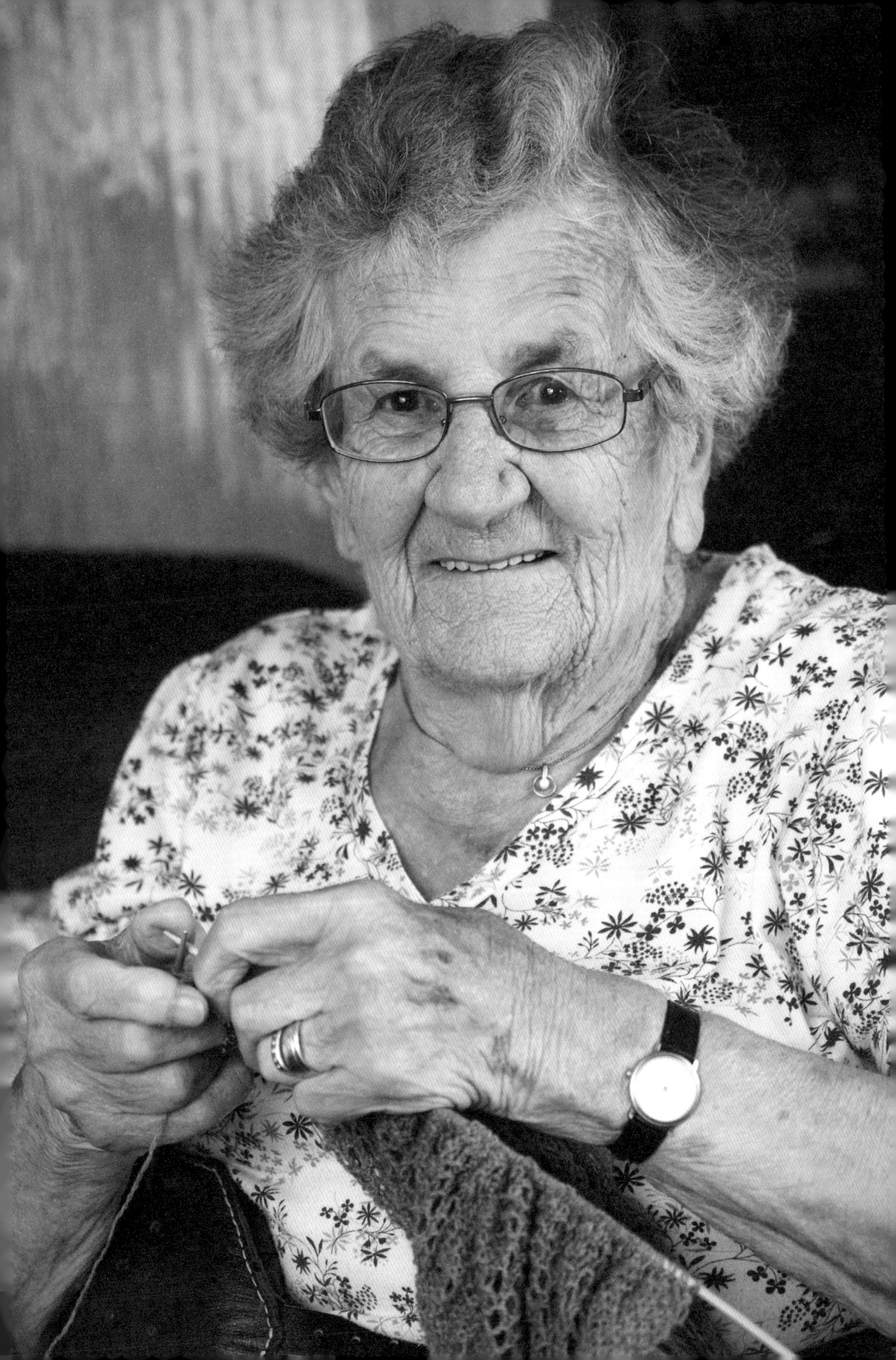

# Emma Isbister
## Lace Knitter

Emma Isbister has been knitting for most of her 96 years. Born in a tiny croft near Sand on Shetland's west side, she recalls being given the plain centres of haps to knit after her mother had completed the lace edging and border. Her deft hands were soon capable of knitting simple spencers (vests), and Emma sold her finished knitwear to the grocery van that visited her small community once a week. Just like her mother, her grandmother and her siblings, from an early age the work of Emma's hands supplied her family with basic necessities like sugar, flour and tea. Later, Emma's hands raised four of her own children, and were crucial to her work in nursing. Emma's hands made a hap for each new baby in the family that arrived, and kept on knitting through the generations and across the decades. As lace of startling beauty and complexity emerged from the quick movement of her needles, so the landscape of Shetland changed: war, electricity, roads, oil. Like the majority of Shetland knitters, Emma follows her own instincts rather than charts or patterns, and she does not regard her skill as in the least unusual or unique. Working to order or commission, Emma's hands have shaped hundreds of wonderful haps, shawls, cardigans and jumpers, and this work has shaped her hands in turn. Emma Isbister's creative, beautiful and mischievous hands pay testimony to a lifetime's work of knitting.

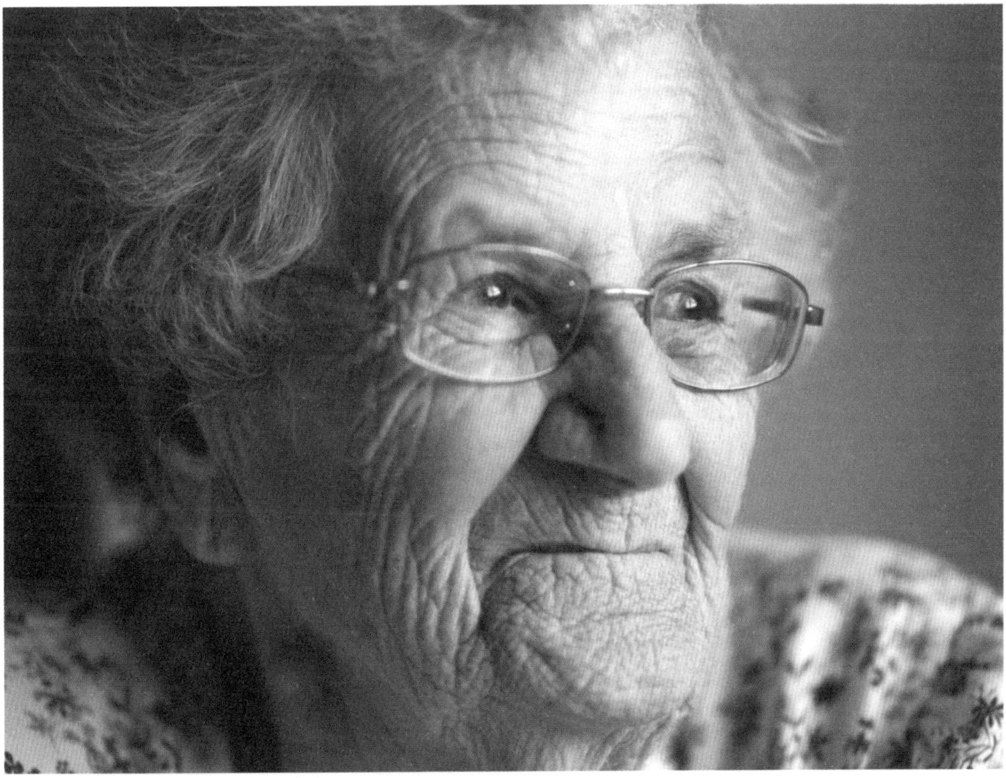

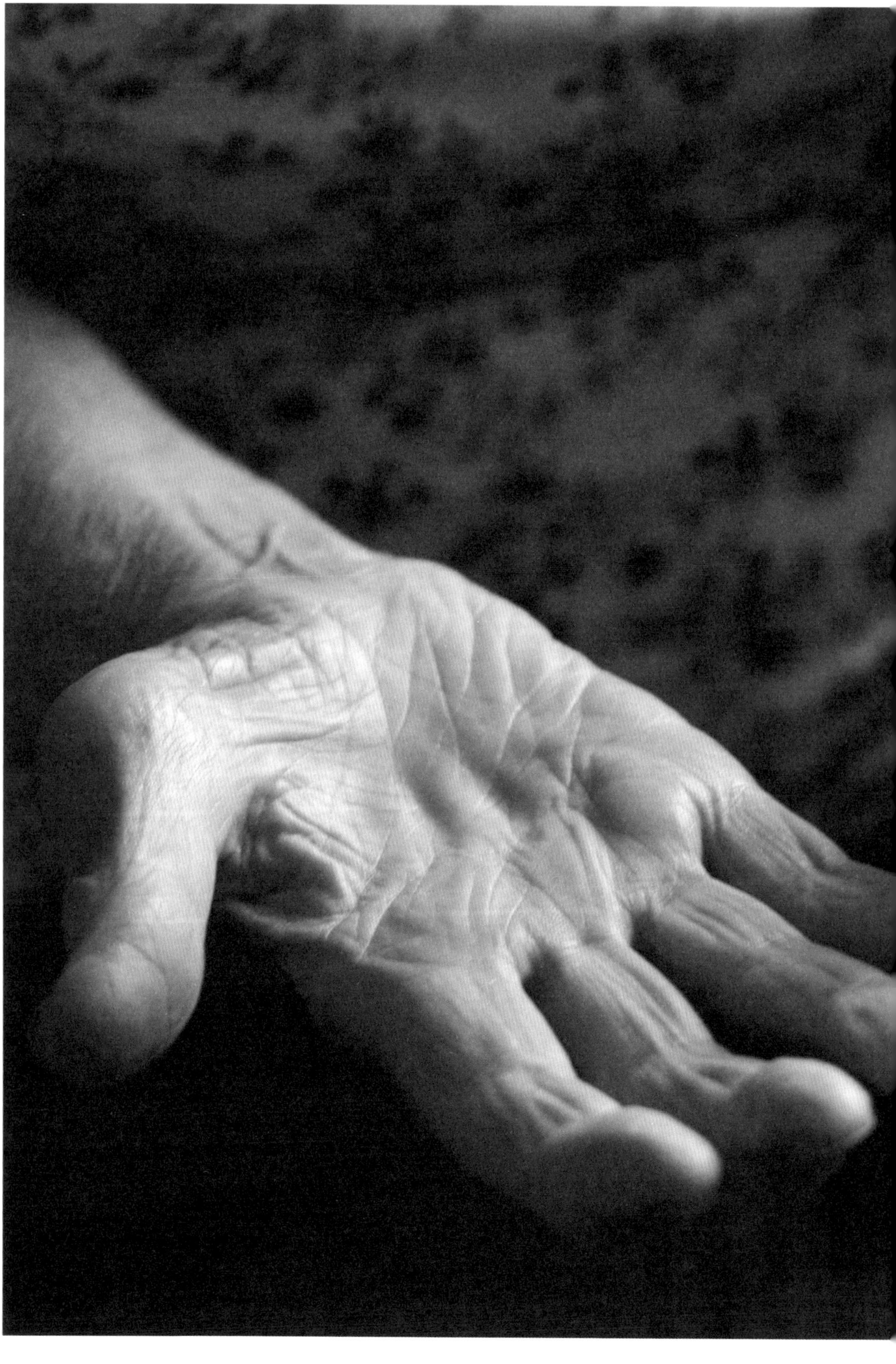

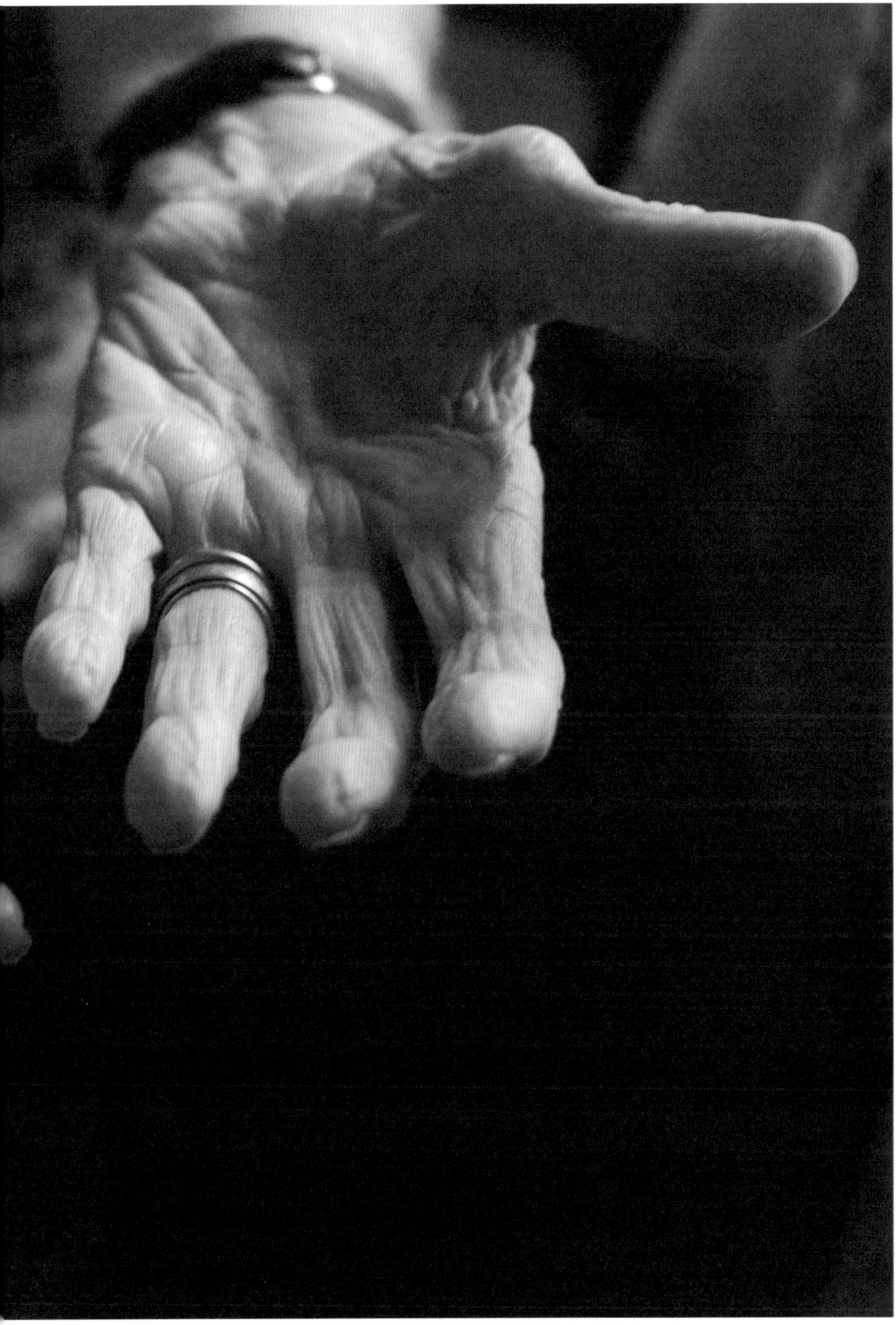

# Shetland PeerieMakkers

## Whalsay's Young Knitters

Under pressure from UK government cuts in 2010, Shetland Islands Council withdrew funding for the knitting tuition which all children once received as part of the primary school curriculum. Concerns that this move would distance the next generation from their important local heritage and skills had an intriguing effect, immediately prompting a renaissance of hand-knitting among those Shetland children who really wanted to learn. With the energy and experience of committed volunteers, the support of yarn provided by local company, Jamieson's, and under the umbrella of the PeerieMakkers scheme, hand-knitting thrives once more in lunchtime and after-school clubs around the islands, of which the group on Whalsay is one of the most successful. Working in the traditional way with long wires (needles) and belt, Whalsay's young knitters begin by making a pincushion, before moving on to learn how to work in the round with two colours, and to chart out and knit their own Fairisle designs. With the support of their tutors, the young knitters follow their own creative paths, developing individual ideas about pattern and colour, and producing pieces with which they compete in Shetland country shows. Building confidence through their own styles and preferences, consolidating their sense of community and local pride through working together, and communicating their skills by instructing younger learners in their turn, the inspiring example of these girls reveals the truth of what all knitters know in their hearts already: this craft is so much more than just a hobby.

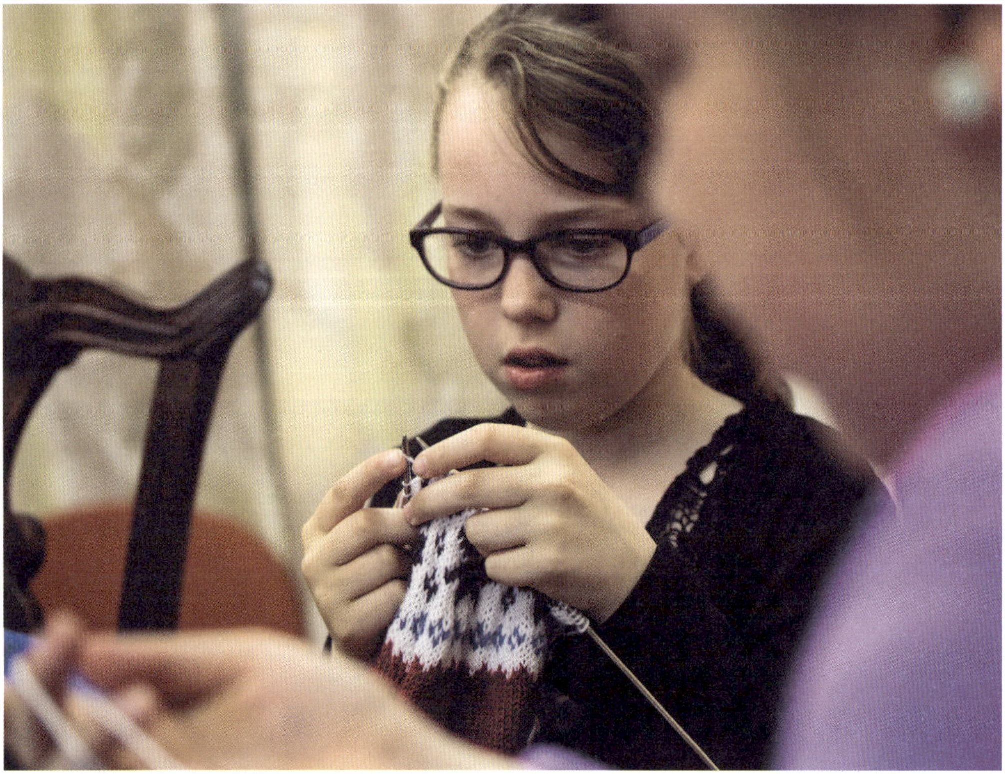

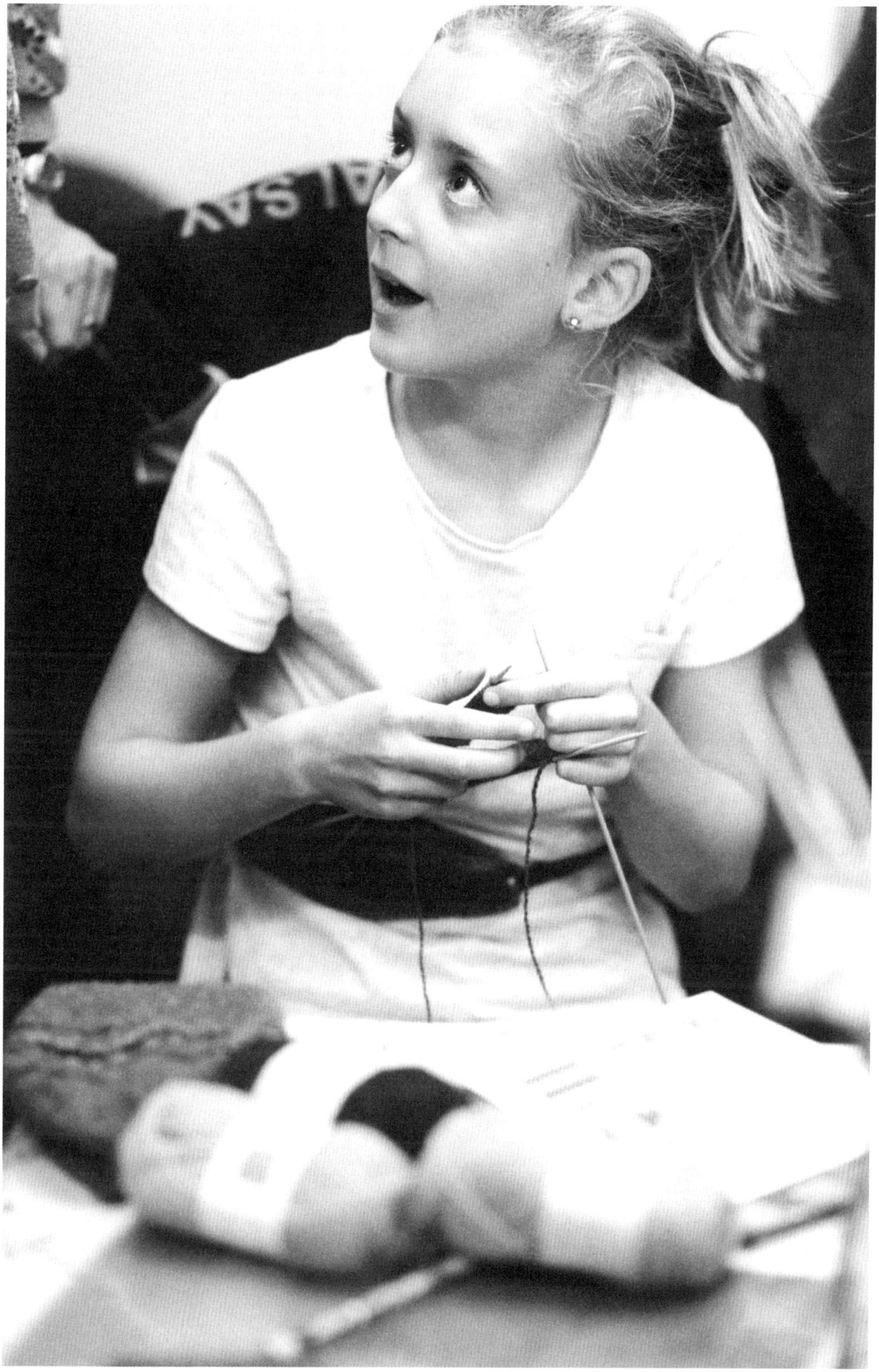

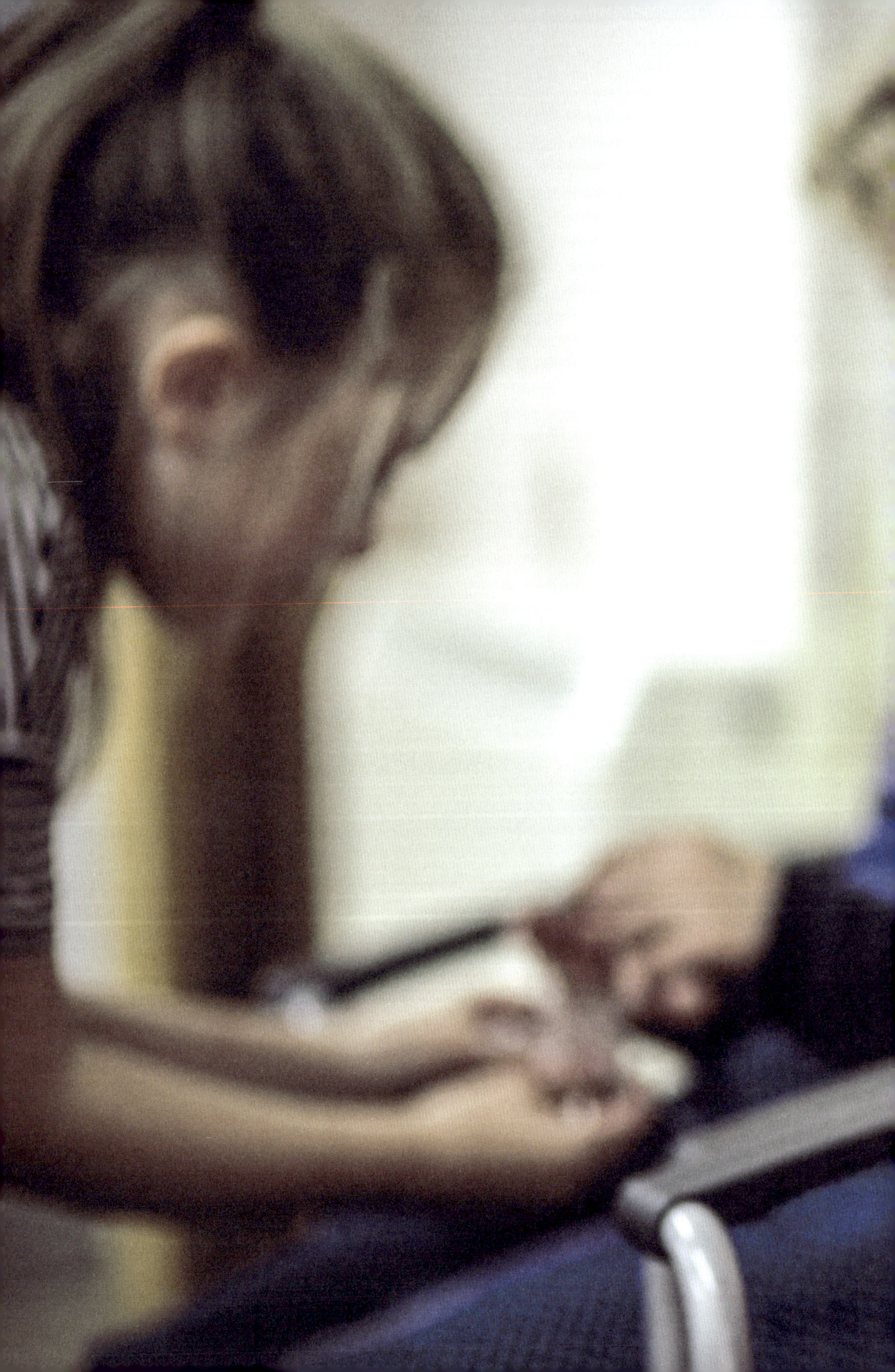

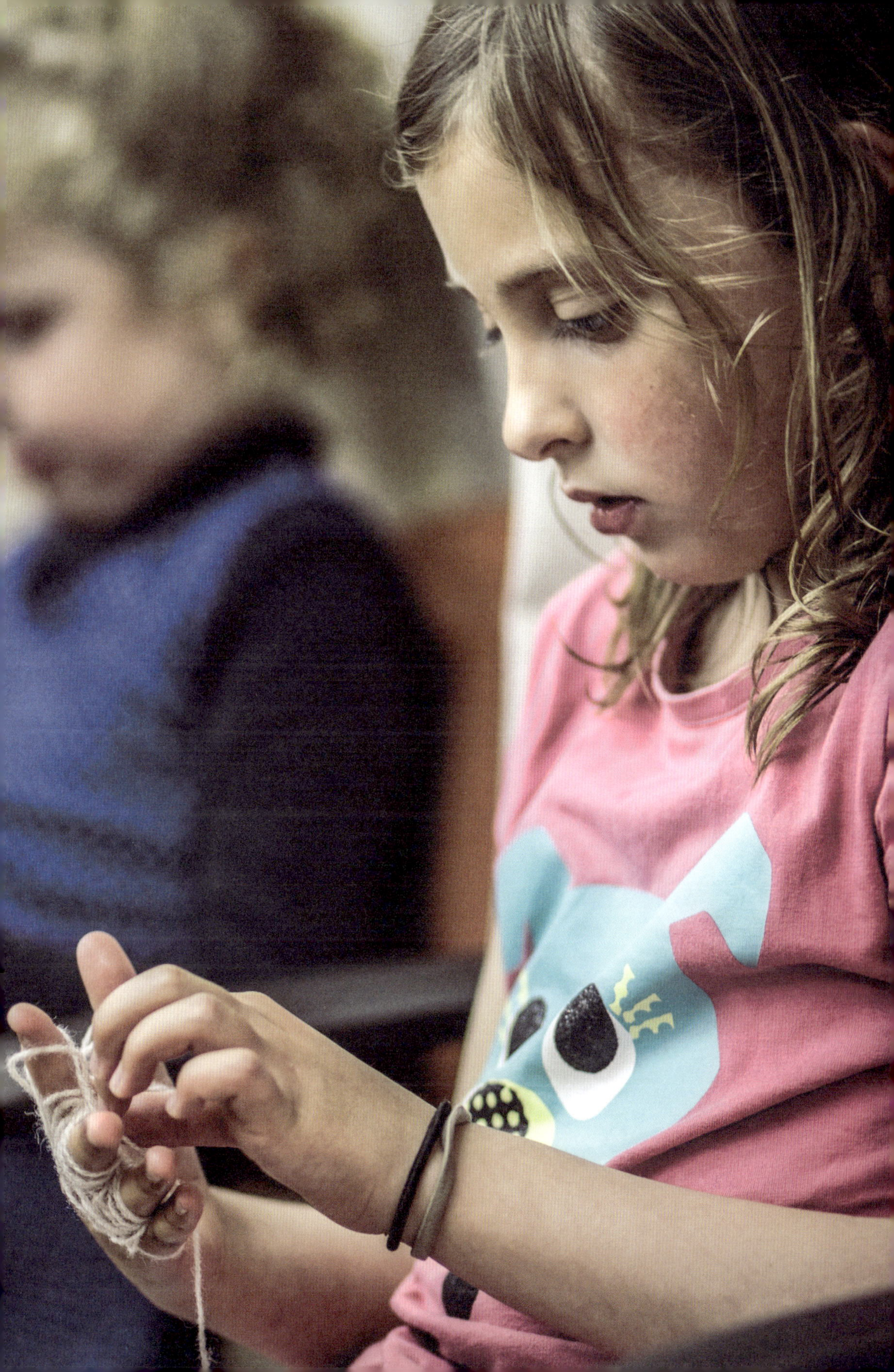

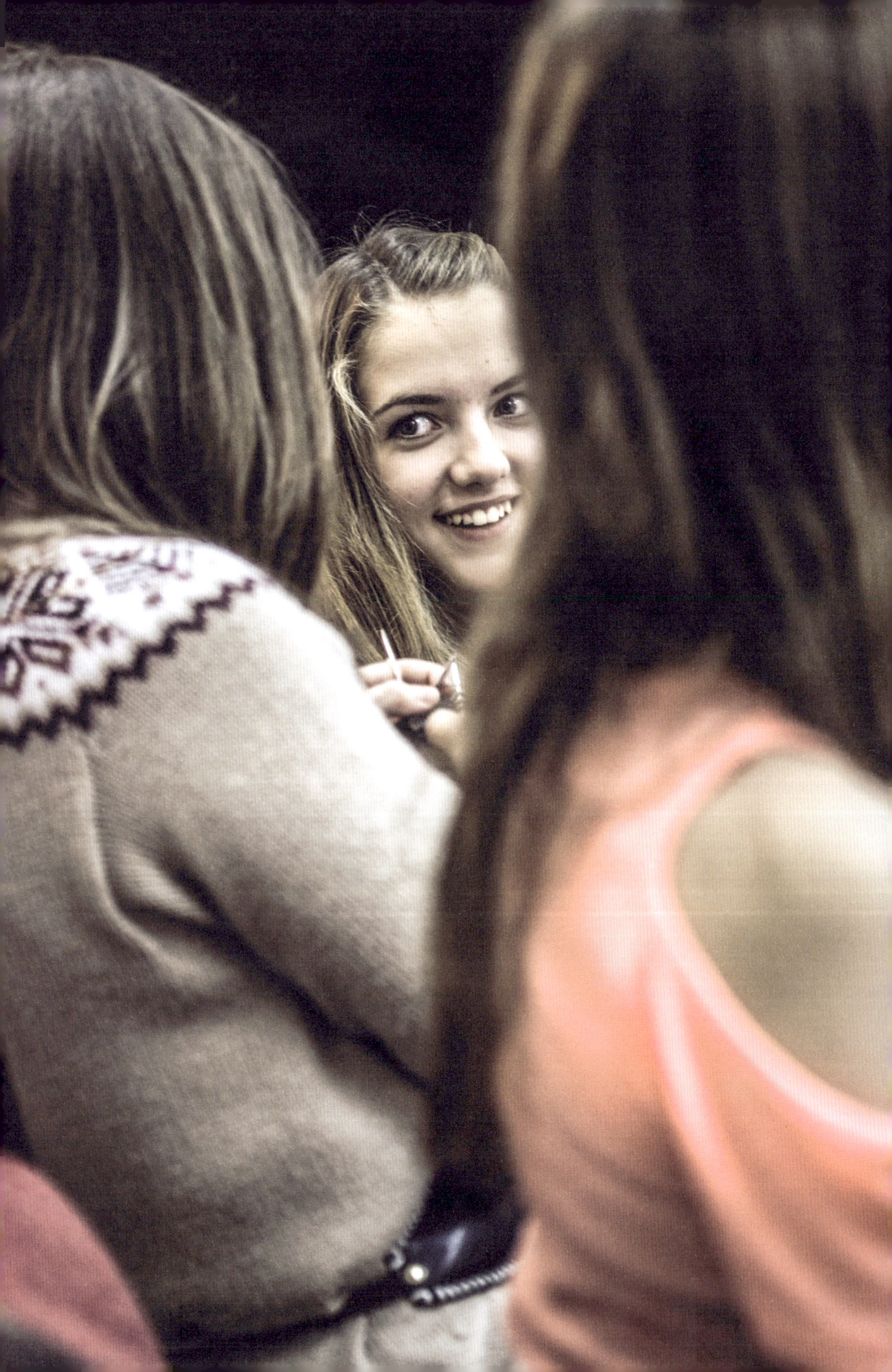

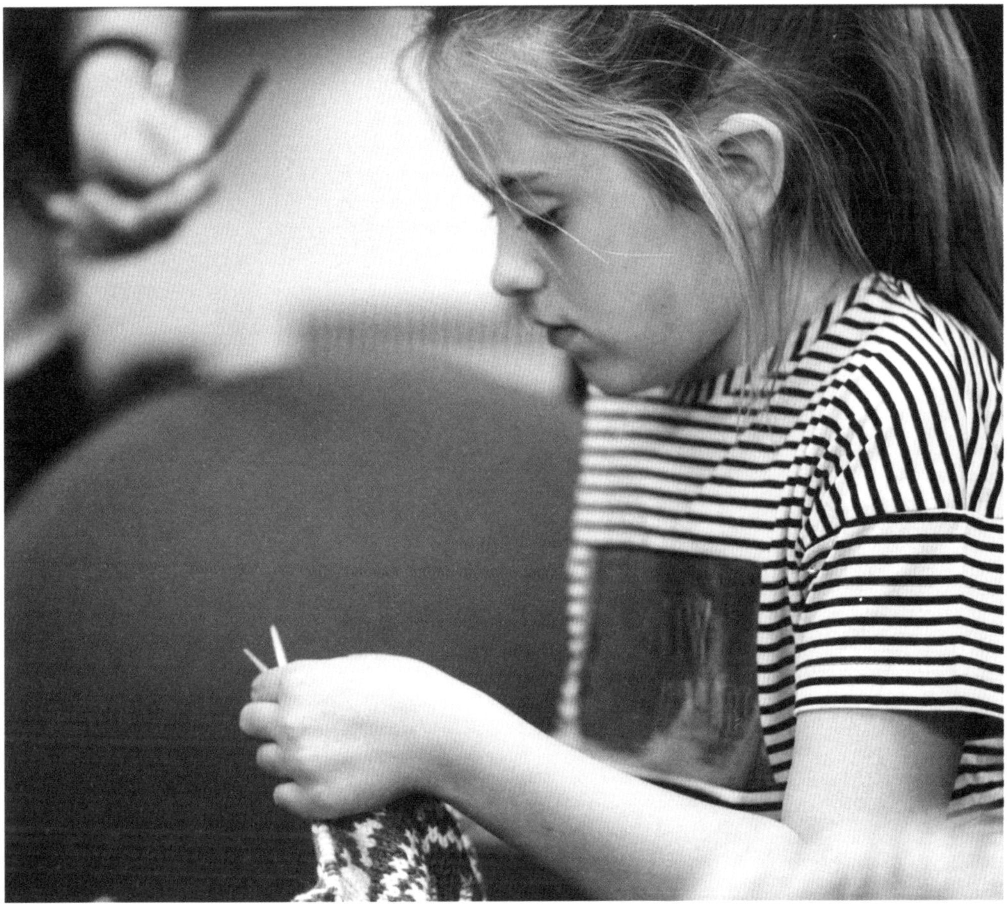

*"Seeing a young knitter's interest develop, supporting them as they move onto a more challenging project, watching them persevere as they learn new techniques, and finally being able to congratulate them years later when they win a trophy at an agricultural show is a real privilege. We are the lucky ones to have the opportunity to work with these bairns."*

*Whalsay knitting tutors Anne Anderson, Amanda Pottinger and Linda Shearer*

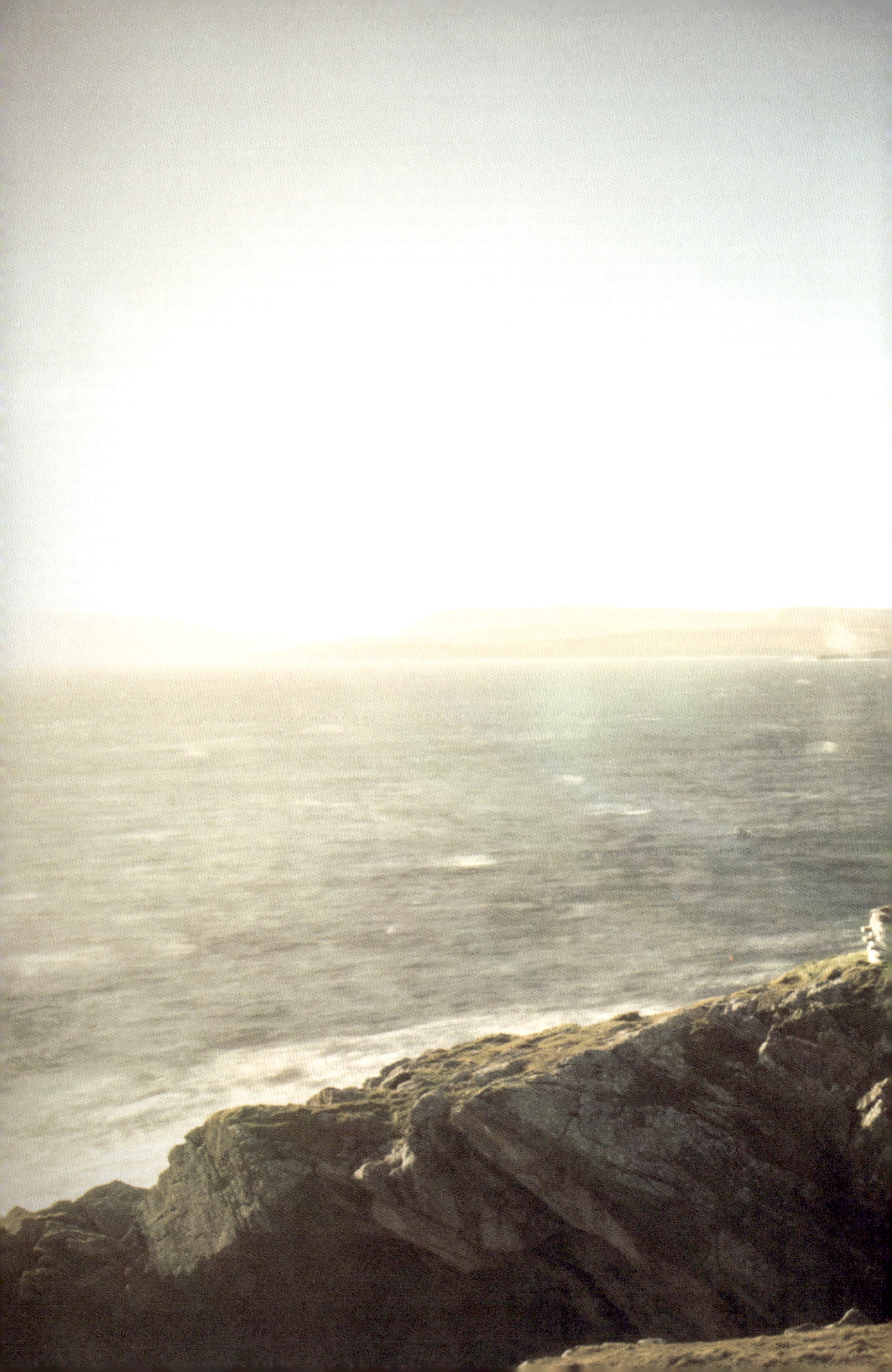

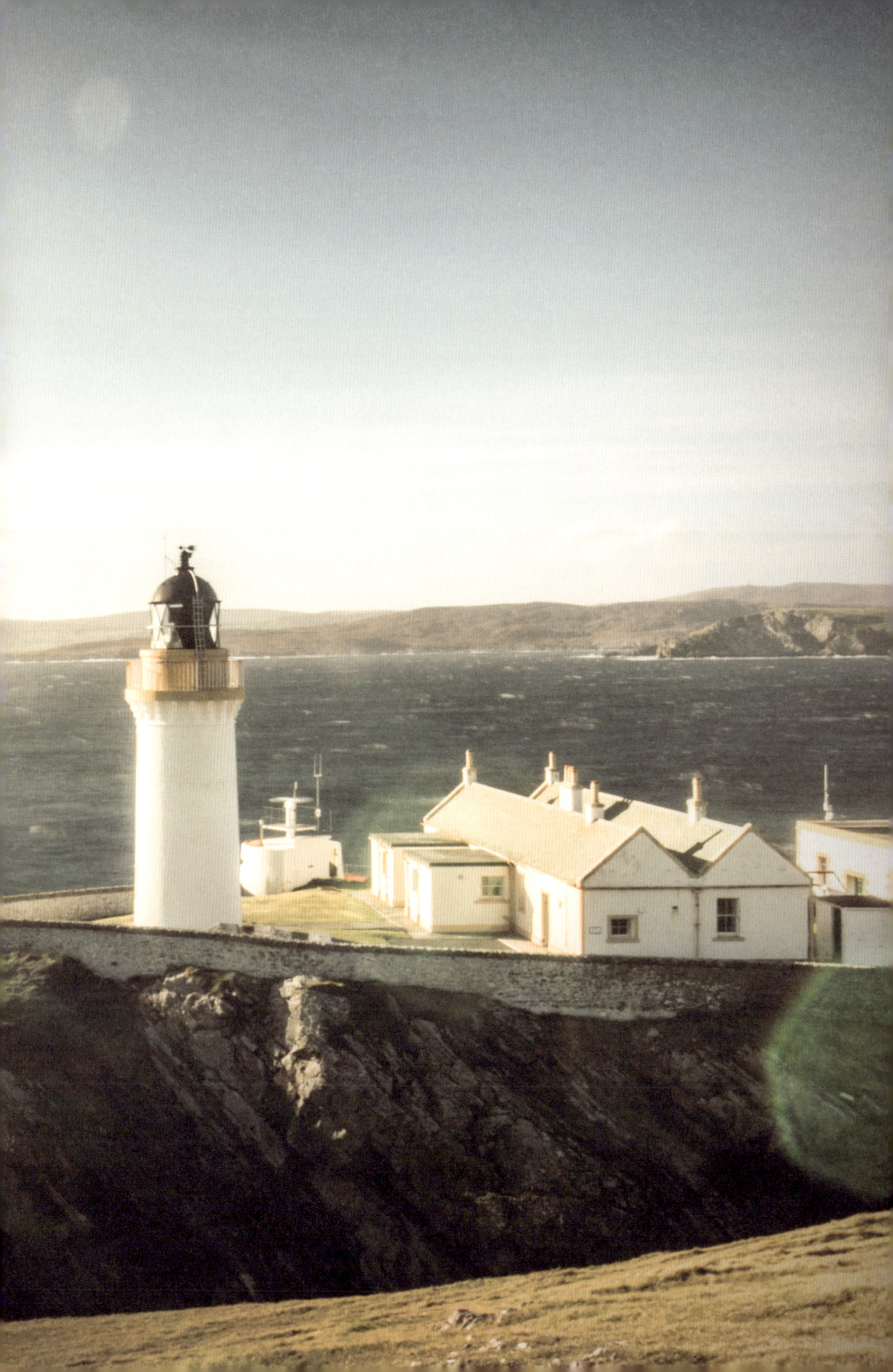

## Further Reading


Lynn Abrams, *Myth and Materiality in a Woman's World: Shetland 1800-2000* (2010)

Alastair & Adaline Christie-Johnston, *Shetland Words* (2014)

Carol Christiansen, *Primitive Wool and Early Textile Production in Shetland* (2003); *Taatit Rugs: The Pile Bedcovers of Shetland* (2015)

Kate Davies, *Colours of Shetland* (2012); *Yokes* (2014); *The Book of Haps* (2016)

Linda Fryer, *Knitting by the Fireside and on the Hillside: A History of the Shetland Hand Knitting Industry 1600-1950* (1994)

Jakob Jakobsen, *An Etymological Dictionary of the Norn Language in Shetland* (1985)

Sarah Laurenson, ed., *Shetland Textiles: 800 BC to the Present* (2013)

Shetland Guild of Spinners, Knitters, Weavers and Dyers, *A Legacy of Shetland Lace* (2012)

Brian Smith, *Toons and Tenants: Settlement and Society in Shetland 1299-1899* (2000)

Various authors, *Shetland Breeds: Ancient, Endangered and Adaptable* (2003)


## Links

Donna Smith Designs (Donna Smith) www.donnasmithdesigns.co.uk

Ella Gordon Designs (Ella Gordon) www.ellagordon.wordpress.com

GlobalYell / Shetland Weaving Company (Andy Ross and Kirsty Jean Brabin) www.globalyell.org

Hazel Tindall www.hazeltindall.com

Helen Robertson www.helenrobertson.com

Home is an Island (Kharis Leggate) www.homeisanisland.co.uk

Jamieson's of Shetland www.jamiesonsofshetland.co.uk

Jamieson & Smith www.shetlandwoolbrokers.co.uk

NielaNell (Niela Nell Kalra) www.nielanell.com

Ninian (Joanna Hunter) www.ninianshetland.co.uk

Shetland Designer (Wilma Malcolmson) www.shetlanddesigner.co.uk

Shetland Handspun (Elizabeth Johnston) www.shetlandhandspun.com

Shetland Livestock Marketing Group www.slmg.co.uk

Shetland Museum and Archives www.shetlandmuseumandarchives.org.uk

Shetland Organics www.shetlandorganics.com

Shetland Tannery (Natalie Cairns-Ratter) www.shetlandtannery.com

Shetland Wool Adventures (Misa Hay) www.shetlandwooladventures.com

Shetland Wool Week www.shetlandwoolweek.com

Uradale (Ronnie Eunson) www.aalmerk.com

Whalsay Heritage Centre www.whalsayheritage.co.uk

For general information about many different aspects of Shetland life and culture, visit www.shetland.org

## Photographing Oo

I enjoy photographing people and I like being outdoors. Given that, this project has felt like a great gift to me, as I explored parts of Shetland I'd never previously visited, spoke to so many wonderful people, and learnt much more about how crucial wool is to life in these islands. It has been both fascinating and inspiring for me to find out about the different kinds of work that wool involves, and meet the committed Shetlanders for whom, in a wide variety of ways, sheep and wool are a passion as much as they are livelihood.

For those interested in the technical aspects of my photography: everything in this book was shot using Canon equipment. The majority of portraits were shot using a 5D mark III body equipped with 100mm or 50mm prime lenses (EF 100mm f/2.8L macro IS USM or EF 50mm f/1.4 USM). Landscapes were photographed using a 70D body and either an EF-S 17-55mm f/2.8 IS USM or EF-S 10-18mm f4/5-5.6 IS STM lens. For film work, I used a Canon EOS 30 and Ilford HP5 plus 35mm film. Film was developed by Ilford laboratories. The people you'll meet in the pages of this book deserve enormous respect for the work they do with sheep and wool. This book is dedicated to them.

*Tom Barr*

## About Tom and Kate

Tom Barr is a photographer who enjoys taking pictures of people. Through his images he aims to celebrate the varied dignity of human work and the beautiful landscapes and spaces of Scotland. When he isn't out and about with his camera, he is usually to be found on a bike, or in a pair of fell shoes, somewhere on a Scottish hill. You can find galleries of Tom's photographs, and purchase prints of his work, at photos.ootlier.com.

Kate Davies is a writer and designer, with a deep love of all things Shetland and woolly. She's the author of *Colours of Shetland* (2012) *Yokes* (2014) and *The Book of Haps* (2016), and produces Buachaille—her own brand of 100% Scottish wool yarn for handknitting. Kate blogs at www.katedaviesdesigns.com, and you'll find her books and yarn at www.shopkdd.com. You can follow Kate on Instagram (@katedaviesdesigns) or Twitter (@KDaviesdesigns).

Tom and Kate live together on the edge of the Scottish Highlands with their fun-loving labrador, Bruce.

## Shetland Oo

First published in 2016 by Kate Davies Designs Ltd, 17-19 East London Street, Edinburgh, EH7 4BN, UK.

Photography by Tom Barr

Words by Kate Davies

Design and Layout by Tom Barr

Edited by Ivor Normand.

Printed in the UK by Bell & Bain, Glasgow.

**British Library Cataloguing Publication Data:**

A catalogue record for this book is available from the British Library.

ISBN 978-0-9574666-4-7

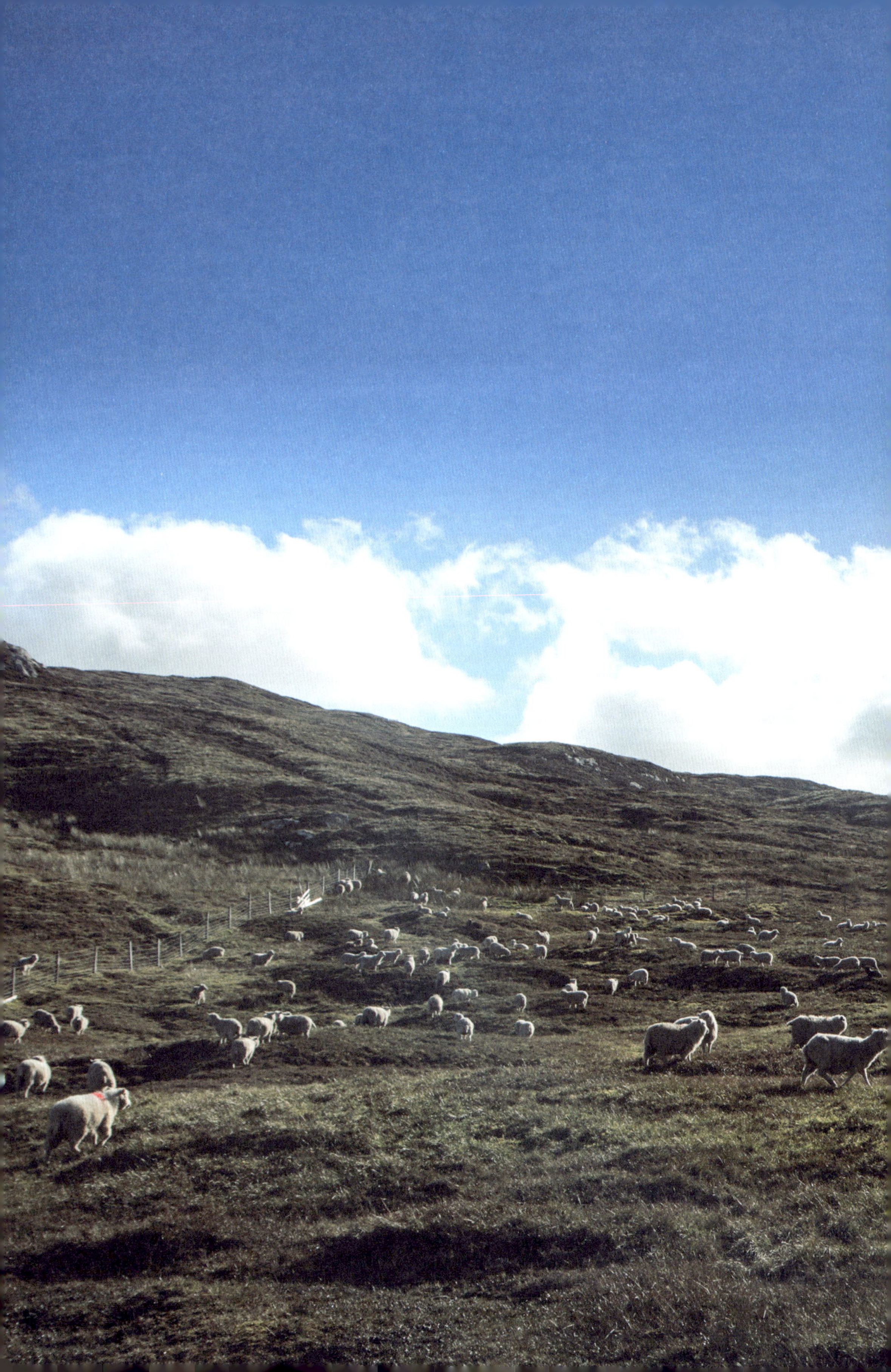

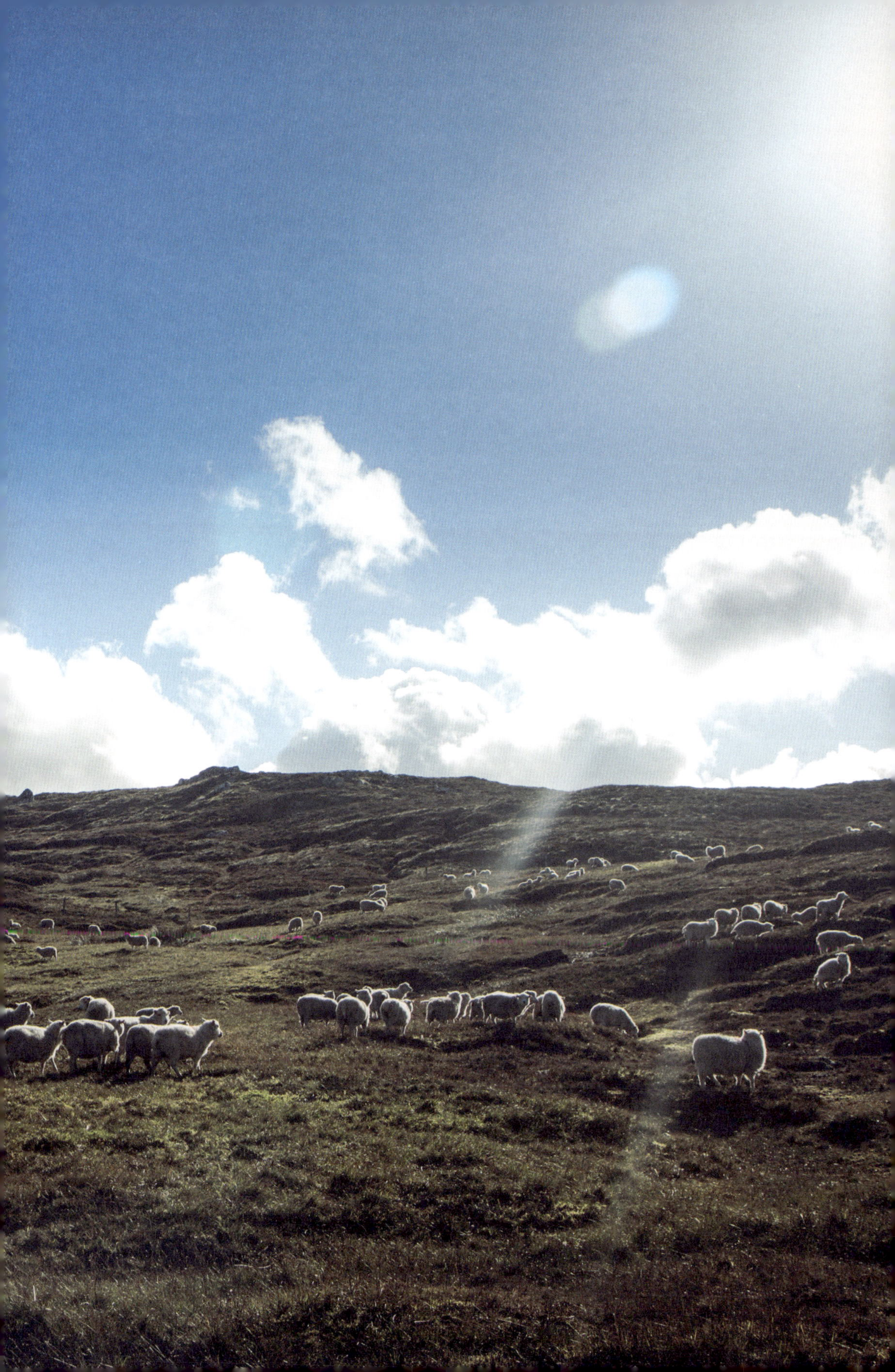

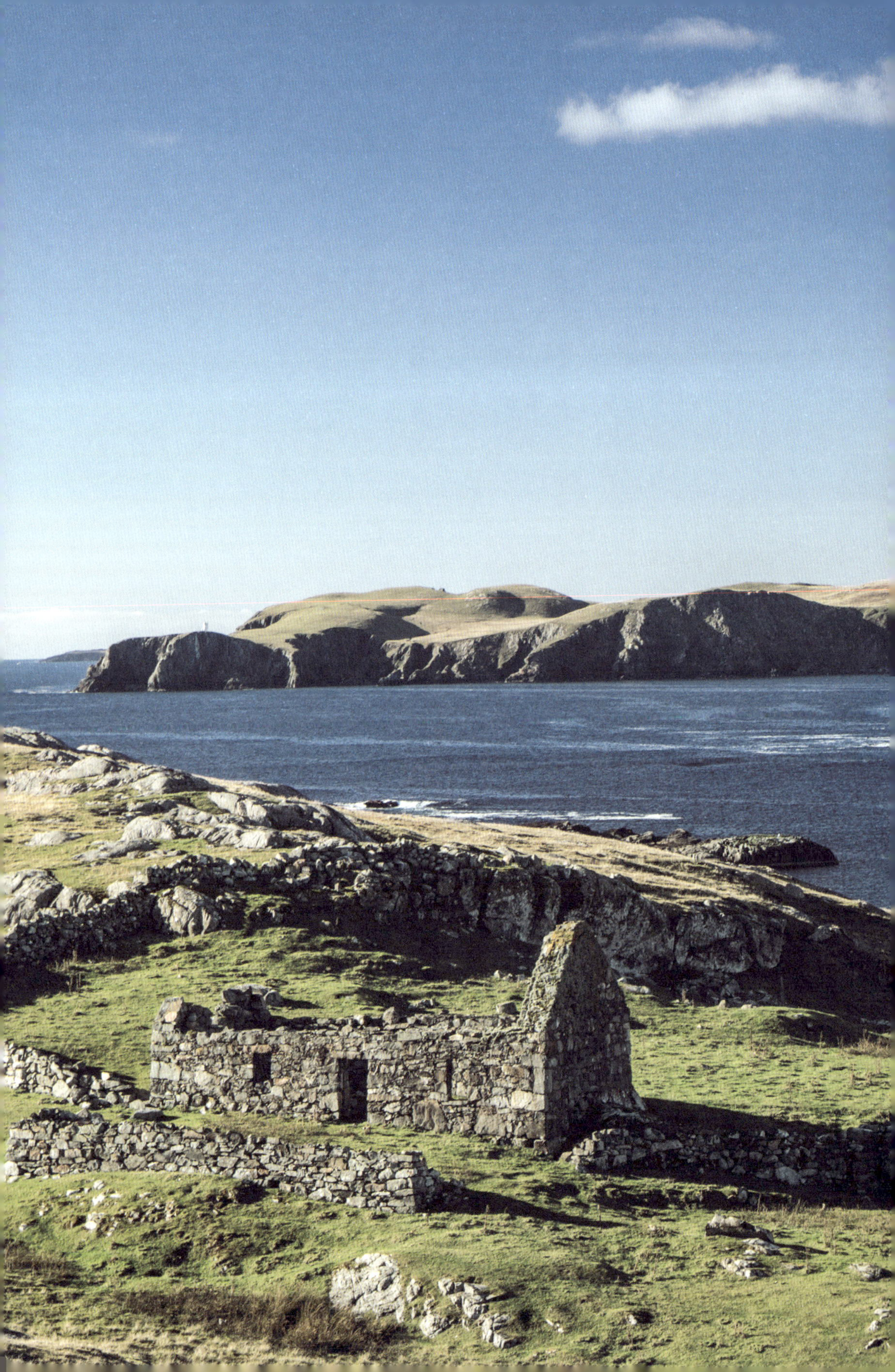

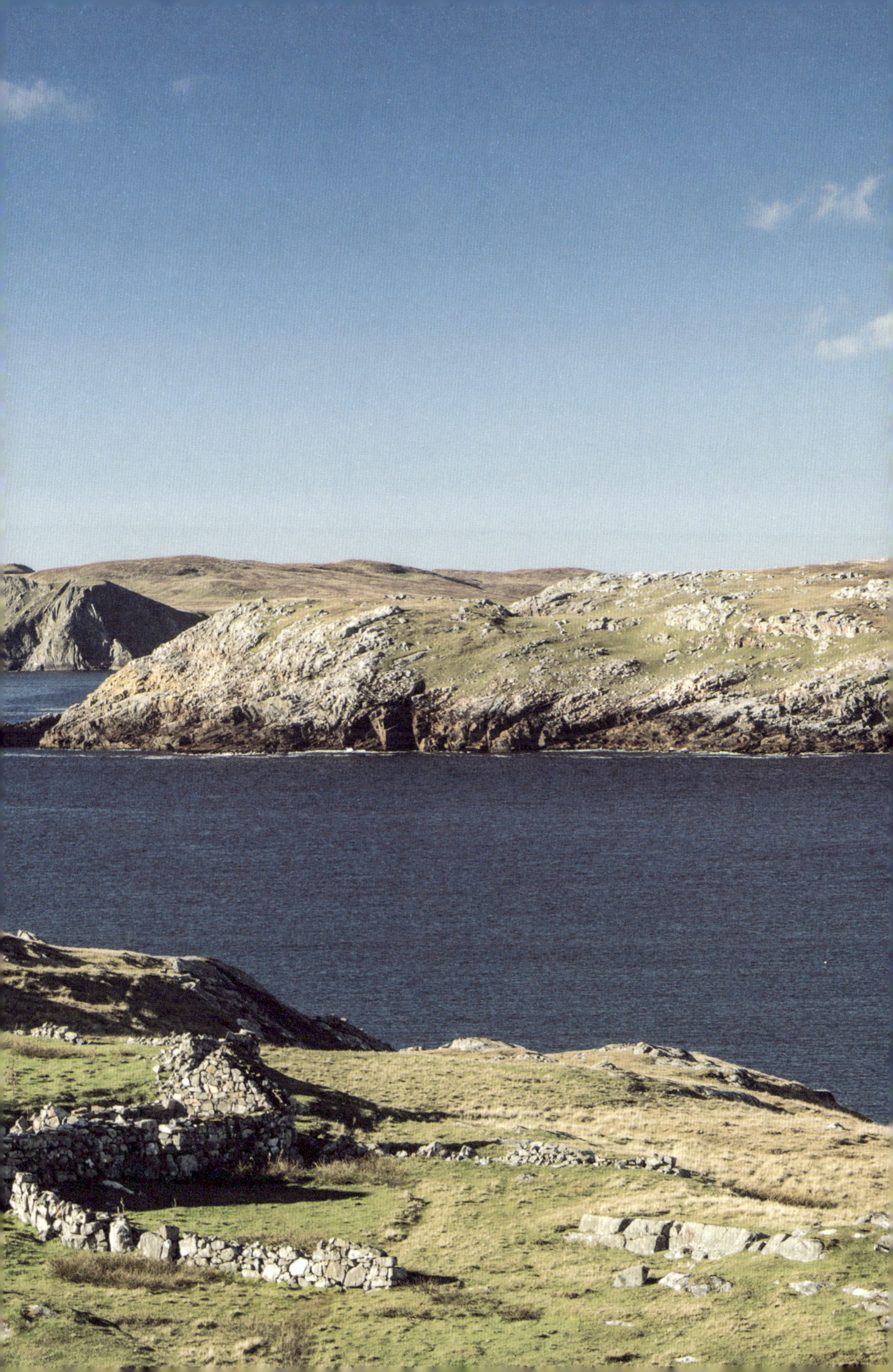

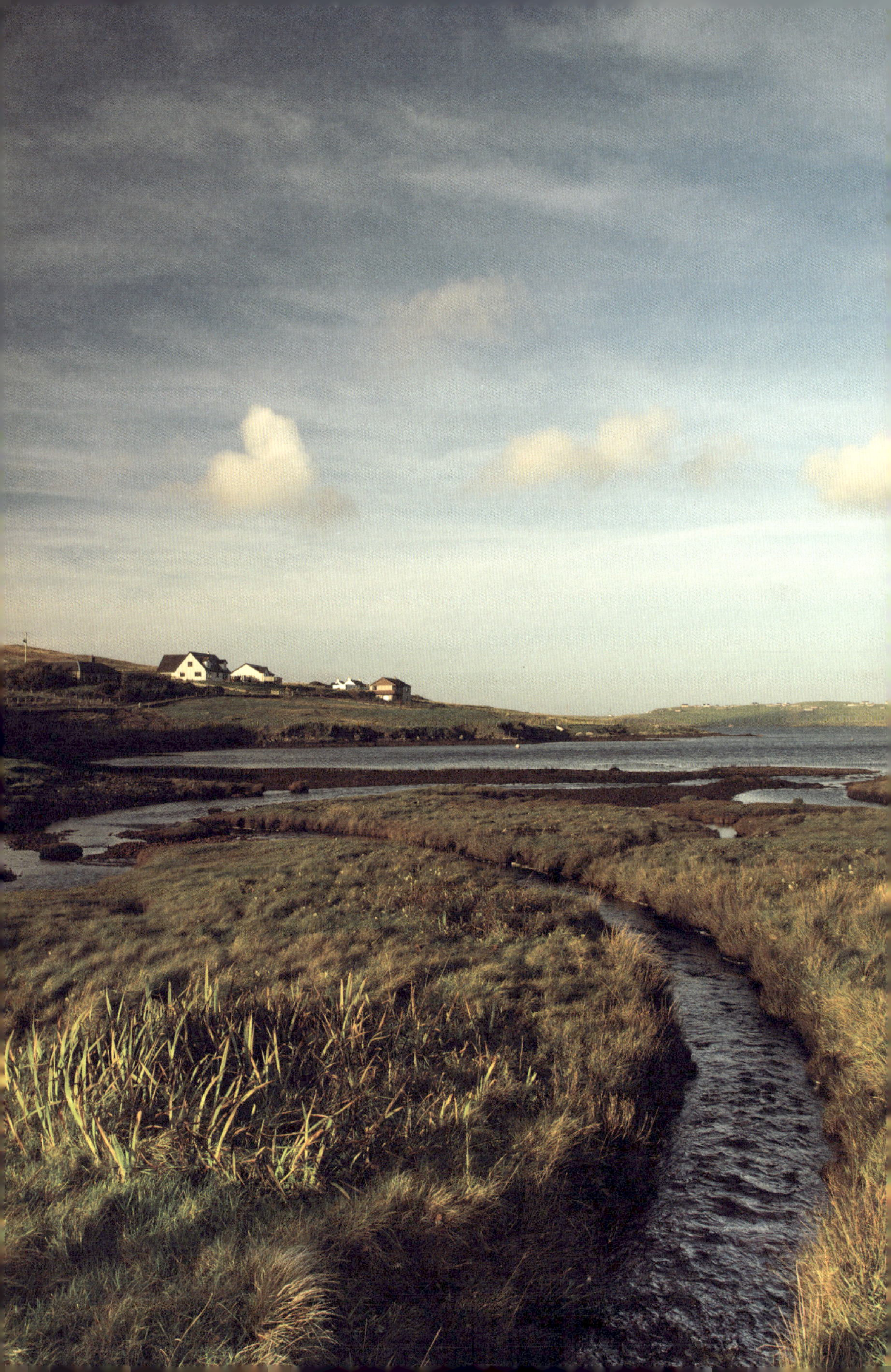

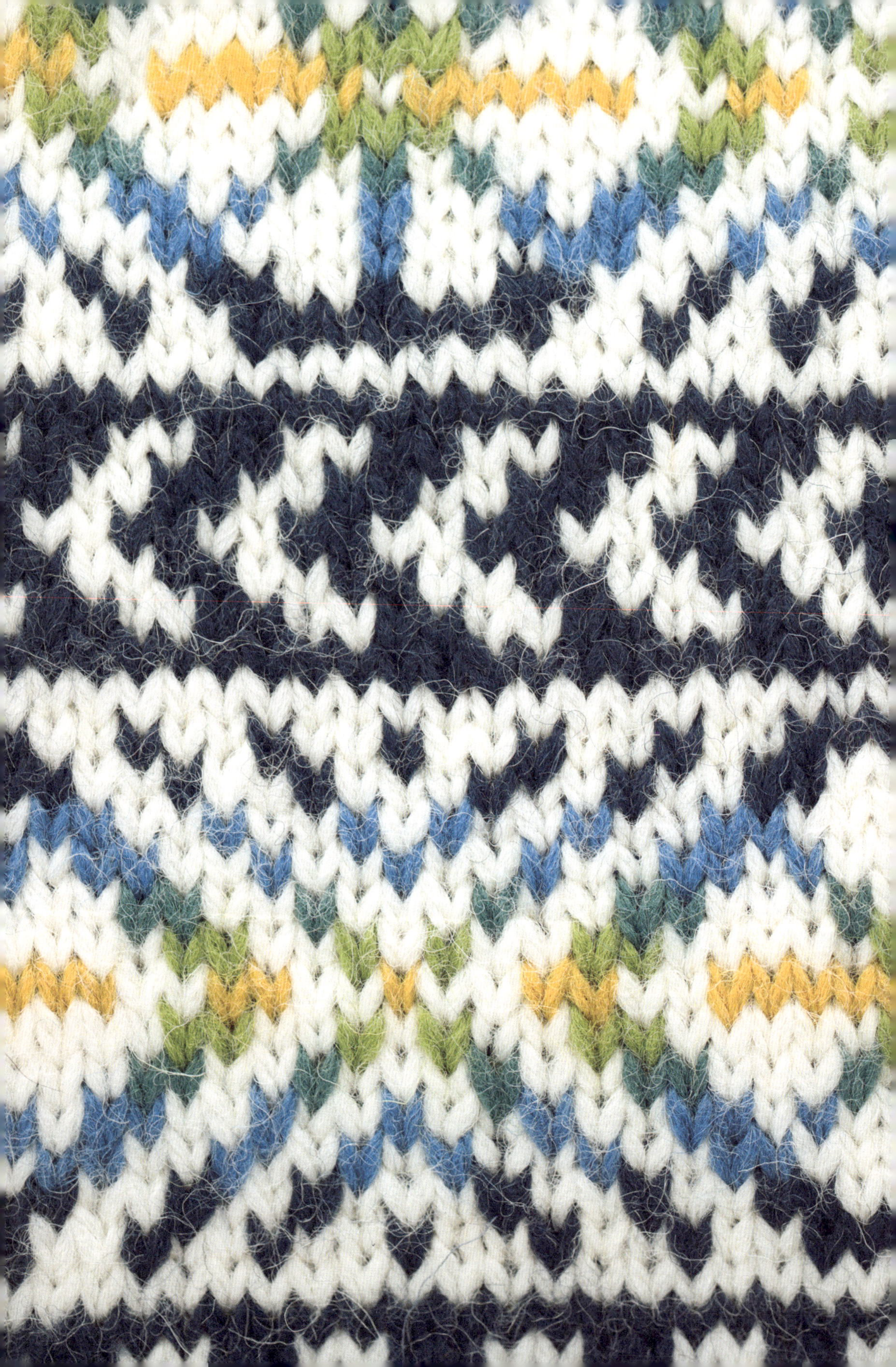